"A NEVER-BEFORE-TOLD STORY THAT DOESN'T SLACKEN FOR A MOMENT!"
—KIRKUS REVIEWS

"Now for the first time the full story of the Hammelburg Raid is told, by Major Abe Baum and many of the others who took part, and by Richard Baron, who was one of the prisoners waiting to be rescued"

—MILWAUKEE JOURNAL

"The full story of one of the most controversial actions of World War II . . . a story of loyalty, devotion, bravery . . . Once you start it, you will not be able to put it down!"
—Hal C. Pattison,
Brigadier General, U.S. Army, Ret.

"Dramatic . . . gives new insight into Patton!"
—IRISH ECHO

"RAID! *IS ONE HELL OF A BOOK . . .*
AS GOOD AS ANYTHING WRITTEN
BY CORNELIUS RYAN OR JOHN TOLAND!"
—James C. Pollock,
author of
MISSION MIA

"We picked up a copy and started to read it. We were unable to lay it down until it was finished. It's that kind of story!"

—THE STAMFORD ADVOCATE

"If truth is stranger than fiction, it can also be more dramatic and exciting . . . this story of an American military nightmare pulses with the power of human courage in war!"

—SAN DIEGO UNION

THE UNTOLD STORY OF PATTON'S SECRET MISSION

RAID

RICHARD BARON, MAJOR ABE BAUM AND RICHARD GOLDHURST

BERKLEY BOOKS, NEW YORK

To those brave men of Task Force Baum who risked their lives to save their
brothers in arms at Oflag XIIIB

This Berkley book contains the complete
text of the original hardcover edition.

RAID!
THE UNTOLD STORY OF PATTON'S SECRET MISSION

A Berkley Book / published by arrangement with
G. P. Putnam's Sons

PRINTING HISTORY
G. P. Putnam's Sons edition published 1981
Berkley edition / March 1984

ISBN: 0-425-05937-5

A BERKLEY BOOK ® TM 757,375
Berkley Books are published by The Berkley Publishing Group,
200 Madison Avenue, New York, New York 10016.
The name "BERKLEY" and the stylized "B" with design
are trademarks belonging to Berkley Publishing Corporation.
PRINTED IN THE UNITED STATES OF AMERICA

Contents

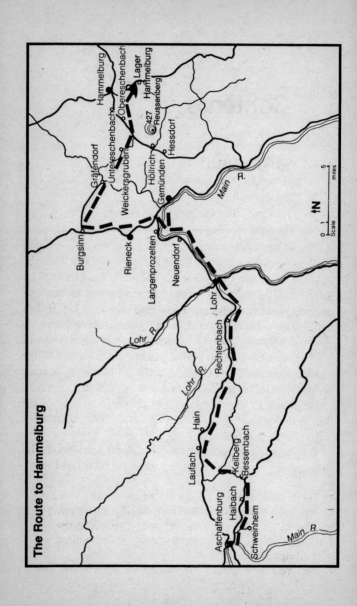

The Route to Hammelburg

Prologue

On 22 March 1945 General George S. Patton, Jr., ordered one of the divisions of his Third Army across the Rhine at night in small boats. The bold move caught the Germans by surprise. The Germans were used to enormous buildups before attacks. Not only had Patton beaten his British counterpart, Field Marshal Bernard Law Montgomery, to German soil but he had accomplished this with the loss of only twenty-eight men. Two days later, Patton drove to the river and stopped his jeep midstream on the newly erected pontoon bridge. He leaped out to piss, a broad, arrogant smile breaking over his face. On the German side of the bridge he scooped up two handfuls of dirt in emulation of William the Conqueror.

Patton was at the summit of his glorious powers. In the Third Army General Orders, he told his officers and men:

In the period from 29 January to 22 March, you have wrested 6,484 square miles of territory from the enemy. You have taken 3,072 cities, towns, and villages including . . . Trier, Coblenz, Bingen, Worms, Mainz, Kaiserslautern, and Ludwigshafen. . . .

You have captured 140,112 enemy soldiers and have

9

killed or wounded an additional 99,000, thereby eliminating practically all of the German Seventh and First Armies. History records no greater achievement in so limited a time. . . .

The world rings with your praises: better still, General Marshall, General Eisenhower, and General Bradley have personally commended you. The highest honor I have ever attained is that of having my name coupled with yours in these great events.

Indeed he had more honors than that. President Franklin D. Roosevelt sent Secretary of War Henry L. Stimson to Patton's headquarters to tender personal congratulations. Dwight D. Eisenhower, commander of the Allied forces sent Patton a note "to express to you personally my deep appreciation of the splendid way in which you have conducted Third Army operations from the moment it entered battle last August 1." Prime Minister Winston Churchill commended Patton publicly.

But Patton was notorious for taking the extra step. On the day that the Third Army was across the Rhine, Patton wrote his wife, Beatrice, "We are headed right for John's place and may get there before he is moved."

"John" was Patton's son-in-law, Lieutenant Colonel John Waters. His "place" was the Hammelburg prisoner of war camp 80 miles east of Mainz on the Main River, which Patton's troops crossed on 25 March. On that day, Patton wrote Beatrice, "Hope to send an expedition tomorrow to get John."

He knew if he failed, he would be severely criticized. "However," he wrote, "I do not believe that fear of criticism should prevent my getting back American prisoners, particularly as in the last death struggles of the Germans, our POWs might be murdered." In authorizing the Hammelburg raid, Patton later said that part of his plan was to create a diversion to confuse the German High Command.

But he was careful enough to clear the raid with higher authority, General Omar N. Bradley. In the war diaries of Bradley's aide, Colonel Joe Hansen, there is an entry dated 28 March: "When Patton ran off on his mission the other day, Brad told him he would allow it provided Patton did not become involved. He was ordered to withdraw if he did to prevent him from becoming entangled in the wrong direction."

It is easy to read Bradley's motives. Saying "yes" to George S. Patton was easier than saying "no." In March 1945, George S. Patton was the most popular and admired field commander since Ulysses S. Grant. Many felt his tanks had won the war in Europe.

Reading Patton's motives is not as easy as it seems. To expose men to peril and death by sending them to rescue a member of his own family seems cruel and selfish. Patton later claimed there were other considerations, some of which were realized though the mission itself failed. And Patton was far from simply a selfish and cruel man. His endurance, stamina and uncomplaining nature, his willingness to do more than was ordered endeared him to his soldiers. Patton never tired of proving his courage to himself. Perhaps that is why he sent men on the Hammelburg Raid—because he would have wanted to go himself, would have gone if he hadn't been a three-star general. Patton knew what he was about. He was an American and as Alexis de Tocqueville wrote in *Democracy in America,* "No kind of greatness is more pleasing to the imagination of a democratic people than military greatness, a greatness of vivid and sudden luster, obtained without toil, by nothing but the risk of life."

:: 1 ::

We've Got Our Orders

The order to form a task force to go to Hammelburg, 50 miles behind enemy lines, began its journey down through the chain of command of the United States Third Army late on the night of 25 March 1945. The order originated with Lieutenant General George S. Patton, commander of the Third Army, who sent it to Major General Manton Eddy, commander of XII Corps. Eddy, in turn, chose the 4th Armored Division to carry out the mission and drove over to the division's forward command post.

The 4th Armored was the best division in Eddy's command. It had seen a lot of action and had always succeeded brilliantly. Because it had spearheaded so many of Patton's spectacular attacks, it was called "The Point." The 4th and the 101st Airborne were the only divisions in the European Theater of Operations to have been awarded the Distinguished Unit Citation by order of the President. Every member of the 4th felt that the division was invincible.

Major General John "Tiger Jack" Wood had trained the division. He believed in planning armored attacks carefully and executing them violently. The purpose of an armored force, he taught, is to terrify enemy infantry. A

line of fifty attacking tanks is infernal. It comes upon
soldiers with treads grinding, uprooting defenses, the big
guns booming destruction, the machine guns spraying a
deadly barrage. Behind the armor infantry follows to mop
up anyone who escapes the tanks. Even an enemy unit
armed with a *Panzerfaust* (bazooka) or an antitank gun is in
danger of annihilation. If it does succeed in knocking out a
tank, another forty-nine are left to grind inexorably toward
its position. The armored force also has the advantage of
surprise because of its extreme mobility. General Wood
never let his command forget that the Nazis had conquered
Europe by virtue of the *Blitzkrieg,* lightning fast attacks of
armor with air support. In order to increase speed and
maneuverability, American tanks carried much lighter armor plate than their German counterparts.

Now the 4th had a new commander. He was Brigadier
General William M. Hoge, fifty-one. A tall, spare, blue-
eyed Missourian, Hoge was a stern and demanding officer.
He had been given command of the 4th Armored Division
only four days before, after serving with distinction in the
9th Armored Division. When Eddy explained Patton's
order to form a task force, it angered Hoge. Not only had
his division finished thirty-six hours of intense combat
taking the Aschaffenburg bridge across the Main River, but
he had also received the order to move the division north
along with the rest of the Third Army. It was too much.
How was he to move his battle-depleted force and, at the
same time, put together a special task force (which would
have to consist of exhausted troops) and send it 50 miles
eastward? Hoge told Eddy that the order was impossible to
obey. He assumed that that was the end of the matter.

Manton Eddy returned to Third Army headquarters
and explained Hoge's reluctance to General Patton. Patton
called Hoge directly. "Bill," Patton announced without

preamble, "I want you to put this little task force together. Now get on it."

Hoge resisted. "We'd be encroaching on the Seventh Army zone."

"I've cleared this with Bradley," Patton countered, citing the authority of General Omar N. Bradley, 12th Army Group commander.*

Stubbornly, Hoge tried again. "My people are exhausted. The division is only at half strength as it is."

Patton's tone changed abruptly and he utterly surprised Hoge by saying, "Bill, I promise I'll replace anything you lose—every man, every tank, every half-track. I promise."

Hoge had never liked Patton. He found the controversial commander to be mean and vainglorious, his habit of browbeating his subordinates unnecessarily a nettlesome, distracting waste of time. Hoge knew replacements were not the equal of tested troops. Green troops were more easily disoriented by the confusion of battle and more likely to become disheartened. Seasoned, battle-tested combat groups also owed much of their effectiveness to the confidence they had in their comrades and in the units around them.

But Hoge was acutely aware that he was a new division commander, junior to other division commanders. There was no way he could succeed in resisting the will of George S. Patton. He capitulated and told his caller, "I'll get Abrams of Combat Command B right on it, sir."

Lieutenant Colonel Creighton Abrams, thirty years old, was one of the youngest combat commanders of ground forces in Europe. Many swore that the burly, intense soldier with the cherubic face *was* the 4th Armored Division. He

---

* General Hansen's *Third Army Diary* confirms Patton's position, although Bradley contradicts this statement in his autobiography.

was tough, brave, resolute and aggressive in battle, yet humane; his desire for success was coupled with a genuine concern for the welfare of his men.

When Hoge called Abrams, he knew that the young officer would raise many of the same objections he himself had raised. Sure enough, when he described the mission, Abrams resisted.

"Fifty miles is a long way to go, sir, for that small a force. If we have to go that far, I want my whole command to go. Hell, a combat command can go anywhere." Indeed it could. Varying in strength from 3,500 to 5,000 men (depending on the rates of casualties and replacements), it consisted of a battalion each of infantry, armor and artillery, plus medical, engineering, reconnaissance and service elements—a formidable force.

"No," Hoge replied, "it has to be a small force. And Army says it has to go tonight."

"I'd like to talk to Army, sir."

"Don't worry, you'll get your chance," Hoge said. "General Patton is planning to come down to your command post later this morning."

While waiting for the visit of General Patton, Abrams realized that his objections and suggested alternatives would be overruled. Still, he would try. In the meantime, he began making plans. He started by reviewing the casualty reports and equipment status of his command in the aftermath of the battle for the Aschaffenburg bridge. After considering his battalion commanders, Abrams chose Lieutenant Colonel Harold Cohen of the 10th Armored Infantry Battalion to lead the task force.* So that Hal would not be

---

*West Pointer Lieutenant Colonel Graham L. Kirkpatrick, the former CO of the 10th AIB had resigned from the army for several years, and had entered the business world, where he had

totally surprised by the order and so that he could begin resupplying his units, Abrams sent him a brief message. "Prepare your battalion for a special combat mission for General Patton. ETD 1700."

Cohen was exhausted. In the last five days, his 10th Armored Infantry Battalion, following the 37th Tank Battalion, had found three bridges across the Main River. Cohen had watched helplessly as the Germans blew each bridge when the column started across. On the third one, a tank was in the middle of the bridge when it collapsed. Cohen tried not to think about the five tankers falling, falling, falling inside their tank to their deaths in the river below.

At Aschaffenburg, Cohen's troops had found a fourth span, this one a railroad bridge. Many of his infantrymen crawled along under the bridge cutting the wires of aerial bombs that the Germans had lashed together there. The lead tank cautiously led the way riding over the railroad ties. Behind it came engineers laying boards over the ties to facilitate the passage of the other tanks.

Cohen ordered his jeep to follow. The bumpy trip forcibly reminded the young lieutenant colonel of his piles, and he gritted his teeth. He sat on an inner tube in the jeep and needed help in getting out. Piles, Cohen knew, were as much a part of war as drowning or blown kneecaps. But the

----

been favorably impressed by the ability of the many Jews with whom he had come in contact. When he rejoined the army, before the outbreak of the war, he tried to utilize as many Jewish officers as he could on his staff. He was wounded shortly after his unit landed, but this accounts for the preponderance of Jewish officers in his battalion. General Arthur West of the 4th Armored Division had similar feelings as he was aware that Jews had more motivation and hatred for the enemy.

colonel was not so philosophical that he couldn't curse his affliction.

The bridge was theirs. Cohen, tall, lean, with a face like a triangle, was pleased. His eyeglasses were covered with grime. They had been flecked with grime or dust or rain since he had landed in France on D Day plus 36 with the lead combat command of General Patton's army.

As his troops fought their way into Aschaffenburg, Cohen received a radio call from Abrams, CO of Combat Command B, who directed the infantry and tank battalions as well as the artillery and support units. Cohen and Abrams had become friends in the past nine months and were to remain friends all their lives, even when Cohen was a wealthy apparel manufacturer in Spartanburg, South Carolina, and Abrams the United States Army Chief-of-Staff. There was no "Able, Baker and Charlie," between them, no "Red Fox to Kangaroo." It was "Cohen, this is Abrams," or "Abrams, this here is Cohen."

"What can I do for you?" asked Cohen.

"I want you to disengage and withdraw," said Abrams.

"I ain't never heard you talk like that since I've known you," Cohen drawled.

"Disengage and withdraw," ordered Abrams, the West Pointer.

"I'm in the middle of this goddamn town," Cohen shouted. "How in hell can I do that?"

"I am telling you in plain talk," said Abrams. "The army boundary has been changed. You get your ass out of there. You are now in the Seventh Army zone under the command of Lieutenant General Alexander Patch. I just sent you a message to prepare for another mission. How are you going to do that without withdrawing?"

Cohen ordered his infantrymen to withdraw. But since an armored force is safer when it is moving forward fast than when it is backing away slowly, the 37th lost some tanks in the disengagement and the 10th some men.

We never did learn about turning the enemy loose, thought Cohen. Once you get ahold of the enemy, there's not supposed to be any more enemy.

But he kept the bridge over the Main and moved his battalion to a reverse slope where it was out of mortar range, though still vulnerable to artillery. Then he tried to get some sleep. There was never enough time for sleep, but, for Cohen, simply lying down provided relief for his pulsing hemorrhoids. After a few hours' rest, he was awakened by a runner with the message from Abrams.

At 1000 hours, General George S. Patton appeared at Abrams's command post. He wore the famous varnished helmet with the three stars gleaming brilliantly, a beribboned Eisenhower jacket, carefully tailored jodhpurs, and the abbreviated boots worn by tankers. He was accompanied by his aide, Major Alexander Stiller, and by General Hoge.

In his high-pitched voice, Patton asked who was going to lead the task force.

"I am," Abrams ventured, "and I want to take Combat Command B."

"You are not going and neither is your combat command. This is to be a small force. Now, answer my question. Who is going to lead it?"

Abrams knew that any argument was over before it began. Reluctantly, he answered, "Hal Cohen, 10th Armored Infantry—if he's well enough. His piles are giving him a lot of trouble."

"Piles," Patton interrupted. He seemed amused. "Get a doctor in here. Then we'll go see if Cohen is well enough."

After Abrams had dispatched an aide to get the physician, Patton said, "I don't want any damned hemorrhoids lousing up an important mission. Napoleon's hemorrhoids defeated him at Waterloo. He couldn't sit a horse for long and had to direct the battle from his tent. If Cohen's ass is hurting, I don't want him going."

A few minutes later, Patton, Hoge, Stiller, Abrams and the battalion surgeon were on their way to Cohen's headquarters. As they entered, Cohen and his top officers—Captain William Dwight and Major Willian Hunter of the 37th Tank Battalion, and Captain Abraham Baum of the 10th AIB—came to attention and saluted. They had been assessing their situation and making plans for a small combat mission, wondering how they were supposed to do that without knowing the mission's purpose.

Patton began, "I understand you may not be physically up to taking on any extracurricular activities. I hear you have a very sore ass."

"That's right, sir. It is kind of sore," Cohen replied.

"Would you step in the other room? The doctor and I want to have a look," Patton said. Once inside, Patton ordered, "Drop your pants and grab your ankles." When Cohen had followed the orders, he heard the doctor whistle in disbelief. The hemorrhoids looked like a half dozen eggs.

Patton, too, seemed impressed with the severity of Cohen's condition. "That is some sorry ass. Terrible. Thank you." It must be remembered that Patton was a cavalryman and he had probably inspected as many sore asses in his time as George Washington had inspected sore feet. Rejoining the rest of the group, Patton told Abrams, "You were right. Cohen can't go. You and he pick someone else and have him get over to Hammelburg tonight. And remember, no more than 300 men."

"Excuse me, sir," Cohen said, "but I already have

someone in mind and I'm sure Colonel Abrams will approve."

"Well," Patton asked impatiently, "who?"

"Captain Baum," said Cohen, gesturing toward the young officer standing outside the circle of commanders.

"Excellent! Very impressive combat record."

Suddenly, Patton motioned Baum to step aside with him. Away from the others, the general spoke conspiratorily. "Listen, Abe—it is Abe, isn't it? I thought so. You pull this off and I'll see to it that you get the Congressional Medal of Honor."

"I have my orders, sir. You don't have to bribe me," Baum said calmly.

Rejoining the others, Patton headed for the door. General Hoge followed to accompany Patton back to his headquarters. At the door, Patton turned and said, "Major Stiller will fill you in on the details." The legendary commander was fully confident that his men would accept this mission and exert themselves to the fullest to make it successful.

Abrams and Cohen stared at each other, both wondering what possible goal the mission could have.

"What's so special about Hammelburg?" Abrams at last asked Stiller.

"There's a POW camp there with 300 American officers in it."

"And?" prompted Cohen.

"And," Stiller said, "Patton wants them liberated."

The major ignored the sceptical expressions on the faces of the two and proceeded to take a map from his briefcase, unfold it on the table and begin tracing out the route to Hammelburg, located 60 miles east of their present position.

"You know, Major Stiller," Cohen said, "our vehicles

don't have that range. There's no way they can go that far and still get back."

"I would suggest carrying as much extra fuel as you can, and it should be possible to capture fuel at or near the objective. It will also be necessary to procure some enemy vehicles in order to transport that many POWs back to our lines." He then added, "Have you decided on the composition of the task force, Colonel Cohen?"

"Yes. There'll be a company of armored infantry, a company of Shermans, plus a platoon of light tanks, a platoon of 105mm assault guns and a recon platoon. That'd make about fifty vehicles in all and about 280 to 300 men."

"Sounds good."

Captain Baum, who was studying the map closely, asked, "Where is the POW camp in relation to the town? It's not indicated on the map."

"Don't know, Captain," Major Stiller responded, "but General Patton says you ought to be able to choke that out of some civilian when you get there."

"Where's the division going to be?" Baum asked innocently.

"Well, Abe," Colonel Abrams replied, wishing there were another answer to the question, "you'll be on your own. The division—the Third Army is moving. This area and the area you're going into are now a part of the Seventh Army's command zone."

Major Stiller could see the chagrin in Abrams and Cohen's faces and the surprise in Baum's. He quickly added, "The task force will be getting whatever air support it needs, weather permitting, and General Patch, who's head of the Seventh, will be ready to help out when the task force returns from Hammelburg." Pausing for a few moments, he then asked, "Are there any questions?" and deciding that there were none, he prepared to leave. "One more thing," Stiller added, "I'll be accompanying the task force."

Baum looked from Abrams to Cohen, who were almost as surprised as he was by this new development in an already highly extraordinary mission. "I thought I was to be in command of the task force," Baum asserted.

"You are," Major Stiller replied.

"You're damned right you are, and don't you forget it," Abrams said forcefully to Baum, but it was clear that he was also giving Stiller fair warning not to get any ideas. Nevertheless, Baum was suspicious. He knew that aces were made to take kings and that majors were made to command captains.

By way of explanation, Major Stiller said, "The general wants me to get a taste of combat. I'm only going along for the laughs and a high old time."

"This isn't my idea of a high old time," Cohen commented dourly.

Baum was not reassured. He understood that generals often sent their aides out to the front lines just so they could decorate them—generals had a real fondness for decorating their aides—but this mission would be more than a "taste of combat"; this mission was perilous, as perilous as any mission in the war. And Stiller in fact had crossed the Rhine in the first boat a few nights ago. Something was up. Yes it was. Furthermore, Baum doubted that Stiller would be able to pack his authority away in his mess kit and not use it until the task force had returned.

When Stiller was gone, Baum voiced his doubts. "Something's fishy. This doesn't make sense."

"Can it, Abe," Cohen shot back. "We've gotten our orders. If I was well, I'd be leading the mission and you'd be going along. At least, this way you're in command and you don't have to put up with any shit from me. And if Stiller says he's going along for the ride, you don't have to put up with any shit from him either. You got that?"

During all of this, Creighton Abrams stood motionless. He was furious. His cigar was clenched hard between his teeth and his hands were balled into fists. "Damn," he muttered finally, frustrated that his duty required him to sacrifice such good men—he didn't know how many—on such a mission. He and Cohen wished the young captain good luck.

Baum looked at them cockily and replied, "Don't think you can get rid of me this easily. I'll be back." Then he, Dwight and Hunter left the command post.

When they had gone, Abrams slammed his fist down on the not so steady folding field table that Cohen had been using as a desk. "What the hell is this all about?" he growled. "It just doesn't make sense. Did we ever do anything like this before?"

"Never," Cohen answered, keeping his anger and frustration more under control, as was his way. "Any time we ever sent someone out through the lines into enemy territory, we damn sure followed, and in force."

Abrams stalked up and down the room, lamenting bitterly. "So we have to send them out, while the rest of us pack up and take off in the other direction. Damn, I just don't like it." He kicked the chair, not bothering to watch it skid across the floor and crash into the tent flaps. "We are always asking men to take risks, but they are calculated risks. They know they have a chance. This mission doesn't have a chance and we both know it. If this task force does make it back, it'll be a miracle."

"Look," Cohen said, "we've already upped their odds of succeeding."

"How's that?"

"We gave them Abe Baum. If anyone can get them back, Abe can."

:: 2 ::

Task Force Baum

Captain Abe Baum, upon receiving his orders, began preparing the task force for its mission. There was the extra fuel to be put in jerricans and loaded on the vehicles. There were supplies and ammunition to be gathered and loaded. There were officers, NCOs and enlisted men to be supervised to make sure each did his job.

As he went about these tasks, Baum was disturbed. Normally, he didn't reflect much on orders he was given; orders were to follow, not reflect upon. This is not to say that if the orders were flawed, he wouldn't object. He would and had on several occasions. On 6 December 1944, the division was trying to build a pontoon bridge across the Eichel River in the heart of the Maginot Line in eastern France. Colonel Cohen was given the task of eliminating the harassing fire coming from the nearby river town of Voellerdingen. Rather than use the road winding down the hill into the town, Cohen decided to send his troops down a steep wooded incline.

"I think we should take the road," Baum objected.

"The road might be mined," answered Cohen.

"You can't take that town at night by dropping men off

a cliff," Baum countered stubbornly. "Besides, I doubt that the road is mined."

"Get 'em ready, Abe. And tell them they're going down that hill if I have to stand at the top and kick their butts over the side."

Even though under artillery fire, the men were able to advance until they were stopped by a mine field. The two officers leading the way were badly wounded. Baum volunteered to go in to rescue them.

The men of the attack force were grouped on the perimeter of the mine field, frozen by their fear. The two officers lay writhing, farther on, both bleeding profusely. The field was filled with antipersonnel mines triggered by small charges. The mines were shaped like fountain pens and detonated when a wire was tripped. They flew up from the ground and exploded metallic fragments at the height of a man's balls.

Baum told the medics to wait and began to work his way into the field to set a safe path. He had nearly reached the moaning officers when he heard a click. He whirled, taking the charge across his buttocks. But he had cleared the path and the medics rushed to the three men and carried them to safety. Despite his wounds, Baum was able to direct the rest of the men back to safe ground as he lay on his stretcher.

The doctors at the aid station spent hours picking out the splinters. More than a week later, Baum rejoined his unit, with as sore an ass as Hal Cohen's. He had also suffered a damaged testicle—which, fortunately, never dimmed his romantic eagerness. And he had earned his second Silver Star and an apology from Cohen, who had indeed finally used the road and taken the town without loss.

As a result of these actions, the division was able to complete the pontoon bridge, cross the Eichel River, breach the Maginot Line and begin its assault on the Siegfried line, the perimeter of fortress Germany.

It was not that Baum had never been in command of special missions before. He had led spearheads into enemy territory, armed reconnaissance missions, even a special task force. As operations officer of battalion headquarters—S-3 in military nomenclature—he was responsible for planning the details of attacks. Based on all this experience, he was acutely aware that this order was unlike any he had ever received or even heard about. The stated objective was not militarily significant. The force assigned was probably insufficient to do the job. And there was Major Stiller, whose inclusion in the task force had not been adequately explained. Finally, the fact that the division was not to follow or in any way provide meaningful backup to the task force was unprecedented. If I didn't know Cohen better, Baum thought, I'd say he was trying to get rid of me.

Despite his doubts and his growing cynicism about the mission, Baum continued his preparations. At the assembly area, he looked over the vehicles composing Task Force Baum. There was C Company of the 37th Tank Battalion, commanded by Second Lieutenant William J. Nutto and consisting of ten medium tanks. Designated the M4, but called the Sherman, these were the main battle tanks of the United States Army; 57,027 of them were produced, as compared to the 21,000 tanks produced by Nazi Germany. The Sherman was clumsy. For example, to make a sharp turn, it often had to proceed part way, then back up and go forward again to complete the maneuver. It was manned by a crew of five (driver, assistant driver, main gunner, loader and machine gunner). It was armed with a 75mm main gun (late in the war, a few

Shermans had 76mm guns and before the war ended, some mediums had been mounted with 90mm guns), a .50-caliber machine gun mounted on the turret, and two .30-caliber machine guns mounted in front. All the machine guns were air cooled.

There was a platoon of five light tanks from D Company of the 37th, commanded by Second Lieutenant William Weaver. The M3 (and later the M5) tank weighed 15 tons, not much for a tank. Because it was lightly armored, it was extraordinarily maneuverable and fast, cornering easily and depending upon its speed to escape destruction. It was used for reconnaissance, to support heavier tanks and to establish roadblocks. Manned by a crew of four (driver, assistant driver, main gunner and loader), the light tank was armed with a 37mm main gun and three .30-caliber air-cooled machine guns.

There was a platoon of three self-propelled assault guns under the command of Technical Sergeant Charles O. Graham. The assault gun was actually a Sherman tank adapted to carry a 105mm gun that could be used either as an antitank weapon or as an artillery piece. Next to the main gun was the vehicle's single .50-caliber air-cooled machine gun, mounted in the gun turret. Like the Sherman tank, the Sherman 105mm assault gun had a crew of five.

The bulk of the task force would consist of twenty-seven half-tracks, Company A of the 10th Armored Infantry, under the command of Captain Robert Lange. The White engine-powered half-track, with heavy-duty wheels in front and endless rubber treads in the rear, was 21 feet long and could carry thirteen infantrymen in addition to the driver and the radio operator who rode in the front. It was normally armed with one .50- or .30-caliber air-cooled machine gun. On this mission, some of the half-tracks were used to carry spare fuel and extra supplies and ammunition. One of them was a service vehicle equipped to provide maintenance for the tanks. Another was the battalion S-4 half-track equipped with a special radio too big to be carried by a jeep. The radio had a broad enough range of frequencies to reach Third Army headquarters from Hammelburg, and it was manned by the battalion radio operator, John Sidles. This radio was not voice powered but was operated with a Morse key, i.e., messages were transmitted in dots and dashes.

Finally, there was part of a reconnaissance platoon— nine men in three jeeps—under the command of Second Lieutenant Norman Hoffner. Included in his group was an interpreter, Private First Class Irving Solotoff. There were also a medical jeep, Baum's command jeep, his assistant's jeep (commanded by Sergeant Ellis Wise), a maintenance jeep and Major Stiller's jeep. At the final count, Task Force Baum would set out with fifty-three vehicles carrying 294 men.

Task force commander Abe Baum was born on March 29, 1921, in the Borough of the Bronx in New York City. He was the son of a Russian-Jewish immigrant, Harry Baum, a hard worker who married an American-born woman. Harry Baum wanted his sons to grapple with unpleasant, difficult situations. Harry applied iodine to a cut instead of Mercurochrome because iodine stung. The sting helped a boy learn how to deal with momentary pain. Harry wanted his sons to apply logic, good judgment and self-control in crucial moments. While the Great Depression of the 1930s did not devastate the Baum family, it damaged it. Abe's father, deep in debt, lost his business, but he refused to declare bankruptcy. Instead, he went back to work as a pattern maker in the garment district in midtown New York City. And he paid back his creditors every dollar that he owed.

At sixteen, Abe decided to drop out of James Monroe High School and learn a trade so he could support himself and no longer burden his family. He studied at the McDowell School of Costume Design and then his father wangled him a job as a pattern maker and a cutter in the factory where Baum Senior was the production manager. Abe made $12 a week in 1937 and a year later was up to $17. When he locked the boss in the designing room and demanded a raise to $37, the boss gave in—principally because the prevailing wage for Baum's job was $90 a week and he was paying Baum less because he was underage.

Joining a long line of volunteers at 39 Whitehall Street in downtown Manhattan, Abe signed up the day after Pearl Harbor. He failed the eye test for the Army Air Forces. A sergeant figured that Baum's profession as a pattern designer qualified him for the Engineers, not realizing that while a pattern designer might produce tools and dies, this pattern designer cut ladies' apparel. Nevertheless, Abe went off to Fort Belvoir, Virginia, for basic training with the Engineers.

At twenty, Abe was tall (6 feet 2 inches), thin (167 pounds), stubborn, tough, articulate and proud. And like countless boys from urban, industrial America, he found the army tough going. The Regular Army had a distinctly southern and rural cast between the wars. Even in war time, the rural South still contributed a proportionately higher number of volunteers than industrial and urban areas. Rural and small town America does not like urban New Yorkers. Rural and small town America, as represented in an army barracks, can make life miserable for urban New Yorkers.

From Belvoir, Abe went to Fort Benning, Georgia, for

duty with the 17th Engineering Battalion, a component of General Patton's 2d Armored Division. Patton required each unit to schedule two hours a day for boxing, wrestling or judo. The noncommissioned officers used this schedule as punishment. They mismatched the enlisted men they didn't like. One of these NCOs disliked Baum, who constantly defended an undersized Jewish-Dutch diamond cutter from his harassment and bullying. The NCO put Baum in the ring with a 250-pounder who liked the bout no better than Abe; the two men faked their fighting. The enraged NCO got into the ring with Baum to demonstrate the finer points of boxing, not realizing that Abe was a good boxer. Abe broke his jaw.

In his next bout, Abe's opponent was smaller than he and had a bent-in nose and cauliflower ears. The scuttlebutt had it that he was Johnny Cook, a former welterweight contender. In the first round, Baum kept him away, but near the end of the second, Cook gave him one in the balls. When Abe doubled over in agony, Cook laid a left across his mouth.

The next day, Abe was called to headquarters where he once again met Cook, this time in company with a man who he was told was the famous wrestler Man Mountain Dean, who was in charge of the division boxing program. "Dean" and Cook wanted Abe to box for the 2d Armored, but he refused, saying, "I came to fight the enemy, not other Americans." The NCOs promptly increased his shit details.

In 1942, there were only two ways out of an armored unit. One was to volunteer for paratroop training; the other was to apply for officer candidate school. Abe applied for OCS. On the day he had to face his examiners, the NCOs deliberately assigned him to garbage detail, and so he appeared in his malodorous fatigues. Nevertheless, he passed muster; he felt it was because he had such a booming voice that he made the windows rattle when he delivered marching commands.

Abe found OCS difficult. It was seventeen weeks of rigorous field and classroom training. He did well enough in the field but he was lost in the classroom. He studied the subject instead of studying for the test. A college graduate put him wise. The grad showed Abe how to anticipate questions from past tests. Thus, Abe was able to pass the course. He was commissioned a second lieutenant of armored infantry at Fort Knox, Kentucky, in the late summer of 1942. Baum was assigned to the 4th Armored Division as a replacement officer and sent to the California desert near Needles. He shipped with the 4th overseas to England in the spring of 1944.

The 10th Armored Infantry Battalion, of which Abe was a member, left Dorchester, England, on 9 July and boarded a Liberty ship the following day, the half-tracks swinging on high as they were hoisted aboard. On the 11th the ship arrived at the Normandy beachhead. Abe saw the horizon festooned with silver antiaircraft balloons. For a radius of 10 miles, freighters, corvettes, destroyers and convoy ships were waiting to unload or preparing to return across the Channel. Hundreds of LCIs, LCVPs and LSTs chugged through the water. Utah Beach was a frenzy of bulldozers and trucks, jeeps and tanks; crates of ammunition, clothing, rations, bedding and shoes were stacked like haphazard pyramids. Rails glistened in the sunlight. Field artillery pieces, packed cheek by jowl, awaited gunners, their shells stacked alongside on the sand. Utah Beach, Baum thought, had become the Times Square of Europe.

The men and half-tracks of the 10th Armored Infantry Battalion were put ashore on D Day plus 36 and proceeded to move inland with the division. On 17 July, the 4th Armored Division took over the front held by the 4th Infantry Division south of Carentan in the apple orchard country of Normandy.

The countryside was divided by endless numbers of hedgerows, mounds of earth packed 8 to 10 feet high and made compact by the tentacle roots of hedges. The 4th Armored went over to the attack at once. To clear the hedgerows they fought dismounted as ground infantry, footsloggers, while German mortar shells danced along the parapets. Artillery pounded incessantly. Baum urged his men forward, feeling a confidence and a strength he had never before known. He was a competitor by nature, a combatant. He was patriotic, coming from an immigrant milieu that never doubted the sanctity of the American way.

As he and his men went forward, he knew he could do what the army had trained him to do—fight intelligently and fiercely. Baum saw that some officers lacked the will to fight while others sometimes lacked expertise and confidence. He was nicknamed "Able" and he won two Bronze Stars in the fighting in France, and a Silver Star at the Battle of Troyes.

In December, Baum was given joint command of a task force and ordered to make his way into Bastogne during the fighting to encircle it.

Baum saw panic on his way in: artillerymen deserting their guns under small-arms fire, lines of soldiers who had thrown away their rifles, jeep drivers searching frantically for a headquarters. When Baum reported to the G-3 of the 101st Airborne Division, that officer turned him over to the combat command of another armored division whose colonel didn't know where his troops were.

In rushing to Bastogne, Baum's task force had crossed into another army's zone. When he learned this, General

Patton said, "I want that son of a bitch back here. I want him back as fast as shit goes through a sick duck."

Baum complied and drove back at a high rate of speed while German infantrymen took potshots at his careening jeep. A week later, the 4th Armored had to fight its way along the same route into Bastogne to relieve the 101st, which was almost out of food and ammunition, and in dire straits despite the legendary reply, "Nuts!" sent by General McAuliffe to the enemy when the Germans demanded his surrender.

The constant fighting took its toll on the men of the 4th Armored. From July 1944 to late March 1945, eight months, it had been constantly engaged. It had lost over half of its original personnel, and even with replacements, most units were far under strength. By the time the division had reached Aschaffenburg, the men were exhausted, punchy from endless exertion and fear.

Baum was bone tired, too. Like the other men, he craved sleep. Whenever there was a short lull in the fighting, he napped, sleeping wherever he could. Abe's former commander, General Arthur West, has written, "Even though he was a staff officer, Baum was always out front. There were occasions when he, by example, shamed me into doing things on the battlefield that I otherwise would not have done."

The 10th Armored Infantry was about to ask Baum to set another example, this one impossible.

In the summer of 1944, young William Weaver graduated from the Armored School at Fort Knox as a second lieutenant and volunteered immediately for paratroop training at Fort Benning. Bill was twenty-one years old, handsome and blue eyed; his father was a West Pointer, Major

General William Weaver, who commanded the 8th Infantry Division in combat in France.

Young Weaver despaired of seeing action and wrote his father that the "damn war will end before I ever get to Europe." Shortly thereafter he received orders to report to the Third Army as an aide-de-camp to General Patton. On his way there, he got leave to visit his father at the front. It was there that he learned he wasn't going to be Patton's aide; he would be working for Patton, however, but in D Company, 37th Tank Battalion. And the very next morning, he found himself in the lead tank on his way, penetrating Germany, his platoon sergeant having informed him it was SOP, standard operating procedure, for the platoon leader to be in the lead tank. Ruefully the sergeant had added that the platoon had lost three lieutenants in the past month. War was far more dangerous than Bill Weaver had imagined. On his first day of combat, the afternoon of 25 March, his lead tank approached the railroad bridge leading over the Main River to the city of Aschaffenburg. He ordered an immediate halt on the west bank when he spotted two 500-pound bombs lashed to the underpinnings of the bridge with wires leading to the east bank. He radioed Colonel Abrams for instructions.

Abrams replied tersely, "You've done an excellent job. Proceed."

Weaver took off his headset for a moment and stared at it. He couldn't believe he had heard right. He fitted the headphones over his ears and asked, "May I have clarification of my orders, sir?"

"Get your ass over the bridge, sonny."

Weaver went over the bridge slowly, hoping the infantry had dismantled the bombs properly.

*   *   *

During the afternoon of 26 March, Captain Carter Ogden, the 37th Tank Battalion supply officer, was sitting in the mess with Major Alexander Stiller to whom he had been assigned as liaison while the preparations for Task Force Baum progressed. Ogden remembered the story of Stiller's association with General Patton. He had first served with Patton in World War I. Between the wars, he had been a Texas Ranger. He had reenlisted with the outbreak of war in 1941 in hopes of fighting again with Patton. Stiller said he had written asking for an assignment. The general approved. Stiller expected to drive a tank. Instead, Patton had made him one of his aides; Stiller had been with him throughout the war in Africa, Sicily, France and now in Germany.

Knowing this, Ogden ventured to say to Stiller, "I guess you'll get your fill of action and excitement on Task Force Baum." He then added the observation that such a small force wouldn't have much of a chance to succeed.

Stiller replied, "Abrams wanted to send a whole damned combat command. Maybe he's right, but the general is convinced that a small task force will be sufficient."

"And he asked you to go along as insurance?" said Ogden joking.

"No," Stiller replied. "Patton asked me, all right. He asked me to volunteer for the trip, but when a general asks an aide to volunteer, he's ordering the aide to go along."

"Why?" asked Ogden.

The leathery major stared at the horizon and then turned his pale blue eyes on Ogden. "Patton wants me to go along because I'll recognize Johnny Waters, his son-in-law. He's a prisoner at Hammelburg."

Carter Ogden wasn't sure what to say, so he said, "And

you're going so they don't bring back the wrong man."

Stiller nodded. "Do you remember about Waters being taken prisoner in Africa and Little Bea, that's Patton's daughter, saying, 'Pappy'll get him back'?"

"No," said Ogden. "I don't know anything about Patton's family."

"There might be another reason, too," said Stiller. "George would like to show MacArthur that he also can liberate prisoner of war camps."

Ogden understood this immediately. In January in a glorious exploit, General Douglas MacArthur had authorized a special raid that had liberated 5,000 American prisoners of war from two Japanese camps in the Philippines.

"Patton says he wants to make Cabanatuan [where 500 of the POWs were] look like a Boy Scout hike," Stiller added.

After Second Lieutenant William J. Nutto, CO of the 37th's C Company, pulled his medium tanks back from Aschaffenburg to the bivouac, he checked his casualties and inspected the damage to his vehicles. One of his tankers offered him a drink from a canteen. Nutto swallowed several generous pulls of green, sweetish liquor and sat down on the rear deck of one of his tanks. He promptly fell asleep. He had been in battle for three days straight.

Sometime later, a messenger woke him to say he was wanted at headquarters. Nutto got in the jeep with the runner, and as they drove he hung his head over the side to let the wind blow in his face to counter his fatigue and the effects of the liquor.

When he walked into the 37th Tank Battalion headquarters, he saw several officers, including Major Bill

Hunter, the new battalion commander, who asked him directly, "How many tanks do you have?"

"I have eight, with two more to get ready," Nutto replied. "One is stuck and one has a track off."

"Your company is assigned to Task Force Baum," said Hunter.

As Nutto turned to leave, Captain Richard Pancake, CO of B Company hugged him. "Thank God you have more tanks than me. They were going to send my company until you got here."

Nutto still didn't know where he was going, but he knew he was going in place of Pancake, the best company CO in the battalion. Nutto was sure Pancake would do a better job even with fewer tanks.

Nutto went back to his unit and got the men working on the tank with the track off. He crawled through a ditch with a cable to the stuck tank. Sniper fire started. Nevertheless, Nutto got the cable secured and another tank pulled the stuck tank free.

It was growing dark. Nutto went to headquarters for his briefing.

Captain Ogden stopped him after the briefing. "Just get back from Hammelburg," he said, "and you'll get the Silver Star." At the time, Nutto thought it was a hell of a silly remark.

Private First Class Irving Solotoff was a member of a reconnaissance platoon, and had been for so long he had become a very nervous man. The duty of a recon platoon is to take the point, draw fire, reconnoiter and report what the battalion is up against. In doing this, the platoon is a constant target and frequently takes heavy casualties. Three or four months is a long term of service in battle. Solotoff was thankful that the war was drawing to a close and that he was going to make it home.

He was also the battalion headquarters' interpreter. He was born in Vienna of Jewish parents who immigrated to the United States when he was four years old. Fluent in German, one of Solotoff's jobs was to go to the farms and villages and arrange billeting in German homes for the top brass. He relished the job because it meant he was one of the first men into a captured town and could exercise first choice in buying valuable souvenirs.

On 26 March, Solotoff was on the outskirts of Aschaffenburg informing German families that they could either evacuate their homes or make arrangements to accommodate Americans. He rarely got an argument. But he did at the last house. Two young girls objected to both alternatives. They couldn't leave the house, they said, because their parents were dying upstairs. Solotoff said he would have to see for himself; he had heard this story before. The daughters countered by saying that their parents' condition was too critical for inspection. Looking around, it suddenly occurred to Solotoff that the parents were dying in unaccountable luxury. Then he understood: this was a whore house.

There were three more whores in the place. Adamantly, Solotoff ordered them to leave. The madam appeared and promised that if Solotoff let the girls stay, he could come back that night with five of his buddies. The house had everything for a good time—schnapps and sausage and pleasure beyond description. Solotoff allowed that there were already too many homeless Germans and agreed not to add this little group to their number. "Oboyoboyoboy," thought Solotoff as he raced back to the camp to inform his buddies of the evening he had planned for them.

At that point he was interrupted by his CO, Lieutenant Norman Hoffner. Hoffner had selected five men for a mission that night. Solotoff wasn't included. Instead, he was to report to Captain Baum. Solotoff's fantasies about the whores lasted only as long as it took Abe Baum to order him on the mission as an interpreter. Baum proved steadfastly unsympathetic to Solotoff's entreaties, saying simply, "Look, Irv, don't bring any of your junk along—especially that Luger. Just bring your own gun and ammo."

Solotoff's anticipation of a night of earthly delights quickly turned to dread. Captain Baum's reputation for advancing fearlessly under fire, even behind enemy lines, was well known. Indeed, Solotoff had some firsthand experience of action under Baum's command. To himself, he said, It's suicide to go with Baum on a mission like this.

Uncertainly, Solotoff entrusted his souvenirs—two cameras, some bottles of perfume, a bolt of lace and some Lugers—to a buddy who wasn't going.

"If anything happens to me," said Solotoff, "see that my mother gets these."

"Don't worry about it," said the friend solemnly. It was, of course, the last Solotoff ever saw of his things. The only souvenir he kept was a small mezuzah he had purchased in Paris and carried in his wallet.

While Baum was inspecting the components of the task force, Creighton Abrams and Hal Cohen were planning an attack to breach the enemy line so that Baum's column could get through. Although the bulk of Combat Command B was across the Main River, it still faced tough and experienced defenders. They did not want the task force depleted by forcing its own way through, so another force would have to break open a passageway for it. This, too, was a difficult operation.

They had to move soon—tonight, 26 March—and the breach had to be made quickly, in no more than an hour, or else Baum wouldn't be able to reach Hammelburg under the cover of darkness. If Baum were to succeed, if he were to have any chance at all, the task force had to get by the enemy before the enemy knew it was coming.

Cohen and Abrams drove along the line. To their direct front was Aschaffenburg, by now probably reinforced by German infantry. It was also a large city, which meant GIs would have to fight through a maze of narrow, curving city streets, each intersection defended by experienced German troops.

To the south of Aschaffenburg, less than a mile away over a road in American possession, was the smaller town of Schweinheim. Intelligence said the town was minimally fortified and had few defenders. Its streets were probably narrow, which afforded hard passage, but once through Schweinheim, Baum was only eight miles from the highway that led to Hammelburg.

But there were serious misgivings. Armored units almost never fought through enemy towns at night, and finding a route in the dark over unfamiliar terrain was a challenge for any task force leader. Baum, the two colonels remembered, had guided task forces through equally confusing geography before. Unfortunately, all that Baum had for guidance was a simple road map with no indications of terrain and, of course, nothing about the placement of enemy defenses.

Abrams and Cohen finally decided to punch through at Schweinheim because it looked like the easiest way. While they stood near their jeep discussing the attack, they heard a strange noise behind them. They turned and were amazed to see, barely 200 yards away, a large door opening to reveal an underground German aircraft hangar that had been dug into a hill. They saw the propellers of an Me 110 revolving faster and faster until they spun like two great merciless lathes. The pilot jockeyed the Messerschmitt out and gunned it for takeoff. It lifted into the air, its prop blast blowing the Americans' clothes back. As the two colonels watched the plane, they realized the pilot was getting away while the getting was good.

"I hope there are no more surprises like this," said the breathless Cohen as he and Abrams dashed for their jeep, the driver of which was still covering his head with his arms.

:: 3 ::

Delay at Schweinheim—

We're Going Through!

Cohen and Abrams chose B Company (medium tanks) of
the 37th Tank Battalion, commanded by Captain Richard
Pancake, and B Company of the 10th Armored Infantry,
under Captain Adrian Tessier, to prepare and secure a
route through Schweinheim. Tessier and Pancake had
simple orders: secure the main street of Schweinheim, clear
it of obstacles, and station a tank at each intersection to
protect the flanks of Task Force Baum as it sped through.

Tessier and Pancake were two of the most efficient
officers of Combat Command B, and their companies were
often paired in combat. The radio code names the two used
were original: "Chicken, this is Shit," was Pancake communicating with Tessier. Pancake had been the executive
officer of A Company until the CO of B was killed and
Abrams moved him over, promoting him to captain. Tessier
had been a first sergeant until he won a battlefield commission. A few weeks before, Tessier had shot a German
Feldmarschall (field marshal) who refused to surrender to a
captain. Tessier's ultimatum to the *Feldmarschall* was to
surrender or stay where he was forever. The *Feldmarschall*
said he would stay. Tessier made sure of it.

The two captains briefed their noncoms at 1700 hours

and moved their companies to the assembly area, an orchard between Aschaffenburg and Schweinheim. At 1800, both companies began rolling over a small dirt road through the fields toward Schweinheim, a red-roofed farm village.

Before they left, Baum said, "Pancake, Tess, I've got to get through there fast. You've never let me down. Get me that goddamn street as fast as you can." A quick start on the night of 26 March seemed to be a reasonable expectation.

The attacking units moved toward the village in a single column, tanks in the lead with infantrymen riding them and half-tracks behind carrying still more infantrymen and ammunition.

An artillery barrage boomed at 2030. The guns of the 22d Armored Field Artillery fired on Schweinheim so that all their shells landed at the same time—called "time on target" or TOT. The purpose of TOT was to pin the defenders down, allowing an attacking force to close on an enemy position.

At his jumping off point, which was on a hill overlooking Schweinheim, Pancake arranged his tanks into three platoons: four in the first, which would lead the attack; three in the second; and two in the third, which formed the reserve. The lead platoon was to proceed through the main street destroying roadblocks and tank traps and then it and the second platoon would secure the intersections to keep the Germans from mounting attacks through the side streets.

Tessier put a squad of infantry on each of the first seven tanks. Other infantry waited with the reserve tanks. When the tanks met resistance, the infantry dismounted and moved alongside, clearing pockets of defenders from houses and emplacements along the way.

Pancake said to Tessier, "The main street is a half mile

long at best. It won't take us an hour." At 2100 hours, the artillery barrage lifted and Pancake moved out immediately.

"Get in there, get in there," shouted Tessier, spurring his riflemen forward. But the two companies came upon the unexpected, and war and its exigencies once again thwarted and disappointed reasonable expectation.

For the past several weeks, the 4th Armored Division had passed through towns and villages where ashen-faced civilians with white flags stared impassively as the tanks and the half-tracks rolled by. But Schweinheim and Aschaffenburg were reinforced by determined German units, including cadets and staff from the SS officer candidate school in Aschaffenburg. Although Patton's army had conquered vast territory, the Germans had resisted all the way, always retreating in order.

German units on the Western Front were seasoned troops, well supplied and well trained, fanatical and brave. These troops lent their vigor to the populace of Schweinheim, where civilians unattached to military units also fought courageously. Old ladies dropped grenades from rooftops and young boys and old men manned machine guns with the cold fury of experienced killers.

The area was under the command of Major von Lambert, the commandant of the SS officer candidate school. This loyal Nazi summarily executed soldiers and civilians if they abandoned their posts or tried to surrender. These tough soldiers and grim civilians brought Pancake's tank column under fire when it had proceeded no more than 200 yards into Schweinheim. And the main street measured appreciably more than a half mile.

A *Panzerfaust* knocked out the first tank and set it afire, blocking the road and halting the column in its tracks. Pancake tried unsuccessfully to raise its crew on his radio.

He leaped from his own tank, the last in the column of the first platoon, and ran forward. German civilians, whom he could see hiding behind a white fence, were firing at him. Somehow Pancake had to get the lead tank out of the way. If he ordered the second one to bump it over, there was a chance it would be lost as well. Pancake ran to the jeep driven by Corporal Lester Powell. "Get that tank out of there," he said.

Powell was the company clerk, but in his native Indianapolis, he had been an undertaker, an auctioneer and the proprietor of a bookstore selling questionable literature. The men of B Company called him an "operator."

Powell gunned his jeep forward at high speed and headed for the burning Sherman. Then he clambered up its tread and dropped inside the turret. He found four dead men and a fifth unconscious with his leg blown off. After he steered the blazing medium tank up onto the right sidewalk close to the building, he hoisted the wounded man up through the hatch and lowered him to the ground. As he followed, Powell was hit and seriously wounded.

Hauling the unconscious tanker to his jeep, Powell draped him across the hood and sped back past Pancake to the rear. Pancake saw that Powell's jeep was red with blood. The next thing Powell remembered was awakening in a hospital in England several weeks later; his actions at Schweinheim earned him the Silver Star and a Purple Heart.

Although Pancake's platoon was stalled, Tessier led his infantrymen in clearing the main street house by house.

Their job was made more difficult because it was dark, the streets, narrow and winding. It was difficult to know which way to turn at the end of a street because the main route through the town was not easy to see. As if this weren't enough, Tessier's men had to fight the fanatical SS cadets and staff from the school at Aschaffenburg. Much of the antitank fire came from the cellars of the houses the GIs passed. The tankers weren't able to depress their guns sufficiently to attack these well-positioned enemy gunners who were most proficient with their *Panzerfäuste*. It therefore fell upon Tessier's infantry to keep the enemy so occupied that they couldn't fire effectively against the Americans. Often it was necessary for a squad to run through withering fire close enough to a house to lob a grenade through a window. Many didn't make it.

Tessier couldn't send his men too far forward until the halted tank column moved again. Finally, Tessier saw Pancake return to his tank and the column begin to advance.

On the small hill that overlooked Schweinheim, the tankers of the third platoon awaited their orders. Among them were tank commander Technical Sergeant Charles Paulus, maintenance Sergeant John Cortese and radio operator Technician 4th Grade Ken Jefferis. Over the radio, Jefferis heard Pancake order Sergeant Homer Miller, now the lead tanker, to get going.

Paulus, Cortese and Jefferis called the intercommunication between Pancake and Miller the "Amos and Andy Show" because each had a pronounced southern accent— Pancake was from West Virginia and Miller from the swamplands behind Mobile, Alabama.

One of these waiting tankers, using a stubby pencil and the back of a maintenance pad, recorded the following radio dialogue which he later mimeographed and circulated to division members:

"Mill-ah, you pullin' the string. Get your ass in geah. Heah?"

"Ah'm movin'."

"Whut's takin' you so long?"

"Takes time, Cap'n Wretched, takes time. They shootin' at us up heah."

"You gettin' raffle far?" asked Pancake.

"Sprinkle a little ovah heah," said Miller to his gunner. "Sprinkle a little over theah."

"Panzerfaust on yore raht flank, Mill-ah?"

"Yes, Cap'n. Either that or bull with a bugle down his throat. Sprinkle 'em some moah."

Meanwhile, Tessier had run back to the reserve tanks, which were dotted with infantrymen. These were replacements, newly assigned to the division, and this was their first combat. Tessier stalked along the road as he ordered them forward. The men moved slowly. At that moment, Lester Powell passed them in his jeep, the wounded tanker still over the hood, both bleeding badly.

"Look at that," said Tessier to the replacements. "He's wounded, but he's rescuing another wounder soldier. Everybody's got a job to do, so you sons of bitches are going down there or I'll shoot you right here in the road."

The men went down the road. They believed Tessier.

Pancake ordered his second platoon of Shermans into Schweinheim to begin sealing off the side streets. As they started moving, however, the Germans attacked their rear. Mortar fire scattered the infantry and one of the tanks dodged into a side street. From a rooftop, a German dropped a grenade which exploded next to the turret, although it did not puncture the armor. To a tanker, from inside his vehicle, however, a grenade sounds like a

Panzerfaust. Members of 4th Armored were trained to abandon their vulnerable tank as soon as it was hit; if it didn't blow up, they got back in and continued. The tankers squirmed through their hatches and the turret, dropped to the street and crawled away. The German grenadier dropped from the roof and disappeared into the turret. Somehow, he was able to kidnap the tank, a brand-new one, received by the battalion only the day before. The tank clattered up the street, then turned around and began firing toward the Americans.

The mortar fire in the rear had a paralyzing effect on the infantry and Tessier could see that it was bogged down in a small field near the edge of town. Tapping six of his men to follow him, Tessier crouched low, ran hugging the buildings, then cut through an alley, hoping to hit the enemy's flank. He and his riflemen came upon four Germans assiduously working an 8.1cm mortar. Tessier's men leaped in, rifles at the ready. One of them kicked over the mortar and Tessier herded the four Germans, three privates and an SS lieutenant, toward a wall 50 yards away. The Nazi lieutenant spat in Tessier's face and said, *"Amerikanisch* swine."* Tessier knocked his helmet off, grabbed his blond hair, forcing his head back. With his free hand, Tessier pulled his trench knife from his boot and cut the lieutenant's throat. The blood splattered the American captain's uniform. The three privates fell to the ground, hands still clasped behind their heads, two of them shouting, *"Kamerad! Kamerad!"* ("Comrade!"), the third weeping uncontrollably.

Tessier sent the Germans to the rear with a GI guard; then he worked his way back to the main street. The kidnapped tank was still firing, its machine-gun bullets loudly ricocheting off stone buildings and cobblestone street.

On the hill midway between Aschaffenburg and Schweinheim, Abe Baum waited near the front of his task force, pacing back and forth like a panther around a kraal. He saw buildings burning in the village and the flashes of gunfire like monstrous fireflies, the brightness contrasting starkly with the heavy darkness.

Mentally he reviewed the men under his command and tried to judge how they would respond during this mission. Lieutenant William Weaver, platoon commander of the light tanks, was new, brand-new. The division had received many new lieutenants and many of them were good officers. As was to be expected, it took a while for the noncoms to orient new lieutenants to the standard operating procedures that were followed by successful units. The main problem, however, was that they lacked confidence and therefore were not unreservedly aggressive. To get in and out of Hammelburg, Baum had to have scrappers. He hoped Weaver was that kind of officer.

William Nutto, who led the medium tanks, had been with the outfit for a while, but Baum knew that he had only recently taken over as company commander. Baum trusted Abrams's judgment and if Abrams thought Nutto was a good company commander, he was probably a crackerjack.

Captain Robert Lange, CO of Company A, was a recent replacement infantry officer and therefore an unknown quantity to Baum.

Baum knew Lieutenant Norman Hoffner of the recon platoon. They had worked together before and Baum was one of the officers who spoke on Hoffner's behalf when the battalion commander issued battlefield commissions. Hoffner, however, had been leading the recon platoon for a long time and Baum, knowing it was the most trying work in an infantry outfit, hoped he was not burned out.

Baum had specifically requested Technical Sergeant

Charles O. Graham's assault gun platoon. Graham was a country boy who could do what he was told. He was easily the most competent noncommissioned officer Baum had known. And Graham knew his guns; he was the premier technician in the battalion.

And there was Ellis Wise, Baum's operations sergeant who had been with him since England. Baum had trained Wise, who was especially good at reading maps. Baum depended upon Wise to orient the rest of the men for a mission.

Yes, he trusted his force, trusted it because he had to trust it and because he trusted himself.

Baum glanced at his watch again, its luminous dial mocking him. Time was his preoccupation and it was now after 2100. He climbed on the front of the lead Sherman and tried to read the action below through his binoculars. He couldn't and swore in frustration.

The men in the outfit watching Baum knew he was tough, aggressive and easy to anger if frustrated.

Baum jumped down and stalked off toward the battalion CP (command post) where Hal Cohen, still nursing his painfully throbbing butt, was monitoring the radio communications in Schweinheim. To Baum's unspoken question, Cohen said glumly, "They're stuck." Impatiently, Baum returned to his jeep.

Baum's driver and Private First Class Irving Solotoff, the interpreter, sat as quietly as they could while Baum kicked the tires and again began pacing back and forth. The delay seemed interminable.

At 2300, Stiller left his jeep to join Baum. Baum wondered if the major felt uncomfortable being a part of the mission but having no job, no role—at least no role of which Baum was aware.

"We're late," said Stiller matter of factly.

"I may not be able to reach Hammelburg before dawn. We need the cover of darkness," said Baum, his voice steely with suppressed anger. "We gotta get through and back before the Germans organize reinforcements."

"Is there another way to Hammelburg?" asked Stiller.

Baum shook his head and stared at the major, still wondering why he was going. "What's so important about those POWs in Hammelburg?" asked Baum finally.

"It's important to General Patton," said Stiller, staring straight ahead.

"We've come hundreds of miles without liberating camps," said Baum.

"Colonel Waters wasn't in any of them," said Stiller.

"Who's Colonel Waters?" asked Baum.

"He's Patton's son-in-law. Didn't you know that?"

"No. How does Patton know he's in Hammelburg?"

"He knows," said Stiller. "Johnny's been a prisoner of war for over two years and Patton has kept track of his movements all along. We're going in to get him out. I'm the only one who knows what he looks like," he added.

"Is that why you have your own jeep? To drive him back?" asked Baum.

"We've got to get there first," said Stiller.

A cold fury washed over Abe Baum. Men were dying in that town down there to break his task force out, and more would die on the way to Hammelburg—all to bring back *one* man. What difference can one man make in this war? thought Baum. For an instant, he considered aborting the mission then and there as futile, a waste of good men. And now he had to worry that word about Waters would get to the men. Solotoff had heard. Radioman John Sidles, in his nearby half-track, had heard. Soon everyone else would know why their lives were being risked. The effect on morale could be disastrous. Baum only hoped that his men would see it as he did—a job to be done.

With an effort, Baum collected himself. Cohen and Abrams had picked him because they knew he wouldn't quit. He had his orders. Baum was the kind of man and soldier who was compelled to do his best. He hoped his men would follow his example.

He looked at his watch again. Stiller did the same. It was past 2330. Baum ordered Sergeant Wise: "Tell Weaver, Nutto, Lange and Graham to get their people mounted up and ready to roll. I'm going into Schweinheim. When I get back, we're moving out."

Baum's jeep sped toward the embattled village. He saw GIs dashing from house to house, outlined by the flames. Tanks were jerking like startled beetles as their gunners fired furiously. He worked his way from tank to tank until he found Pancake, afoot again.

"I've got to go through," shouted Baum.

"It's no good," said Pancake. "I've got resistance in ten houses up ahead. Take another hour, I reckon."

There were hard words between them.

"Goddamnit, Pancake, listen to me. I can't wait any longer. Get your tanks up on the sidewalks—about every twenty yards. We'll use 'em like signposts. We're barrel-assing through. Got that? Get those damn tanks going."

Baum ran back and found Tessier. "Tess," he shouted, "get your men back. I'm coming through in five minutes. Pin down as many of the enemy as you can."

Back in his jeep, Baum raced out of the village. When he returned to his place behind the sixth tank in his column, the motors of the tanks and half-tracks were rumbling and ready. The ground vibrated and the cold March night was warmed with exhaust fumes.

On his radio, Baum gave his final orders. "We're going through. Don't stop to shoot. Bypass crippled tanks. Bulldoze them if they're in the way. Sirens, but no lights except the blackout lights. So stay close and follow the vehicle in front of you. Let's go."

Slowly the column began moving, the lead tank first, followed as soon as there was room by each succeeding vehicle. The column was arranged with the light tanks in front, then the jeeps (Baum's, Stiller's, the recon platoon's jeeps, the medics' and Sergeant Wise's jeeps), the medium tanks, the half-tracks, the assault guns and the maintenance and service vehicles.

Tankers of the 37th rode with their hatch covers open, as a moral obligation to their infantry comrades. The tankers under the command of Creighton Abrams rarely "buttoned up," that is, closed their hatches, because he believed that if a foot soldier could accompany a tank protected only by his combat jacket, then a tanker at least owed the foot soldier the advantage of tank crews with full vision. Traveling at night without lights also required the best possible view for the driver.

The sirens of the tanks were like the rebel yells of the Civil War. These, along with the thunderous roar of the engines and furious clanking of the treads, were meant to terrorize and immobilize enemy infantry. The confusion and consternation Baum hoped to create might just give him the edge he needed to cleave his way through Schweinheim. It was a dangerous tactic made worse by the hazards inherent in traveling over unknown territory in the dark.

As Task Force Baum entered Schweinheim, there was a momentary halt to the shooting—the Americans stopping to allow the column to pass, the Germans responding in turn to the slackening fire—but the unholy clamor of Baum's force made the night even more menacing. The armored column was as relentless as the waters of a flash flood coursing through a dry creek. It was a dangerous tactic. Baum knew it. The driver of the lead tank had to be cool and right, for the drivers behind him had nothing to follow but the dim specks of the blackout lights and the exhaust of the tank ahead. That exhaust glowed as bright as an acetylene torch.

There was some small-arms fire from the buildings and side streets. Tessier's men suffered. One fell. Another. But the task force was through.

:: 4 ::

Oflag XIIIB

The town of Hammelburg was founded as Hamulo Castellum in A.D. 716. In 777, Charlemagne made it part of the Carolingian Empire. Men fought over the city many times, especially during the Thirty Years War (1618–48). As the central city in the Rhön Valley, the corridor which leads into Bavaria, it was used by the Hapsburgs to defend themselves against the incursions of petty German princes and the armies of France, Sweden, Denmark and England.

The Hapsburgs erected the wall fortifications around Hammelburg in 1242 and a few years later its great Gothic cathedral was erected. With its quaint stone houses, gabled roofs, and its Renaissance-style market fountain in front of the town hall, Hammelburg was the ideal subject for a tourist postcard. In 1945, it had 6,000 inhabitants.

A mile south of the town, in the rolling, peaceful hills, green pastures, and forests, crisscrossed with narrow winding country roads, is the small hamlet of Pfaffenhausen, and less than a mile farther is the Hammelburg *Lager,* or camp, an extensive military complex built in 1918 by the German High Command as a training center.

During World War I, a small portion of the *Lager* was set aside as a POW camp for Allied soldiers, for which forty to fifty stone and wooden barracks were constructed, barracks that were not dismantled after the Armistice. In the 1920s and early 1930s, the Hammelburg *Lager* served as a school for a German work corps similar to the Civilian Conservation Corps in the United States. In the mid-1930s, Hitler secretly transformed the *Lager* into a military camp in violation of the Treaty of Versailles. The Hammelburg *Lager*, including the nearby villages of Hundsfeld and Bonnland to the south, became a training area for panzer units; the surrounding countryside became a range where German infantry was trained, particularly in antitank warfare.

With the beginning of World War II, the Germans again used part of the *Lager* as a POW camp while continuing to use the rest as a military training facility. By the end of the war, there were two separate POW camps in the hills in the northern part of the *Lager*. There was an enormous stalag, short for *Stammlager*, housing thousands of Russian, French, American, English, Canadian and Australian enlisted men. On the other side of a hill, the side facing the towns of Pfaffenhausen and Hammelburg there was an oflag, short for *Offizierslager*, housing more than 5,500 Allied officer *Kriegsgefangener* (prisoners of war) who called themselves "kriegies." At one end of the oflag was a water tower; around the barbed wire perimeter were twelve towers, each containing a machine-gun unit.

The first POWs to arrive at Oflag XIIIB were 4,000 Serbs, captured in 1941 during the Nazi invasion of Yugoslavia. Ironically, one of these men had spent four long years as a POW behind the same barbed wire during World War I. They would be joined throughout the war by a steady stream of officers from nearly all the Allied countries, including most notably the son of Soviet Premier Joseph Stalin.

The Serbian POWs constituted a significant part of the Yugoslav General Staff and officer corps and were aristocrats, a social distinction typical of the armies in many middle European countries. In March 1941, a cabal of these officers had staged a palace revolution when Prince Paul and his government signed the Axis Tripartite Pact with Nazi Germany. The generals organized a coalition government and proclaimed eighteen-year-old Prince Peter as King Peter II. On 6 April, Hitler invaded and the Serbian officers mustered to repel the invasion. Thousands boarded trains in order to be transported to their respective units. But the invading Germans were too fast and easily captured the trains with hardly a shot fired.

Since most of these Serbs were Royalists, the Germans offered them their freedom if they would fight against Mihajlović or Tito. To a man, the Serbs refused. Despite this patriotism, the postwar Communist regime in Yugoslavia confiscated their property and proscribed them. Few returned; those who did were either executed or imprisoned.

On 18 January 1945, the first of about 1,500 American officers captured in the Ardennes during the Battle of the Bulge in Belgium arrived at the camp. The Serbs were moved into another section of the camp, separated by barbed wire, to make room for the Americans in the cold, drafty, crudely constructed barracks. Each barracks, heated quite inadequately by a single stove, had forty two-tiered bunks. Although captured on 20 January, another group of twenty officers, which included young Second Lieutenant Richard Baron, arrived during the last week in February. Also in January 1945, 800 prisoners left a POW camp in Poland because of the approach of the advancing Red Army. They arrived at Oflag XIIIB in early March. The Serbs were inordinately generous with the American kriegies, sharing rations, blankets, razor blades and clothing with them.

From one of the windows of the oflag barracks, Second Lieutenant Richard Baron could see a small saucerlike depression between the hill on which the camp was located and another gentle hill rising toward Pfaffenhausen and Hammelburg. Like the other kriegies, Baron was in bad shape. Life in the camp meant unending cold, disease and hunger. Before his capture, he had been healthy, vigorous, handsome, with hazel eyes and curly hair; he was 6 feet 1 inch tall and had weighed 170 pounds. Now, though his morale was good and he was faring better than many, he was debilitated; sickness, exposure and malnutrition had left him weighing 130 pounds.

Dysentery was the scourge of POW camps. When the Germans locked their prisoners up at night, there were two pails, one for defecating and one for urinating. Each morning, a detail of kriegies cleaned the area around the overflowing cans. Typhus was common.

Like many kriegies, Baron suffered from pyorrhea induced by the lack of vitamins in the diet. He found he could endure his puffy and bleeding gums, but he despaired whenever his tongue warned him how loose his teeth had become. There was virtually no medication available except a small amount of sulfanilamide for dire emergencies.

The cold was relentless. The small, square, squat stove in each barracks threw off a low heat at best and the ration of charcoal and coal was always meager. Baron and his barracksmates rearranged their bed slats so they could secretly burn one or two at night for added warmth. In fact, any nonessential wood was sure to be scavenged for the stove.

Overshadowing these hardships, however, was hunger, constant gnawing hunger. Each barracks received a ration of dark bread in the morning. Depending on the supplies the Germans themselves had and their ever-changing attitude toward the kriegies, as well as the behavior of the prisoners, the ration ranged from one loaf for five prisoners to one loaf for twelve; the ration averaged one loaf for every eight men. On rare occasions, the kriegies were given a treat—a cubic inch of lard or margarine. Lunch and dinner consisted of watery soup made with turnips or rutabagas or even dandelion greens. It was easy enough to divide the loaves evenly, but severe anxiety gripped the men when the soup was distributed. Would one man get more than another? Would the mess detail favor its friends?

To lessen the tension, the kriegies put their bowls on the serving table and allowed the detail of ranking POWs in each barracks, who brought the pot of steaming soup from the cookhouse, to ladle it out. From across the room the waiting kriegies watched closely to see that each bowl got a dollop of the solids from the bottom of the pot. In addition, the order of the chow line was changed each day—alphabetical one day, reversed the next. Sunday dinner was a particularly excruciating ordeal (which was nevertheless exciting) because the soup contained tiny bits of horse meat. All the kriegies were extremely attentive to the distribution process, watching for any irregularity.

In fact, the diet was so meager that it was supplemented by whatever came within the grasp of the hungry kriegies; nothing—from roots and greens to rats to cockroaches—was safe.

Baron and his fellow officers rarely thought about women, but they thought, talked and dreamed about food incessantly. They made solemn resolutions that once they were free they would never go any place without a chocolate bar.

One of the officers in the barracks was Henry Baier whose family owned a bakery in Chicago. The men listened in longing silence as Baier enumerated the baked goods his family produced. Another had managed a Horn and Hard-art Automat in Philadelphia and often entertained the men with detailed descriptions of the menu.

To Richard Baron, baked Alaska and baked macaroni with cheese were as chimerical as the El Dorado. So were steaks and trout mousse. The only food he could remember vividly was army K rations. K rations came in boxes like Cracker Jack, wrapped in heavy-duty brown waxed paper. He could feel his fingers tearing the carton open.

There were K rations for breakfast, lunch and dinner. He longed for the breakfast carton, the ham-and-egg mixture, which came in a short, squat can, and a chocolate bar. Some men boasted that they earned a Purple Heart as a result of opening their ham and eggs with a bayonet. In the lunch carton was a tin of American cheese, as soft and smooth as moonlight, as yellow as processed cheese always is. In the dinner packet was a tin of Spam and a prune bar. In all three were crackers that resembled RyKrisp, and pouches of lemonade powder, coffee and sugar.

Richard Baron was no stranger to delicacies, despite his present preoccupation with K rations. The nearly twenty-two-year-old lieutenant was the son of an upper-middle-class Jewish family whose wealth derived from the paper business started by his grandfather. Baron grew up in comfortable surroundings in New York City, first on West End Avenue, then on Central Park West and then in a luxurious apartment on Sutton Place overlooking the river.

Neither the paper business nor discipline particularly

appealed to young Richard. His father, who prided himself on both, decided to ship his son off to Manlius, a select military prep school near Syracuse. Baron was graduated in 1940 and entered the University of North Carolina. He was a superior student who did well on his exams. Unfortunately he was also bored with the day-to-day classwork, and quickly used up his allotment of class cuts. Also, having come from the cloistered life at Manlius and the ever-watchful eyes of his parents at home, the freedom of college life—and the presence of coeds—went to his head. His late night activities, coupled with his aversion for early rising, kept him from doing his daily assignments. After nine months, the university expelled him. Returning home to a disappointed but still determined father, Baron was promptly enrolled at New York University where he majored in business administration.

When the war started, Baron was eager to go. He wanted to fight for his country and was beginning to feel uncomfortable staying behind as more and more of his friends signed up. Besides, the service would provide a welcome escape from the drudgery of college work. As a Manlius graduate, Baron qualified to be commissioned as a second lieutenant in the reserves after graduating as a special cadet from the Infantry Officer Candidate School at Fort Benning. However, it took Baron longer to win his commission than the other special cadets.

Baron didn't graduate with his class at Fort Benning; he had been caught in an off-limits gambling hall in the nearby sin capital of the South—Phenix City, Alabama. The price was immediate dismissal from OCS. After months of badgering the commanding officer, his staff and some of the instructors for a second chance, Baron was reinstated, the main reason being that he had been such an excellent student. While campaigning for reinstatement, Baron had to work off a $1,300 debt at one of the gambling houses; he did that by working as a shill at the rate of $75 a night, a task he thoroughly enjoyed. Once reinstated, however, he never repeated his mistake, and avoided Phenix City assiduously.

After he was commissioned as a second lieutenant in late 1943, his first assignment was to Camp Wheeler in Macon, Georgia. This was one of the five basic infantry replacement training centers (BIRTC) where new infantry draftees and enlistees received their basic training. After a stint there, he was transferred to the Shenango, Pennsylvania, staging area, then to the Hampton Roads port of embarkation in Newport News, Virginia, preparatory to being shipped overseas.

The staging area at Shenango was known to be under tight security. Baron had heard that once inside the installation, there were only two ways to get out: a death in the family, or to dispose of your car before embarkation. Baron made sure he arrived at Shenango with a car, thus to be able to get one last emergency leave.

On Mother's Day 1943, Baron sailed for overseas on the troop transport *Santa Rosa* as an infantry replacement officer. During the crossing, as part of one of the largest convoys yet to cross the Atlantic, the ships were under repeated U-boat attack, despite a huge destroyer escort. The troops, of course, had no idea of their destination until they saw the outline of Gibraltar and then the coast of North Africa. Once the convoy entered the Mediterranean, it was also subject to air attack, and a number of ships were sunk. The Allied command believed German agents in neutral Gibraltar reported all convoys to the enemy.

When the convoy was not under attack, Baron enjoyed

life at sea. He ate relatively well in the officers' ward room. There was the proverbial poker game every night. He also became friendly with the ship's supply officer, an old acquaintance from school, with whom he spent much time playing chess. This renewed friendship was to be helpful to Baron subsequently.

The destination of the convoy turned out to be Algeria. The ships disembarked their troops and matériel at Mers el-Kébir, some 6 or 7 miles from Oran. While waiting for further assignment, the troops were sent to the hated first IRTC, the infantry replacement depot in Canastel, also just outside of Oran.

During the six or seven weeks while at Canastel, Baron was often in Oran and, because of his fluency in French, he met and became friends with many families in the European quarter. In particular, there was the Zemor family, French Jews who allowed Baron to use their car because he could get gasoline for it. After the final liberation of North Africa by the Allies, General Charles de Gaulle drove through the streets of Oran in an open touring car. Baron, who was visiting the Zemors, stood with them on the balcony and waved. It was an unforgettably thrilling and exciting experience to cheer the living symbol of the Free French and to share the joy of this family at the liberation of their country.

A second, even more transforming experience for the young Baron was attending the first postliberation Rosh Hashanah services with the Zemors. All the Jews in the city went to Oran's only temple, one of the oldest synagogues in the world, overflowing it and filling up the streets outside. And, as the first religious holiday that they could celebrate as truly free, the Nazi-inspired anti-Jewish regulations of the Vichy French government now being all rescinded, the holy days were charged with extra meaning for all. Baron, who had never been a practicing Jew, was suddenly acutely aware of his heritage and what thanking God for one's blessings really meant.

Baron and several other lieutenants were assigned to bird-dog hundreds of enlisted men to Tunis via Algiers on a narrow-gauge railroad. The GIs often disembarked to push the train up hills, and whenever the engine stopped for fuel or water or at stations, hundreds of Arabs clustered around, bartering fresh water for cigarettes, clothing or candy. A GI could sell a mattress cover, which the Arabs used as a caftan for $20. The Arabs stole as much as they bartered and they had no compunction about offering their daughters or their sisters for a pair of GI socks.

The GIs gave as good as they got. Baron saw soldiers carefully fill an empty cigarette carton with pebbles or newspaper, put two packs on top, and haggle with Arab traders until the engine began grinding forward. The deal was only consummated when the train gathered enough speed to leave the Arabs without redress. Often enough, the melons for which the cigarettes had been traded were made juicy by Arab piss.

Baron saw a GI palm off a bottle of Atabrine, an antimalarial medicine, to an Arab as bonbons. Atabrine, an artificial substitute for quinine (supplies of which from Malaya had been cut off by the Japanese), was issued in GI chow lines throughout the Mediterranean area. It was so bitter that it was best to take it with food to mask the taste and to cushion the effect of the drug on the stomach. Many soldiers preferred to risk malaria rather than take the foul-tasting, bitter Atabrine. The Arab who received the Atabrine "bonbons" poured half the bottle into his hand and popped them into his mouth. His smiles almost instantly turned to surprise and his face screwed in horror; he spat the foul medicine on the ground and turned in rage and hatred to curse his tormentor.

Baron crossed to Sicily in a small replica of the *Île de France*. Even on this miniature version, there were excellent cuisine and deluxe quarters.

Upon disembarking, Baron requisitioned a civilian car, a Fiat, for transportation. When the company was put on trains for transportation from Licata to the 45th Division near Palermo, he simply had the car pushed onto the train and took it with him. While such requisitioning was very common during the war, the vehicle was usually returned to the civilian after being used. In this case when it was not, the civilian objected and word was sent to the 45th Division. To appease the local authorities, Baron was sent back to North Africa, to Aïn-el-Turk. There he was given temporary duty as a military policeman, housed at a well-furnished beachfront villa, and performed the essential duty of checking to make sure that the nurses assigned to the area (it was mainly used for rest and rehabilitation) were wearing their dog tags. Occasionally, he was sent into Oran for a desk assignment, disposing of cases involving drunk and/or disorderly GIs. At every meal at the luxurious officers' mess, Italian prisoners of war provided chamber music, thus giving young Baron his first taste of European culture, fine food and wine.

There had never been consideration given to any serious punishment of Baron and after a few weeks he went into combat. In October 1943, he rejoined the 45th Division.

The 45th was the Oklahoma National Guard division, but it included men from Colorado, New Mexico and Texas. Justices of the peace were colonels, gas-pump operators were majors and promotions for officers who did not come from the Southwest were slow. Nevertheless, combat soon winnowed the ranks of the political appointees, and soon only the best field officers remained, the rest being shipped back home and replaced with able officers who were promoted from within the division.

The 45th's shoulder patch consisted of a yellow thunderbird against a red shield and its motto was "These colors don't run." It was an appropriate tag for a great division. It was cartoonist Bill Mauldin's original division, and journalist Ernie Pyle had spent time with it. As a vital part of Patton's Seventh Army, it had invaded and fought through Sicily. It was transferred to the Fifth Army under General Mark Clark and established the beachhead at Salerno at the beginning of the Italian campaign.

Baron was assigned as a rifle platoon leader in L Company of the 3d Battalion, 157th Infantry Regiment, and his first taste of battle in Italy was near Venafro in the rugged mountains around Cassino, in what the Allies called the German Winter line. He was fortunate to have as his platoon sergeant an American Indian, Van T. Barfoot, who later received the Congressional Medal of Honor and a battlefield commission. Barfoot was the best possible model of a combat soldier and Baron quickly learned the ropes.

For the next four months, there were endless attacks and counterattacks resulting only in small advances over the cold, wet, muddy terrain. When the division finally gained one mountain, it found itself staring up at another; and there on the more advantageous higher ground were the Germans digging new emplacements.

Toward the end of January 1944, the 45th, along with the 3d Division (a Regular Army unit) and Darby's First Ranger Battalion was pulled back from the mountains to the Naples area and replaced by French forces. These were Moroccan: fierce, feared troops called *goumiers*. Their specialty was infiltrating enemy positions at night, silently slitting the throat of every man they could find, then slipping away. Ironically, after these troops replaced the Americans, they sustained horrendous casualties at the hands of an American Army Air Forces bomber group who mistakenly bombed the "goums" at Venafro instead of the Germans at nearby Cassino. From a bomber at high altitude, these two mountains, which are near each other, look similar.

The 45th and 3d Divisions, and the Rangers, were rested and resupplied to prepare them for another amphibious landing. On 24 January, D plus 2, the 45th was taken by landing craft to Anzio where the Allies hoped to relieve the pressure on the Cassino line by attacking the German rear. Although there was virtually no initial resistance, the invading forces paused to land and organize reserves instead of striking inland immediately, allowing Feldmarschall Albert Kesselring time to rush German reinforcements to contain the narrow beachhead. The American force was just able to hold on by its fingernails. The Germans in the mountains that ring Anzio directed a fierce and unremitting artillery fire onto the beachhead. The accurate 88mm guns and the even more accurate small-arms fire kept every GI in his foxhole. It was as though the 45th were fighting a war on a pool table where a master cueman sank everything that moved.

Baron sometimes thought of the advantages of being an enlisted man who didn't have the responsibility of sending men every day into mortal danger and exposing them as well as himself to constant peril. Further, he disliked the infantry, especially the marching. He filed applications for transfer to the Air Forces because he could fly a plane, and to the Navy because he was an expert sailor and navigator.

He even tried to apply to West Point. Of course he knew that these applications would never receive serious consideration but he enjoyed the fantasy, which helped amuse him and his friends. What sustained him at Anzio was the knowledge that he was responsible for his men.

He was a canny leader, still ready to take risks. Once he commandeered a DUKW, an amphibious truck, nicknamed "Duck" by the army, motored out to the *Santa Rosa,* which he had learned was in the harbor. His friend the supply officer, who was still on board, loaded the Duck with food for Baron's company. Another time, he led a patrol onto the experimental farm that Mussolini maintained near Anzio and bagged what turned out to be three milk cows. Baron, the city boy, hadn't known there were two kinds of cattle; nevertheless, the week of fresh beef brought no complaints from his men.

On the night of 19–20 March 1944, Baron led his platoon in an attack against a farmhouse. The men crawled through a drainage ditch, raced 1,000 yards to the barbed wire, crawled through and flushed out the defenders.

Baron posted his platoon for the inevitable counterattack. But he had forgotten a detail—the outhouse. And it was from there that a German machine gun opened up, and two of Baron's platoon went down, as did Baron, his left arm torn by bullets. After the machine gunner was killed, Baron ripped off his belt to use as a tourniquet, which he tightened with his teeth and right hand. Ordered to withdraw, he got his platoon back safely, including the wounded.

When he was evacuated on a stretcher-bearing jeep, Baron couldn't help noticing that the vehicle was not fired upon. It was driving across an area where normally if a man held up a finger it was shot off, where men pissed in their helmets during the day and emptied them at night because it was too dangerous to move around. And yet, here he was being driven through the scene as though they were on a Sunday drive.

At the battalion aid station, he received plasma, checked on the other wounded, and then was evacuated to the 10th Field Hospital.* At the field hospital where Baron was sent was a surgical team from the Second Auxiliary Surgical Group. The group was composed of highly qualified medical professionals, all of whom had voluntarily left lucrative practices and top jobs in the U.S. Each surgical team included a surgeon, an assistant surgeon, an anesthetist, two corpsmen and a nurse. Baron's arm was operated on and put in a cast by one of these top-notch surgical teams.

Before he could be moved to a hospital ship to be taken to Naples, the hospital ship was destroyed in an air raid. The raid also killed or wounded a number of doctors and nurses in the hospital on shore. While waiting for the next hospital ship to arrive, Baron was visited by many of his friends who assured him that he had a "million-dollar" wound—one not mutilating or resulting in permanent disability, but serious enough to require him to be sent home.

When he finally reached Naples the next day, there

---

*These field hospitals were mobile units, usually housed in tents near a battalion aid station close to the front lines, so care for critically wounded men was speedy and efficient. (Those men less seriously wounded were sent farther back to an evacuation hospital.) Mobile field hospitals in WWII were the precursors of the MASH (Mobile Army Surgical Hospitals) used later in Korea, only there they were no longer truly mobile because helicopters were used to bring the men to them for medical care and the lines of war were stable.

were ambulances at the dock to transfer the wounded to the hospital area at Bagnoli, the old world's fair grounds outside the city. While they were being loaded into the ambulances, Red Cross girls distributed doughnuts and coffee, a welcome reminder of home.

After more medical treatment, Baron became an ambulatory patient. In his ward, he met Vance Bourjaily, the novelist, who was a volunteer ambulance driver. Baron also acted as the unofficial interpreter for French general Meurice Chevillon—second in command to General Leclerc—who was in the hospital recovering from wounds.

In June, after the final breakout from Anzio and the liberation of Rome, many of Baron's friends from the 45th Division again came to see him. The 45th was assigned to an area near Salerno where it was trained for the invasion of southern France. When his friends complained that they wanted to go to Rome on their passes but couldn't, Baron asked why. The reason was that they had been given responsibility for about twenty captured German vehicles. Baron's response was "Sign them over to me on a memorandum receipt and I'll get rid of them for you."

Later, in Naples, Baron asked a Red Cross worker why it was so hard for them to get ice cream. The worker said he could get plenty of ice cream, but that he lacked vehicles to transport it. Baron offered the twenty captured German cars and trucks. In exchange, he was given a Red Cross sedan for his own use while he was in Naples. Baron had the beat-up Plymouth reconditioned by a friend in ordnance. A new ¾-ton Dodge engine was substituted for the old Plymouth motor. Not only did he now have transportation, but, because it was a civilian vehicle and not an army vehicle, he was allowed to carry nonmilitary personnel in it. During the rest of his convalescence, Baron toured southern Italy, including Sorrento and Capri.

Despite his travels and adventures during his convalescence, Baron was reclassified because of his wounds—he was unable to straighten his arm. He was scheduled to be sent back to the United States. Among his many friends at the hospital was the Chief of Medicine, Dr. Philip Handelsman, who let him use the X-ray lab to develop his 35-mm pictures and invited him to use the beach club restricted to doctors and nurses. When Baron went to say good-bye and to thank Handelsman for his kind treatment, he was in for a surprise. The doctor could tell by Baron's jaundiced appearance that he was seriously ill.

As a result, he was put to bed immediately in a neighboring nonsurgical ward, where he lay deathly ill with hepatitis for the next two weeks.

By the time Baron recovered from the hepatitis, his arm had also recovered to such an extent (he had regained virtually the complete use of it) that the army re-reclassified him and assigned him again to the 45th Division, which was now in France.

He was glad to be back doing what he had been trained to do, and while it meant more war and more fighting, at least it wasn't Anzio. He rejoined the 45th in time for Thanksgiving dinner in Alsace-Lorraine.

Baron was assigned to D Company, the heavy-weapons company of the 1st Battalion, 157th Infantry Regiment, armed with water-cooled .50-caliber machine guns and 81mm mortars. His platoon of machine guns was often deployed in support of C Company, commanded by First Lieutenant John Ernest Floyd and his executive officer, First Lieutenant William Meiggs. Floyd, a mountain boy from North Carolina, knew how to pick his way across terrain, and Baron always had his .50-calibers placed perfectly to provide cover for Floyd and his men. The bond between these officers was more than friendship; it was the deep respect and trust that develops from repeatedly protecting each other in life-and-death situations. Baron provided cover fire for Floyd; in other situations, it was Floyd who protected the machine guns.

The 45th Division was such an effective fighting force, so dependable that the army commanders used it regularly for difficult missions. The men of the 45th resented the fact that they were always sent to do the heaviest fighting. The division retook the Maginot Line, penetrated the Siegfried line and began fighting in the Vosges Mountains, on 12 December 1944. Entering Germany, the 158th Field Artillery had opened the way for the 157th Infantry Regiment. The men were weary, exhausted by the constant fighting in the bitter cold. They had been amazed to see heavy shells bounce off the German pillboxes.

Baron heard about the late December German counteroffensive in the Ardennes region—the Battle of the Bulge—when he was warned about the possibility of Germans wearing American uniforms (taken from newly captured troops) to create confusion behind the lines. Many of the Seventh Army's divisions—and the 45th was a part of the Seventh Army—were transferred to reinforce other areas of the front where the Germans had broken through. This left the Seventh Army spread thin.

When the Germans realized that their advance in the Ardennes had been stopped, they also realized the weakened condition of the Seventh Army in the Haguenau Forest. Thus, on New Year's Eve, they moved south with four rested and well-equipped divisions to try to break the American line. Their objective was Reipertswiller, which controlled the road across the Alsatian plains, giving them clear access to Strasbourg. If they could break through here, they could bottle up the northern American armies by cutting off their lines of supply.

The 45th was moved up to contain the attack. In trying to cross one area of swamp, 2d Battalion found it impossible to use the rubber boats. A company that tried to wade across was turned back by machine-gun fire. Two more efforts were repelled during the night. G Company of the 2d Battalion finally succeeded, and entered the town of Bundenthal, reaching the cemetery area. Machine-gun fire split the advancing column, pinned the two lead platoons down and caused the other platoons to withdraw. Patrols sent in to relieve them were turned back by heavy enemy fire. Nearby, C Company, Floyd with Baron's machine-gun platoon supporting, was ordered to spearhead an attack on Bundenthal to link up with and rescue the two platoons already there. They moved down a hill under enemy fire and began infiltrating toward the town. Most were able to cross the antitank trenches before dawn. When A and B Companies tried to follow, however, they were beaten back. The result was that now there were two platoons (G Company) trapped in the town, and two platoons (C Company) trapped on the edge of the town. Although no patrols were able to reach the trapped men, two GIs from G Company were able to escape; they reported that seventy men were still alive but were out of food and low on ammunition.

Immediate plans to rescue the trapped units were made by Colonel James, the acting regimental commander, and Colonel Ralph Krieger (1st Battalion commander) and Colonel Russell Funk (2d Battalion). They proposed using "boxed" artillery. Exact coordinates of enemy positions and the positions of the trapped platoons were fed to the artillery commanders by spotters and special patrols. In the late afternoon, a squad from Lieutenant Kenneth's B Company, with medics, reached the trapped units, under cover of a heavy artillery barrage. The units were completely surrounded with artillery fire; then the men slowly made their way back to safety, moving inside the "box" of artillery which moved at a walking pace and kept the enemy pinned down.

Over the next two weeks, the enemy consolidated its position. It had strung extra barbed wire, laid mines and erected massive roadblocks of felled trees. The Germans had also, more importantly, punched out the Bitche salient, overrunning the newly placed 70th Division, and exposing the left flank of the 45th Division. It thus became imperative for the 45th to pull back in order to protect its flank. A group of combat engineers tried to cover the retreat by blowing bridges, blocking roads and laying mines. The men of the 157th were bitter; this was the first time they had had to retreat.

On the evening of 13 January, the 157th Infantry moved into Reipertswiller to relieve the 276th Regiment of the 70th Division. The fighting was heavy and the first attack made little progress. On the morning of the 15th, the 3d Battalion was the only one to take its objective. As a result, it found itself on a saddle between two hills some 1,500 yards in advance of the adjacent units, with both its flanks completely unprotected. On 16 January, there were fierce attacks of massed enemy artillery, tank, rocket, mortar and machine-gun concentrations against the 3d Battalion dug in along the salient. In preparation for further counterattack, the 1st Battalion—C Company under Floyd, and Baron's machine-gun platoon in support—was sent to reinforce the 3d Battalion.

Lieutenant Colonel Ralph Krieger from Abilene, Texas, commander of the 1st Battalion, crawled up into a ravine to talk to Baron and Floyd while they were pinned down by mortar fire. After he explained the importance of reaching the 3d Battalion, Floyd responded, "Ralph, we'll sure do our best to get there, but if we make it we'll never be able to get out."

As soon as the next break in the mortar barrage occurred, Floyd and Baron took their men up the ravine under heavy small-arms fire and reached their objective. They lost about a dozen men in this simple last run. The expected counterattack developed, was repelled, but not without leaving enemy troops between the companies. G Company, supported by two light tanks, mopped up these troops and dug in to support 3d Battalion.

With each subsequent attack, however, the enemy increasingly infiltrated the area occupied by the beleaguered Americans, and soon had them virtually isolated from the main American force. Hard fighting throughout the next few days piled up German dead. But by the end of 19 January, the enemy had established itself to the rear of the surrounded men. A three-jeep supply mission was ambushed. Two light tanks were able to fight their way in with supplies of ammunition and food. Nothing else reached the group.

The artillery fire was unremitting and the small-arms fire devastating. By 20 January, there was no more food, no fresh water except what could be melted from snow, no medical supplies and little ammunition. Two machine gunners were killed beside Baron as they swiveled to find the enemy. For a time, Baron himself manned the gun; it was the first time in the war that he felt invincible, raking the forest in a wide traverse. There were now only about 200 survivors of the 1,000 committed to the battle. On both the 18th and 19th, a German appeared with a white flag, asking their surrender. Both time, the white flag was not seen until too late, and the unceasing American fire forced the envoy to retreat.

Early on the 20th, Baron heard the grinding gears and tracks of German tanks moving up. In the morning, the shelling suddenly stopped. German small-arms fire slackened, then ceased. A truce. While the small group of German and American officers parleyed, the GIs got out of their foxholes like men released from dark solitary to fresh air and sunlight. They stumbled on stiff limbs and licked their lips, swollen from thirst. The German demand was that the Americans surrender by 1700 hours. If not, the Germans were going to attack en masse and kill everyone. The enemy also indicated on the map where the American lines were and where the German forces were positioned, trying to show the Americans the hopelessness of the situation. Baron looked around at his shivering men—their clothes were wet, they were gaunt and hollow eyed. They were doing their best to help the wounded, of which there were many.

After the parley, the American officers discussed the proposal. There were no votes for surrender. The main concern was how they were going to escape from the hill and link up with the main force. A radio message from regimental headquarters ordered the group to retreat by attacking to the southwest. As the attack began, full regimental artillery would be used to box them in, pin down the enemy and escort the trapped men, within the ring of fire, back to the lines. Unfortunately, when the maneuver began, the artillery was off target. Bad weather, poor spotter visibility and the difficult terrain led to artillery hits on the Americans and no damage to the Germans dug in around them. As a result the boxed artillery, which had worked so well before at Bundenthal, was called off.

The Germans, who didn't know if the Americas were attacking or surrendering, resumed their fire. Floyd and Baron saw that the GIs who had started over the top of the hill toward the southwest were throwing down their weapons and raising their hands. Leading their men at a run down the other side of the hill in an effort to outflank the enemy, they were also soon blocked and had to surrender.

The enemy who had overcome these six American infantry companies was the 11th SS Regiment of the Sixth Mountain Division, a full-strength assault unit trained in Finland, nicknamed "Nord." The new prisoners were treated with honor and respect, and not threatened, as some had feared. Baron was allowed to lead a squad of men back to collect the wounded and to bury the dead. Later the GIs were led into the woods, where they were fed hot soup and stew from the enemy's company kitchen. The 11th SS had engaged the 45th on many previous occasions and they respected their American foes as soldiers. This was why they treated them so well. Later in the evening, the prisoners were turned over to newly arrived MPs and taken to the rear.

The Germans marched the 176 POWs to a nearby town where they lodged them in a jail. The next morning the captured "Thunderbirds" were paraded around the square for the benefit of German newsreel photographers. Baron, three other officers and a technical sergeant were then separated from the rest of the prisoners. The Germans picked the sergeant because he was an artillery observer who they thought would have information about the new proximity fuze which enabled American artillery to fire repeated midair bursts against which foxholes were no protection. One of the captured men had evidently snitched.

These five were driven in an open car, despite the freezing weather, to a medieval castle in Limburg-Diez. Led to the catacombs below, Baron found himself in solitary confinement in a dungeon. Previous prisoners had scribbled messages on the walls: "Don't talk"; "You get your Red Cross parcel no matter what they tell you"; "Don't worry about the threats"; "The interrogating officers always outrank you." Baron spent five days alone in this cell, not knowing if he would be killed or if his comrades had already been killed, before he was summoned for questioning at two in the morning, when he was groggy. As he was marched across the courtyard, he saw the technical sergeant standing at attention clad only in his underwear. The man was blue from the cold.

A confident *Sturmbannführer* (major), trim in his black *Waffen* SS uniform, greeted Baron from behind a massive desk. The *Sturmbannführer* closed Baron's dossier and said in breezy English, "You're another of those ninety-day wonders, eh, Lieutenant Baron?"

The man did not know as much as he pretended. Baron was not a "ninety-day wonder:" he had been a "special cadet." But the *Sturmbannführer* accurately recited the present disposition of the 45th Division. Baron answered with only his name, rank and serial number. The *Sturmbannführer* offered him a drink. Baron, afraid it was drugged, refused. The *Sturmbannführer* threw the brandy in his face. Baron explained that he couldn't drink because he had diarrhea. The *Sturmbannführer* shrugged and suggested that Baron eat the cocoa out of a Red Cross parcel which he instantly produced. Pouring the cocoa in his palm, Baron

licked the powder up. The *Sturmbannführer* kept threaten-
ing him and asking him questions about other divisions. He
again recited his name, rank and serial number. After many
threats, the *Sturmbannführer* dismissed him. On his way
back to the dungeon, Baron passed the shivering sergeant.
Later he learned the man survived and never talked. A few
days later, Baron was marched to a POW camp a few miles
away.

French POWs were in the camp, but separated by
barbed wire was another enclosure. It was an extremely
overcrowded stalag housing Russian POW's. The two
groups used opposite ends of one latrine building separated
in the middle by a wall. A hole that had been broken
through the wall provided access for trading information
and supplies. Floyd was gravely ill with dysentery, but
Baron was still relatively healthy and was able to keep Floyd
alive by barter. Scrounging whatever he could, Baron was
able to make trade with the Russians and others for extra
food for Floyd.

After three weeks in the Limburg oflag, Baron, Floyd,
Meiggs and some sixty other Americans were crammed into
a forty-and-eight (boxcar). They barely survived several
Allied air raids during the three days the train sat in the
Limburg marshaling yards. A week later—it was now the
end of February—the group disembarked at Hammelburg
and were marched up the hill to Oflag XIIIB.

The first American kriegies had arrived in Hammelburg
several weeks before, on 18 January 1945. They were 1,500
officers from the 106th and 28th Divisions who had been
captured in Belgium during the initial stages of the German
Ardennes offensive. The 106th, whose symbol was a ram-
pant lion, was a green, untried division newly arrived

overseas at the beginning of December. It was promptly moved up on 11 December to relieve the 2d Division in a quiet sector of the line in the bleak vastness of the Schnee Eifel northeast of Luxembourg. Five days later, hundreds of Panther and Tiger tanks leaped from the forests at the "Lionmen." Medium and heavy field pieces, along with railroad artillery, began a massive barrage that snapped trees like toothpicks. One hundred thousand seasoned *Volksgrenadier* inexorably began driving the GIs of the 106th back.

The division took heavy casualties. In five days of fighting, it lost 416 killed, 1,246 wounded and 7,001 missing in action. Men died valiantly in the 106th, fighting until their ammunition and water gave out. But many of the 7,001 who were taken prisoner by the Germans surrendered without fighting. Whole battalions found themselves surrounded before they realized a major German offensive was on the way.

Combat hardens a division, but victory transforms it into a hearty and precise organization. Conversely, when soldiers are driven back by the enemy, often to positions where they cannot dig in and make a stand, when they are separated from their support units and lose communications contact with the flanks, morale fails. The more of his comrades a soldier sees killed, the less his desire to throw himself against the enemy.

This happened to most of the 106th.* The 422d and 423d Infantries with the 589th and 590th Field Artillery

---

*The 81st and 168th Engineer Battalions of the 106th under Lieutenant Colonel Thomas Riggs did hold in front of Saint-Vith until the CCB 7th Armored Division of Brigadier General Bruce Clarke plugged the hole.

Battalions were cut off and surrounded by the German hammer blows. The 424th was thrown back and held the road to Saint-Vith for five days before its colonel, his CP filled with wounded, his men out of supplies and without fixed defensive positions, facing another night of bitter cold, surrendered.

The 7,001 POWs of the 106th were saddened, dispirited, exhausted men with little pride in themselves and less in their officers. One man remarked bitterly that it had taken him less than three weeks to go from Boston to a German oflag. Among these prisoners was Lieutenant Colonel Joseph Matthews, the executive officer of the 424th Infantry. Matthews was a thirty-eight-year-old chemist, a graduate of North Carolina State University in his native Raleigh, who had gone on active duty in 1936. Matthews was in the CP when the regimental commander made the decision to surrender. The colonel gave his staff and line officers the option of trying to work their way back. Captain Anthony Spadola, on the farthest flank, took his company out that night but within an hour ran into an ambush. Half of the men were killed and Spadola lost his leg.

The Germans lined up the captured members of the 106th in several columns and marched them from Belgium toward Germany. The POWs were without food and water and without shelter in the cold night. The winter of 1944–45 was the coldest winter on the continent in twenty-five years. To make matters worse, the 106th had never received its issue of winter footgear. As they trudged along, they saw their own trucks being driven to the rear by Germans.

The column was passing through a small Belgian town near the German border. Suddenly, the guards halted the POWs, pushed them back against the walls of the buildings. They refused to let any of the GIs cross the road to drink water from the horse troughs in the public square. Heavy traffic began churning the mud into a morass. Matthews saw two German *Feldmarschälle* overseeing this traffic, their gold braid still resplendent, but mud up to the ankles of their gleaming boots.

Matthews darted from the column, dodged the trucks, slogged over to the *Feldmarschälle,* saluted, and said, "You Germans are sons of bitches. You won't let my men drink water."

The *Feldmarschälle* turned in surprise toward the peppery light colonel, and with an imperious wave one summoned a guard who roughly escorted Matthews back to the waiting column. "You ought to be shot for talking that way to the German High Command," the guard said.

At Limburg, the officers and the enlisted men were separated and Matthews boarded a train that began moving east. As it traversed the railroad yards, British bombers appeared. One of the bombs blew the doors off Matthews's boxcar and the men tumbled out, dashing for cover. In other cars, the GIs had to tear open the doors from inside. Fifty-seven POWs were killed in the raid, forty of them behind a rock pile that took a direct hit. The Lionmen reboarded the cars after the bombers left and detrained finally at an oflag at Bad Orb, 60 miles beyond Limburg.

Morale was at its nadir. Matthews realized morale is never high when the men are sick, hungry and cold, and the enemy is in charge. But it was to sink even lower because of the weak and vacillating leadership exercised by Colonel Charles Cavender, now the ranking officer of the 106th. Cavender was an efficient training officer who was badly shaken by the Battle of the Bulge and never recovered from the shock of the disaster. The younger officers lost respect for the field-grade officers, some of whom had been captured in their pinks, and Cavender did little to restore it.

On the second day at Bad Orb, one of Cavender's aides came to the barracks and said that the Germans had ordered a list of Jewish officers.

"You just tell Colonel Cavender that every officer in this barracks is Jewish," said Matthews, "and from now on, tell him to stay the hell out of here."

On 11 January, leaving behind the chaplains and the seriously sick and wounded, this contingent of POWs left Bad Orb for Hammelburg.

The cold was relentless. The men doubled up in the bunks to share blankets. The kriegies asked the Germans for all their old and spare copies of the newspaper *Deutsche Allgemeine Zeitung* and *Völkischer Beobachter,* the official Nazi newspaper. The Germans were pleased by the Americans' interest in German affairs, but in fact, the prisoners wanted the newspapers to stuff in the cracks of the barracks' walls, to use as fuel in the stoves and to tear into strips to use as toilet paper. Matthews, who occupied a barracks at the rim of the camp, crawled under the barbed wire every night with two other officers, to a vacant barracks in an unoccupied compound. They gutted the interior of the nearest building for wood with which to keep warm.

When the Lionmen arrived at the Hammelburg oflag the grounds were dotted with the stumps of recently felled trees. By late March, the kriegies had pried these stumps from the ground to fuel the stoves. For shovels, the POWs used KLIM cans. These were condensed milk cans out of Red Cross food parcels—KLIM is "milk" spelled backwards. These cans served many other uses. They were fashioned into cooking utensils; they were attached to the ends of short poles with which the POWs sudsed and rinsed their laundry; the prisoners played with them as with an erector set.

The Red Cross parcels, which came from the United

States, Canada, England, Argentina and New Zealand, contained food and tobacco (see opposite).

The parcels arrived at the camps infrequently. While the Germans let the kriegies supervise the distribution, individuals rarely received one. Instead, the parcels went to a common mess. The Germans always punched holes in the cans to check against contraband as well as to prevent hoarding for an escape. Food often spoiled, even though the mess personnel sealed the holes with oleomargarine.

The boredom and the monotony were unendurable. One lieutenant counted the barbs on one section of the barbed wire fence and then estimated the total number of barbs around the encampment. When he announced this number, his fellow kriegies not only didn't consider him mad, they formed teams to check him out with a barb-by-barb count.

Sleep was ravaged by infestations of fleas, lice and bedbugs. Searchlights constantly played in revolving crisscrosses. The watery diet forced the men from their bunks four or five times a night to relieve themselves. One night a guard shot and killed a POW, a Lieutenant Weeks, on his way to the latrine.

To Matthews, this was a period when morale reached an all-time low: the younger officers held the older ones in contempt; the senior officers found the captains and the lieutenants insolent and disobedient. Colonel Cavender and his staff alienated the German commandant, General Gunther von Goeckel, almost immediately. They told him the Americans would try him as a war criminal as soon as the war was over. Von Goeckel, a Prussian, promptly began withholding Red Cross parcels and made the men answer to an inordinate number of *Appelle,* or roll calls, in the worst weather, late at night and during air raids. The tension this created also

.... 194......

Date of Receipt of Parcel

cknowledge receipt of parcel in good condition. (If not received good condition give details or cross out items missing.)

....

....

(Name in Block Letters)

(Prisoner of War Number)

....

(Former Unit and Number)

....

(Signature of Prisoner Receiving Parcel)

Address of Prison Camp

PARCEL A-1

Commodities

1.	Milk Powder	16 ozs.
2.	Cheese	8 ozs.
3.	Liver Paste	6 ozs.
4.	Corned Beef	12 ozs.
5.	Pork	12 ozs.
6.	Raisins	15 ozs.
7.	Sugar	8 ozs.
8.	Orange Concentrate	8 oss.
9.	Cocoa	8 ozs.
10.	Coffee	8 ozs.
11.	Chocolate	4 ozs.
12.	Candy	6 ozs.
13.	Biscuits	7 ozs.
14.	Cigarettes	40
15.	Tobacco	2¼ ozs.
16.	Matches	40

Form 1631-P
Feb. 1942

American Red Cross
STANDARD PACKAGE NO. 8
for
PRISONER OF WAR
FOOD
CONTENTS

Evaporated Milk, irradiated	1	14½ oz. can
Lunch Biscuit (hard-tack)	1	8 oz. package
Cheese	1	8 oz. package
Instant Cocoa	1	8 oz. tin
Sardines	1	15 oz. tin
Oleomargarine (Vitamin A)	1	1 lb. tin
Corned Beef	1	12 oz. tin
Sweet Chocolate	2	5½ oz. bars
Sugar, Granulated	1	2 oz. package
Powdered orange concentrate (Vitamin C)	1	7 oz. package
Soup (dehydrated)	1	5 oz. package
Prunes	1	16 oz. package
Instant Coffee	1	4 oz. tin
Cigarettes	2	20's
Smoking Tobacco	1	2¼ oz. package

Label from a Red Cross parcel and post card with which to acknowledge receipt of parcel. *(Courtesy Gen. John K. Waters USA, Ret.)*

affected the guards. During an air raid alert, a guard thought that Lieutenant George Vaream was slow in returning to his barracks and shot him in the back, killing him.

The older officers tried to set up classes and study groups; attendance was meager. One of the few classes that did succeed was one organized by Matthews and taught by an engineer who had worked on Boulder dam. It was the only subject to draw a crowd.

Will Michael went into the Army in the first peacetime draft in January 1940. In the succeeding four years, he had slept in some strange places. As an enlisted man, on his way to the relief of the invaded Philippines in early 1942, he slept in the Rose Bowl in Pasadena. When he went overseas as an officer in November 1944, he and three other lieutenants shared a posh stateroom on the *Queen Elizabeth,* recruiting a British military aide to come to their stateroom to tell them what the bidet was.

Michael was captured on 19 December and marched through Belgium to Germany. He slept in the open one night near Malmédy where he saw the frozen bodies of dozens of American soldiers whose shoes were missing.

When he marched into the oflag at Bad Orb, the first thing he noticed in the medieval courtyard was a guillotine with dried blood on it. That night sleep came hard as Michael wondered if the Germans used the guillotine on captured Allied officers.

The worst sleep he would ever have in the army was during the week he spent with sixty-one other men packed into a locked forty-and-eight traveling from Bad Orb to Hammelburg. They had to stand for the entire journey. They slept leaning against one another, waking every few minutes as they were jounced by a rough roadbed, thrown forward by a stop or squeezed to one side by a sharp curve.

No place was provided for the men to relieve themselves. At each end of the boxcar, however, was a small opening, and so the men urinated and defecated in their helmets and passed them hand over hand to one of the soldiers at these openings for emptying.

Michael thought this was as bad as the war could get. It wasn't. Hammelburg was worse. If he tried to save some food or put aside a small treasure, he had to stay awake to guard it or a fellow officer from the 106th would steal it.

Lieutenant Michael's buddy, Captain Benny Lemer from Newark, New Jersey, S-3 for the 3d Battalion of the 423d, tried to avoid capture by working his way out of the Bulge with several enlisted men. They headed west and on the way encountered two black soldiers who developed a surefire technique for flushing German snipers from the trees. Each pulled the pin from a grenade, let the detonating process start, then threw the grenade high in the forest. Twice German bodies came crashing down. But Lemer and his small unit ran into a heavy concentration of Germans who made them, too, march to Bad Orb.

Along with another 100 officers, Lemer was forced by the Germans to strip naked in the snow and stand at attention while German interrogators questioned them. Lemer answered their questions figuring that the Germans knew they were from the 106th and there wasn't anything left of the 106th. What difference did it make what German intelligence made of the news?

Lemer rode from Bad Orb to Hammelburg in a steel boxcar. It was so cold that if a man put his fingers against the metal he left skin behind. Lemer marched from the railroad yard through the town and then climbed up the hill to the Hammelburg camp over a beautiful winding road that reminded him of a country club driveway.

While at Hammelburg, Lemer was one of the burial

party for Lieutenant Weeks, who had been shot the night before on his way to the latrine. The men removed Weeks's boots, put him in a plain wooden coffin and took him to a wooded knoll where they dug his grave. The German guards then directed them to take the corpse out of the box and lower it into the grave; the burial detail carried the empty coffin back to camp as taps was blown. The POWs blew taps for at least fifteen men every week, some weeks for as many as twenty, virtually all victims of sickness and malnutrition.

In January, February and early March other captured officers were incarcerated in Hammelburg. These officers never arrived in as sizeable a contingent as the men from the 106th Division.

Second Lieutenant William Dennis detrained at Hammelburg two days after the men from the 106th were marched in. Dennis was a medical officer who was captured at Bastogne.

A registered pharmacist, he went overseas before D Day as a technician 5th grade, and in England learned he had passed his State Board examinations in Pennsylvania. The army promptly commissioned him and reassigned him to the 327th Glider Infantry Regiment.

Bill Dennis became a paratrooper and was assigned to the 101st Airborne Division, the "Screaming Eagles," who jumped into France on D Day and into Holland a few months later. In December, the 101st was regrouping in France when it received orders to proceed by truck to Belgium to help stem the German advance.

It took the division two days to reach the beleaguered city of Bastogne. The 327th set up its tents and dispensaries at a crossroads 2 miles outside the city. Dennis had learned in training that medical detachments should avoid making themselves a target by setting up as far as possible from crossroads, railroad stations and town squares. In this case, however, he thought the exigencies of the situation required his taking this dangerous position. On the morning of 19 December, his commanding officer sent Dennis into Bastogne to evacuate wounded. Dennis left in a jeep followed by three ambulances and four trucks, all of them bearing red crosses on their hoods and sides.

He started back from the city at night, his convoy laden with wounded. The going was slow. The roads were pocked with shell holes, the night was black, and proceeding without lights, Dennis often had to walk ahead to lead the way. Finally, he spied an MP with a lighted baton who directed him to take the first left to reach the 327th. It wasn't until Dennis had led his convoy past the point of no return that he realized the 327th had been overrun that afternoon, that the MP was a German in an American-issue uniform, and that the tanks facing him were German tanks. The flares made the wooded bower look like a floodlit stage. The machine guns on the panzers opened up. Everything that moved went down.

Dennis drove into a ditch. He wanted to explain to the enemy the rules enacted by the Geneva Convention, but it was too late. The machine guns riddled the ambulances and trucks; the wounded stopped moaning at last.

German infantrymen in white parkas rounded up the remaining members of Dennis's command in the foggy morning, and by 17 January he was at Hammelburg. He had suffered a shrapnel wound in transit and he had trench foot, so he could barely get on his galoshes for the first *Appell*. He was too far away to hear the exchange between the American ranking officer and the German commandant but later in the day he learned that the Germans wanted the names of all the Jewish officers. Dennis was a Jew and considered discarding his dog tags, which were marked "H" for Hebrew, but he decided not to. If he were killed, he wanted his parents and his girl friend to know what had happened to him.

Later that day, when one of the ranking officers' aides appeared and asked the men which of them was Jewish, Dennis said, "I'd just as soon you didn't put my name down." The aide didn't.

Because of his trench foot, Dennis spent three weeks on his back. The hospital guard, named Ostertag (Easter Day), was in his fifties and had lost one son on the Eastern Front and another on the Western. Ostertag liked to taunt a paratrooper lieutenant named Levy, who was as Semitic-looking as Isaiah. "One day we are going to kill you," he said with a smile. The paratrooper, whom Dennis suspected was a street tough, spat. Whenever Ostertag relaxed, Levy would hobble to the window and shout, "Oh my God! Here come Patton's tanks," or "British commandos at twelve o'clock." Ostertag always paled; Levy always laughed.

One day Ostertag inspected Dennis's dog tags and asked what the "H" stood for. From his high school German, Dennis recalled a word and said to Ostertag, "The 'H' stands for *'Heer'* [army]. That means I am not in the navy or the marines or the coast artillery."

"Oh," said the German guard, completely satisfied that an English-speaking nation would use a foreign word to designate a branch of its service.

A German doctor from Hammelburg often inspected the POW hospital. One day as he passed Dennis's bed, he said, "We're going to have to amputate those feet." Dennis had feared this possibility.

An American doctor, Captain DeMarco, asked, "Have you anesthetic?"

"No," said the German.

"Then we are going to treat him with sulfanilamide," said DeMarco.

Fortunately, Dennis recovered and was assigned to the hospital as a medical aide. For reasons best known to themselves, the Germans kept medical personnel isolated and remote from the other POWs. German enlisted men, for example, brought the medical staff its soup and bread. Dennis knew little of what transpired in the rest of the camp, but he learned a great deal about the course of the war from the bombastic Ostertag. The guard boasted that the Germans had destroyed 800 tanks the day before and 1,200 airplanes the day before that, but also revealed that the Allies had taken a bridge over the Rhine.

Ostertag took Dennis over to the Serbian compound every afternoon. The Serbs had a big vat in which they made cocoa. Ostertag liked his daily mug and he arranged for Dennis to have one, too. It was one of the ways men lived through the experience, hanging out with an old, fat German in return for hot chocolate, courtesy of Yugoslavia.

The senior American medical officer at the oflag was Major Albert L. Berndt, an orthopedic surgeon, a graduate of the University of Pennsylvania Medical School. Thirty-seven years old, a native of Portsmouth, Pennsylvania, Berndt was the regimental surgeon of the 112th Infantry Regiment of the 28th Division. He had been captured on 17 December in Ourans, Belgium, during the Battle of the Bulge. Captured with him was Captain Robert Walborn, the senior dental officer of the regiment, a graduate of the University of Pittsburgh Dental School.

With the rest of the regiment, these two medical officers were temporarily confined in the camp at Bad Orb. Walborn was in the mess line the morning a Russian KP almost cut off the fingers of a GI who reached for extra food. The Russian was found murdered the next day. The German guards lined up the senior American officers against a wall, machine guns facing them. A German major ordered the American officers to divulge the name of the man or men who had stabbed the KP. The German promised that if he did not have the name or names within ten minutes he would shoot them all.

Walborn believed him, and so did Berndt, but they did not reveal the names. Instead the murderers, two enlisted men, turned themselves in. Walborn never knew what happened to them and never saw them again.

Once in Hammelburg, Berndt and other doctors worked in the hospital, a prominent stone building near the Serbian compound. Serbian doctors had operated the hospital for four years and the American doctors worked with them. The hospital was strictly for the bedridden. However, Walborn operated a dispensary, separate from the hospital, which served the American prisoners for ordinary sick call. At first, the Germans refused to allow Walborn into the hospital. Eventually, Berndt persuaded them that some of the sick men needed dental treatment and by 26 March, Brendt and Walborn worked together almost every day.

More than 800 POWs arrived at Hammelburg in early March. They had marched from Oflag 64 in Szubin, Poland, to Parchim, Germany, a march of over 300 miles which took forty-five days, one of the epic treks of the war. These men were under the nominal command of Colonel Paul Goode. The executive officer of the Szubin POWs, however, was

Lieutenant Colonel John Waters, a thirty-nine-year-old West Pointer who was captured in Africa on St. Valentine's Day 1943, while serving with the 1st Armored Regiment, 1st Armored Division. Waters was blue eyed and handsome, reserved, self-contained and intelligent, with a high sense of duty. Most of his fellow officers felt that he was bound for high command. They also noted that John Waters had married Bea Patton, the general's daughter.

Waters and Bea Patton met at West Point when he was a stalwart yearling and she was still a teenager. Waters, the son of a Baltimore banker, was on the lacrosse, hockey and soccer squads at West Point. He was also an avid horseman and a superb hunter.

When he was commissioned in June 1931, Waters asked Bea Patton to marry him. Her father, then a major, insisted that the couple wait three years, which they did. Convinced by this time that Waters was no fly-by-night, Patton finally gave his blessing.

Waters admired his father-in-law. Patton was well read, especially in the Bible and history, and could converse in several languages. And Waters found him always a gentle man.

Waters was commissioned in the cavalry, which the War Department later mechanized and converted to the armored forces. In 1942 he was assigned to the 2d Armored Division, commanded by General Patton, which was in training at Fort Benning, Georgia.

Early in May 1942, Waters, then a major, was transferred to the 1st Armored Division and rushed up to the New York port of embarkation where the bulk of the division was to be loaded onto the *Queen Mary,* seeing its first duty as a troop transport. The *Queen* sailed on May 10, 1942, to the River Clyde in Scotland from where the men were transshipped to Northern Ireland.

Major Waters was not to enjoy the luxury of the *Queen Mary* but was sent to Canada whence his unit was shipped directly to Belfast on the *John B. A. Barry,* namesake of a famous U.S. cavalryman, and sister ship to the luxury liner *Morro Castle,* which burned off of the coast of New Jersey. On the *Barry,* less spacious than the *Queen,* it was necessary to double up. That meant that two men had the use of one bunk for twelve hours each.

Major Waters was the executive officer of the 1st Armored Battalion of the 1st Armored Regiment of the 1st Armored Division. This battalion was composed of light tanks. When his unit arrived in Northern Ireland for training for Operation Torch, the invasion of North Africa, his commanding officer was transferred, and Waters was promoted to lieutenant colonel and was appointed battalion commander.

After training all summer, his unit was transferred to England so that his vehicles could be waterproofed for the invasion.

On 7 November 1942, Combat Command B, of which the 1st Armored Regiment was a part, joined the large convoy that was bound for North Africa to launch the attack against the cities of Casablanca and Algiers and the port of Oran.

Combat Command B's objective was Oran. The command was divided into five parts which would strike this large area in five different places. The 1st Battalion was to land on the beach at the neighboring Gulf of Arzew and attack Tafaraoui airport, about 30 miles to the southwest.

Opposed by Vichy French heavy guns and tanks, Colonel Waters led his flying column of light tanks and tank destroyers to the airport and succeeded in taking his objective. This action provided an airfield from which Allied aircraft could fly in close support of the advancing ground forces. Waters thus became one of the first five American commanders to fight in the Mediterranean theater.

Later as part of Task Force Blade, invading Tunisia from Algeria, Colonel Waters ordered his C Company to the airdrome at Djedeida where they destroyed 20 Messerschmitts on the ground.

The German Afrika Korps under Generalfeldmarschall Erwin Rommel had almost succeeded in their attack on Egypt, but they were stopped by Field Marshall Bernard L. Montgomery's Eighth Army at El Alamein.

Rommel realized after the Allied invasion of Algeria, Morocco and Tunisia that his only chance of saving his army from annihilation, now that their supply ports of Tobruk and Tripoli had been captured by the British, was to get it to Tunis and Bizerte where it could be supplied from Italy. This also would provide a port from which to evacuate his army to Europe if it became necessary.

The Afrika Korps fought desperately and well to gain these objectives. They took Sidi Bou Zid on 15 February and tried to smash through quickly.

Colonel Waters was ordered to Djebel Lessouda, high ground about 6 miles north of Sidi Bou Zid. Other units were sent to neighboring hills to help contain the German advance coming from the Faïd Pass. But the Americans on the hills were completely surrounded by enemy tanks, and when the Allied command learned this and realized the size of the enemy forces, orders to evacuate the area were dropped from an airplane. Colonel Waters was captured the first night of this breakout even though 200 of his men were able to slip back through the enemy lines to safe territory. Colonel Thomas D. Drake and Lieutenant Colonel James D. Alger were also captured in this action.

Because the Americans delayed the enemy for two

days and because the Allied command was alerted as to the size and direction of the enemy forces, the Allies were able to reinforce the Kasserine Pass, the obvious route for the enemy, and, after the bitter fighting, stem the German advance and eventually capture a large part of the German Afrika Korps.

Waters and his fellow POWs were transported up the boot of Italy, through Germany, ending finally in the middle of Poland at the Szubin oflag, which contained 1,600 American officers. Szubin was no better than most oflags—desolate, crowded with bedraggled and deprived prisoners. The German name for Szubin was Alt Bergund. The camp's commander was Oberst (Colonel) Schneider. He was thoroughly anti-Semitic. One of the POWs was a Dr. Abrams. Because he was a Jew, Schneider refused to allow him to work in the prison hospital, and as a further insult, forced him to be a "latrine inspector." Waters's immediate superior was Colonel Thomas Drake who was subsequently repatriated under the Geneva Convention because of his serious illness. Drake was replaced by Colonel Paul T. Goode, who had been captured in Normandy while serving with the 29th (Blue-Gray) Division. Waters continued on as the camp's executive officer and helped Goode maintain the military way of life instituted by Colonel Drake. The POWs had their own camp chain of command. The men were fully organized and were required to observe proper military bearing and discipline. As a consequence, they had good morale. They were cohesive, cared for one another, and petty theft just never occurred. Because they had been prisoners for so long, they were better set up than most kriegies to make time pass and had become adept at keeping themselves fit. There were committees for recreation and sports. The YMCA supplied the POWs at Szubin with cards, chess and checkers sets and athletic equipment, the most popular items being baseballs, bats and mitts. The men conducted classes for each other. There was a committee for interrogating newly arrived prisoners to make sure they were not German "plants" and another that planned escapes.

The S-2, Lieutenant Colonel James Alger, was in charge of the escape committee, which engineered an elaborate matrix of tunnels. When the tunnels were ready to facilitate the escape of 100 GIs, Goode learned that Hitler had executed 60 British officers who had participated in a mass escape at another oflag. The news shook Goode; it frightened him in a way that the hedgerow fighting had not. The news of the atrocity took some of the boldness out of him. Goode ordered the American tunnels filled in.

The POW staff saw that their commanding officer had become distressed. A man in distress sooner or later fails to lead and to encourage others. More and more responsibility descended upon Colonel Goode's staff. The POWs knew by the winter of 1944 that the fighting was going well for the Allies, that they wouldn't be in an oflag forever. A secret radio kept them apprised of the war news. The men had high hopes. But Goode remained depressed by the present rather than cheered by the future.

The radio in Szubin was operated by Lieutenant Charles Eberle who had been captured in Africa when C Company of the 168th Regiment, 34th Division, extended itself too far in a counterattack.

Eberle was one of those officers scattered throughout the armed services who had been sent to a special school before combat to learn about planning escapes, special radio codes, and so on. This training was put to good use in the camp. In charge of a smuggled radio (received, like much contraband, concealed in "gift" packages sent from a predesignated person in the U.S.), Eberle was always on call. The electricity in the oflags was so weak that transmission proved impossible, but the radio could receive, and at designated hours Eberle was on the earphones. In itself this was a protracted process. The BBC and the Voice of America broadcast at night when there was less interference. The kriegies had to stand watch to be sure Eberle was awake on time. At least one POW was awake at any hour of the night.

By early January, the POWs at Szubin didn't need the radio. They could hear the big Russian guns to the east and they could detect the edgy nervousness of their guards as the Eastern Front moved inexorably west.

Colonel Goode and his staff knew the Germans were going to move the prisoners. The guards had been bribed with cigarettes, watches and candy to relay the information in the orders crossing the commandant's desk each day. The American command at Szubin ordered the men to repair their clothing and prevailed upon Oberst Schneider to issue the POWs the captured Polish military jackets and greatcoats that the Germans had kept in storage since Poland's surrender. The command worked hard to get shoes for the men through the International Red Cross, which most POWs felt was pro-German. The staff and barracks commanders saw to it that the men ate light rations and began saving food for the march. They also supervised the construction of sleds with wooden runners so the POWs could transport additional supplies.

On 21 January, with the temperature at 20° below zero and in heavy snow, the Germans began to march 1,400 of the American POWs toward Germany. Two hundred sick and seriously wounded were left behind. The German General Staff had determined never to abandon the POWs to the enemy. Whether Hitler planned to keep the POWs as hostages—he did once order Allied airmen executed, an order which General Alfred Jodl refused to implement—or simply as part of his maniacal obsession with subjugation makes little difference. Marching 1,400 Americans away from the Russians in midwinter would mean the death of many of them.

The camp guards were anxious to get under way, fearing the reprisals the Russians had promised to exact. The guards would rather have fled to *das Vaterland* alone and left the prisoners behind, but bringing up the rear of the Szubin column was a contingent of SS.

When the prisoners left Szubin, they had sleds piled high with extra necessities. But they began jettisoning objects after only three hours on the march. The weight was immovable in the heavy snowdrifts. They carried their bedrolls as Civil War soldiers had—over the right shoulder with the ends bound together at the left hip. What they couldn't carry within the roll, they stuffed in their pockets and crammed into ditty bags that they slung from their belts. Soon they began to throw away even their personal possessions as they struggled through the snow.

One of these marchers, however, carried an American flag wrapped around his body. The men had kept it secreted in hopes of raising it to identify themselves as Americans to the Russian troops who must eventually come upon the Szubin oflag. On the march, they would have an even greater need of being able to identify themselves as Americans if they encountered Russians.

On the second morning of the trek, many of the POWs hid in the straw of the barns where they had slept. Some were able to escape in this way, while others simply slipped away from the column. Three escapees played a crucial role in Abe Baum's raid on Hammelburg.

These three were Captain Ernest M. Gruenberg, a medical officer from New York City who had jumped on D Day with the 101st Airborne; Second Lieutenant Frank H. Colley from Georgia, captured in Tunisia; and Second Lieutenant John N. Dimmling, Jr., from Winston-Salem, North Carolina, captured at Anzio while serving with the 3d Division.

Gruenberg, Colley and Dimmling dropped out of the column two days after they left Szubin, hid in the forest, and that night began hitchhiking eastward across Poland. On 24 January they crossed the Russian front lines. Ordinarily, Russian infantrymen would have notified their commissar of the three Americans and the commissar would have notified the NKVD. The NKVD interned American POWs because the Russians did not want them to get a feel for the political situation in Poland. In this instance, however, Dr. Gruenberg spent several days tending wounded Russians. In gratitude, the Russian soldiers arranged transport for the three Americans to one of the eastern rail centers. Riding supply trucks moving to the rear, the trio reached the outskirts of Warsaw where they boarded a troop train that took them all the way to Moscow. A Russian soldier told them how to get to the U.S. Military Mission in the city.

That mission was headed by General John R. Deane, who was deeply annoyed by the Russian practice of picking up arriving Americans, spiriting them to a barracks outside the city and thoroughly interrogating them before release.

In his book, *The Strange Alliance* (Indiana University

Press, 1973), Deane recorded his joy at getting firsthand
information from these three tatterdemalion soldiers who

> . . . represented the thousands of Americans I expected, for
> whom we were prepared to do so much if only allowed the
> opportunity. . . .
>   I learned from them that about two hundred Americans
> had either been left behind by the Germans at Szubin or had
> escaped from the German column before they themselves
> left it. They told me of about thirty Americans who were in
> a Russian hospital at Wegheim. Hundreds of American
> families were relieved of considerable anxiety when we were
> able to send word to the War Department of those who
> Gruenberg, Colley and Dimmling knew had escaped from
> the Germans. Among these was First Lieutenant Craig
> Campbell, one of General Eisenhower's personal aides. We
> were also able to let General Patton know that his son-in-
> law, Lt. Colonel John K. Waters, was in the best of health
> but was still in German custody, being moved to a camp in
> the interior.

Others who escaped from the column did not have as
easy a time as Gruenberg, Colley and Dimmling. Charles
Eberle, the radio operator, escaped after entrusting the set
to another officer. He and three other men made their first
contact with the Russians at the end of January.

The first cry they heard was, *"Halt!"*

"Ich bin Amerikaner," shouted Eberle. When he saw a
Russian sentry approach, he changed this to, *"Ich bin —
Amerikanski."*

He and his companions were packed off to a displaced
persons camp near Warsaw where conditions were more
intolerable than the Szubin oflag. The Americans shared

unheated barracks with Jews, Italians, Poles, Lithuanians—
every one of whom had dysentery, tapeworm or pneumonia. The food was soup; there was no bread, no ersatz
coffee. The Russians maintained a roving bicycle guard over
the camp. Eventually, the Americans were crammed into
boxcars and transported to Odessa, where General Deane
claimed them. By now the general was less than amazed to
learn from his Russian counterpart that there were not 350
unclaimed Americans in Poland and Russia, but 3,000.

Curtis Scott Jones, to whom Eberle had entrusted the
radio, endured the hardships of the march, although once
past the barbed wire of Szubin the POWs felt better. They
had cigarettes and often bartered for food. The Poles along
the way were sympathetic to their plight and often passed
out vegetables from their own sparse larders as well as
medical supplies, such as they were. The POWs carried
their KLIM smokeless cookers and ate warm potatoes in the
barns at night. Now and then, the men scrounged for eggs.
A few even managed one-night liaisons with willing Polish
girls, the men's interest in sex reviving with their improved
diet and morale.

All along the march, the German guards "gave out
addresses," wanting testimony from the POWs in case the
victorious Allies accused them of maltreating the prisoners.

Still the trek was as harrowing and hazardous as any
combat experience. Captain Zoltan Tacaks was one of the
few officers to keep a diary of the journey. Early on the
march, the column passed an outdoor latrine on which sat a
Russian who had frozen to death. The German guards
would not permit the GIs to form a burial detail nor would
they let anyone cover the corpse.

As they moved through the swirling snow, sporadic

small-arms fire could be heard. Up ahead they came upon the corpses of Russian POWs, shot by their SS guards for straggling or falling behind. The SS guards shot the Russians with the abandon and zest with which the crowned heads of Europe once slaughtered wild African game.

In late January, the middle-aged German guards took off, terrified at the rumors of nearby Russian patrols. The SS guards came up. Many of these were teenaged boys, fanatic children who had shot as many POWs at the end of the march as the older German guards had shot throughout the war.

The column reached Stolp where German sailors gave the POWs several baskets of fresh fish. That night they had a fish fry.

When the column crossed the Oder, the kriegies were billeted in barracks at the naval base of Swinemünde. Tacaks thought the men on the line of march must look in worse shape than they actually were because he heard the German sailors condemning the SS men for the way they treated the POWs. Their pity didn't inhibit the sailors from drafting Tacaks and several others to push trucks through heavy snowdrifts.

Throughout the journey, Colonel Goode insisted on carrying his bagpipes. Many men in the column thought the colonel was an accomplished piper. He was not. The bagpipes had come to him in Szubin through the YMCA, and although Goode had mastered only one note, he kept trying—even on the march. One night, a massive German hausfrau appeared at her doorway and ordered him to cease immediately. The war was hard enough on her family without their having to endure Goode and his bagpipes.

Goode's staff thought the colonel's attachment to his pipes quixotic, but they said nothing. They did not want him to give up on the pipes because it would be a gesture discouraging to the other men. And keeping up morale was not easy. The march had a devastating effect and the men needed constant encouragement. The staff patrolled the length of the column, talking to the men, persuading some to carry the kit of an exhausted man, scrounging dry socks from one to help prevent frostbite in another, even convincing the German commander to let Colonel Goode, who was older and severely weakened by the ordeal, ride in one of the horse-drawn wagons that the Germans were using to transport their own supplies. Besides, many men believed that Goode carried the group's clandestine radio in the bagpipes. He didn't, of course, because, as commanding officer of the POWs, he had frequent contacts with the German staff and it was therefore essential that he never carry contraband.

Of the 1,400 men who had left Oflag 64, some 1,200 reached Parchim in central Germany. Along the way they had passed a V-2 rocket installation. The POWs instinctively grasped what devastation these rockets, as big as silos, could wreak. Approximately 400 men were with Goode and Waters and were put in boxcars for the final leg of their trip to Hammelburg. Another 400 who arrived some days later were shipped by train to an oflag east of Berlin. The 400 or so men at the end of the column were marched all the way to Hammelburg. The remaining 200 never reached Parchim. Some were killed, some wounded and sent to hospitals, and the rest managed to escape, avoid recapture and make their way to the Russian lines.

When the first of the Szubin POWs arrived at the Hammelburg oflag, Richard Baron saw them march in. He thought to himself that these new arrivals looked better after their long trek than the Hammelburg kriegies who had spent the last three months in their bunks. Baron was sure he would never see men march as spiritedly again.

At Hammelburg, Colonel Goode found cruel dissension among the three senior colonels of the 106th Division. In fact, in so far as there was any organization at all among the POWs, it was headed by two captains.

"Who authorized you to make these decisions?" Goode demanded, determined to get things straightened out immediately.

"We authorized ourselves," one of the captains replied. "We've been here the longest and we're the strongest."

"Well," the answer came back, "as of this moment, you are relieved of your so-called command. I am the senior officer and from now on this camp will be run with the usual chain of command found in any other army installation."

Goode's own stability, however, was suspect. Above all, he was paranoid about the Germans and was sure the Nazis among them would murder prisoners of war. Nevertheless, he and his staff set about the task of organizing the camp. Most of the men were depressed, shuffling instead of walking, their faces expressionless. They were dirty, unshaven, disheveled. When one was caught digging through the contents of a garbage can, he couldn't understand why he was ordered to stop. He was told, "Because when the guards see you doing that, they find it difficult to believe that you are an officer in the United States Army."

Early on their second day in Hammelburg, Goode, his staff and each of the barracks commanders held an inspection. They reviewed every rank, stopping to order men to shave, to dress in a military manner, to stand up straight.

When asked why his shoes weren't shined, a young, slovenly second lieutenant laughed at the question. He was summarily confined to his barracks for one week. Army discipline had come to Hammelburg and with it morale began to improve.

Goode was well aware of what had happened to the men of the 28th and 106th Divisions and he knew that they felt betrayed. But he also knew that they wouldn't recover their pride and discipline unless they were forced to. He insisted on the army way in everything, standard operating procedure in the mess, the latrine and the barracks. There were classes with required attendance. His orders went through the chain of command, implemented by the barracks commanders (officers of field grade—major or higher) under the supervision of Colonel Waters, his executive.

The kriegies were organized into a network so that what news they received was universally distributed. Teams thoroughly cleansed the barracks every day, including airing the bedbug-infested bedding.

The American command realized they had more than the health of the men to care for. Many men were profoundly depressed. For example, Goode worried obsessively about the threat of German retaliation, that the guards would suddenly shoot the prisoners. Sometimes this worry got the better of him. Goode interrupted a colloquy of four young officers one day to tell them their fate was sealed, the Germans were bound to execute all American prisoners. Some of the more senior POWs thought it was not the kind of information a commanding officer should impart to his subordinates.

Relentlessly, the American command kept working to make the men stop thinking about themselves. As the internal discipline of the camp improved, so did the deportment of the Germans. Commandant von Goeckel relented and no longer called as many *Appelle.* He called none in bad weather. He released more Red Cross parcels. He let the German bishop provide communion wine and wafers for the Catholic chaplain. Von Goeckel even took Goode for rides into Hammelburg. The improved tenor of the camp put the guards more at ease and consequently there were no more shootings.

The change thrilled Richard Baron. From the moment of his arrival at Hammelburg, he had been disgusted and frightened by the conduct of most of the kriegies from the 28th and 106th Divisions. The more they fucked up, the more likely they were to fuck him up. Baron liked prison camp no better than anyone else, but he was a survivor.

:: 5 ::

Attack at Gemünden

When Task Force Baum cleared the small town of Schweinheim on the southern edge of Aschaffenburg, its fifty-three vehicles stretched over a mile, raising a fearsome noise of clanking treads and roaring exhausts in the quiet countryside. Baum, riding in a jeep, had two worries. With so much of the night already passed, how far would the task force be able to get before it lost the cover of darkness? Baum had hoped that the column would be near its objective by dawn, but that was now impossible; the launching of the task force had taken too long. Baum's more immediate worry was to find Highway 26, the main east–west highway.

Task Force Baum had exited from Schweinheim on a secondary road. By looping around Aschaffenburg on a series of such secondary roads, it was Baum's intention to pick up Highway 26 well to the east of the city. He passed through the small village of Haibach-Grünmorsbach without resistance although there was occasional small-arms fire. Heading toward Strassbessenbach, Baum pulled his jeep out of line and sped forward to the lead tank. As the houses of the village loomed ahead like squat little monsters, Baum called out to Lieutenant William Weaver, standing in the turret of the lead tank, that at the next intersection he was to take a left turn, toward Keilberg. Conveniently, there was a road sign indicating the turn— KEILBERG 1½ KM.

Weaver turned and the column followed. Baum waited at the turn in order to inspect the column as it passed. The order of march at this point was as follows: light tanks in the lead, followed by the jeeps (Baum's, Stiller's, Wise's, the medics' and the recon platoon's), the medium tanks, the half-tracks carrying the infantry, the assault guns, and the maintenance vehicles bringing up the rear. When Baum had assured himself that the column was intact and moving along in good order, he sped forward to catch up with the lead tank, reaching it as it entered Keilberg.

Following directly behind Weaver's tank, Baum directed the column through several more turns until it reached a main highway. In the darkness, he could see a road sign. With the aid of his flashlight, shielded with his hand so there was only a narrow beam, he could read the large numerals: 26. He had brought the task force to its first objective. His feeling of relief turned to consternation when he checked his watch; it was 0230 hours.

Negotiating the route at night from Schweinheim to the highway qualified Baum for a decoration. It takes a high order of leadership to keep an armored column moving smoothly in daytime; to keep them moving at night, especially over unfamiliar terrain and with a complicated route to follow, is a supreme test of leadership.

Baum knew that he was venturing farther behind enemy lines than any armored force of this size had before without promised reinforcement. The prospects for success were dim and so, to encourage his men, Baum had his jeep constantly on the move, driving forward, dropping back, then forward again, showing his men that he was there and that everything was under control. He wanted them to believe that they would make it. If they began losing confidence in themselves, they would be doomed.

The late hour preyed on Baum's mind. He knew that the task force would now necessarily have to travel in the open in daylight. But if they moved fast enough they might get by. It was, Baum suspected, a mission bordering on the suicidal, but taking such risks is part of combat.

Baum was not well read, but he thought clearly. It was not only courage that drove him, it was also the challenge of meeting and overcoming adversity. He must have felt much the same way General William Tecumseh Sherman did when the Civil War hero wrote, "To be at the head of a strong column of troops in the execution of some task that requires brain, is the highest pleasure of war—a grim one and terrible, but which leaves on mind and memory the strongest mark."

At Berlin headquarters of the *Oberkommando der Wehrmacht,* staff officers began receiving news about the American events at Schweinheim shortly after 0100 hours on 27 March. The German staff thought that Patton had achieved a brilliant breakthrough. According to the German commander, in his after-battle report:

> This surprise push had been made possible by the fact that the bridge south of Aschaffenburg was still intact and because of the lack of antitank weapons, no local securities could prevent or stop the push. This *coup de main* (in which the hand of General Patton could be recognized) showed us how the enemy understood the situation within the German resistance and knew of the small possibilities for counter-measures. When the Army learned that the enemy task

force despite the immediate alarming of all rear units, securities and duty posts had pushed through . . . the competent *DEP* 13AC was asked to concentrate all available forces to annihilate the enemy task force which had broken through.

Staff Sergeant Robert Vannett from New Era, Michigan, was the platoon sergeant of D Company, 37th Tank Battalion. His light tank, *Conquering Hero,* had led the column through Schweinheim, then along the curving route bypassing Aschaffenburg and finally onto Route 26. They were moving along the side of a hill, the left higher than the right. At the moment, the road was straight, empty and dark.

Vannett's driver was Technician 5th Grade James Mabrey and the gunner was Private First Class Frank Malinski. The tank lacked an assistant driver but the new platoon leader (Lieutenant Weaver), who had taken them over the Aschaffenburg bridge the day before, was riding with them. Vannett couldn't even remember the lieutenant's name. As *Conquering Hero* blasted along at 15 miles an hour, the new lieutenant checked the map under the narrow focus of the tank's interior red dome light. It was a road map with a tissue overlay, already smudged and torn. The lieutenant finally showed the map to Vannett and they read it together. Apparently the lieutenant was no more interested in Vannett's name than Vannett in his. But the route was clear enough. They stayed on the road, keeping the railroad to their left. The lieutenant folded the map and stuffed it in his pocket. Vannett wondered why the army always gave the maps to the lieutenants, because the lieutenants invariably got killed and with them went the map.

Vannett wasn't particularly talkative on the night of 26 March; he simply did his job. Two weeks before, he had been due for rotation. GIs always heard about the policy of sending certain of them back to the States, but so few were ever actually sent that rotation was a long-odds bet. It was something that might happen to you, but it was not something you were entitled to, could plan for or even really hope for. At the pleading of his buddy, the battalion sergeant major, Vannett had traded his rotation spot with another GI so that he and his buddy, who was to be rotated the following month, could go back together. The prospect of wine, women and song portrayed by his friend had been persuasive at the time, although now that he was tearing off behind enemy lines with this crazy task force, Vannett began to wonder if he had done a very smart thing by postponing his trip home.

How had he ended up here? He had been sitting around with his platoon, eating K rations, bullshitting about the French girls they each claimed to have seduced, and hoping for peace, when this new lieutenant came back from a briefing. Grouping the platoon around him, Weaver had given them a sketchy account of the plan and told them to get ready to move out that night. It had all sounded so normal, like every other order to prepare for battle. Now look!

Baum's jeep came alongside and the captain signaled for the lead tanks to knock down telephone poles. Mabrey, the driver, turned *Conquering Hero* to the left and side-swiped one of the short poles, which weren't much higher than a clothesline. It went down. He put the tank in low and shoved over another one. Then he sped back to the center of the road and resumed the lead of the column. The tanks would repeatedly down poles between towns.

Second Lieutenant Allen Moses, leader of the third platoon of the A Company infantry, was riding in one of the half-tracks guarding the rear of the column, followed by a maintenance half-track and the medics. Moses was from Pittsburgh. He had volunteered for flight training in the Army Air Forces after he won his bars in the ROTC at Penn State. However, he washed out as a pilot and the army immediately reassigned him to the infantry. He was shipped to France as a replacement officer and assigned to A Company of the 10th Armored Infantry Battalion in August 1944. Being an infantry lieutenant was a dangerous job, he learned. He had counted twenty other officers as they came and went. He found out that Lieutenant Elmer Sutton, first platoon leader, was the only lieutenant who had survived since the outfit had landed at Utah Beach.

Moses saw Baum's jeep dropping back. Baum wasn't sure that the wires had broken when the short poles were downed. He therefore ordered Moses to have his men cut the wires. Moses bent to the equipment kit and passed out wire cutters. The half-track swerved from the column and the men alighted. Moses hated jumping from the half-tracks, because his helmet always thumped his skull. He thought that hundreds of thousands of men were going to be bald after the war because they had to jump from half-tracks, tanks and 2½-ton trucks so often. His men snipped the wires, remounted, and caught up to the column. They repeated this every time they saw more downed poles.

Sergeant Donald Yoerk of East Aurora, New York, commanded one of the light tanks, the *City of New York,* in which he had been through five campaigns. Yoerk initially thought the mission was easy, but as light began to fill the eastern sky, he began to think differently. When he saw

white sheets hanging from the windows of homes in the
small towns the column passed, he knew they were in
trouble. They know we're coming, he thought. I guess we
didn't knock down the telephone wires soon enough.

His anxiety was somewhat relieved when Baum ordered
the column to hit top speed. Passing near one of the small
towns along their route, Yoerk saw German officers hurrying
along the streets with their briefcases, civilians on their way to
work and German soldiers exiting from bars with girls on their
arms. He saw guards goose-stepping on sentry duty. As his
tank whizzed by a hospital, Yoerk saw the windows filled with
the smiling faces of pretty nurses who waved gaily. The
Germans thought the Shermans, the light tanks and half-
tracks were their own. Yoerk waved back hoping nobody
would notice that there were no German crosses on the
vehicles. In fact, these veteran tankers had smeared dirty oil
on the white star which identified American vehicles; the star
also provided a perfect target for antitank guns and *Panzerfäuste* (bazookas).

Still in the lead tank, Lieutenant William Weaver was
in his glory. Mobility is an important asset of a tank. It
makes it a secure place. He had been at war long enough to
know that no one plays fair with a tank, especially the
German Tiger tanks, which had larger guns and more
armor. The GIs called the 37mm gun on a light tank a
peashooter. But there were no German tanks ahead of
Weaver, only the open highway and he was flying along it.
If indeed he came across a German Tiger, he felt his speed
could get him past it before its crew could zero in their
88mm gun. (Some tankers still believe this.) Weaver suspected Task Force Baum could send any light tanker to hell
with a smile.

In the first light of dawn, as the column sped between the towns of Frohnhofen and Laufach, it passed a German military installation with a large contingent of troops on the parade ground doing their morning calisthenics. Weaver could hear the German officer shouting the commands, but the cadence was interrupted as Sergeant Vannett sprayed them with machine-gun fire.

The exercising Germans had stacked their rifles. When the bullets began decimating them, Weaver saw them running for their weapons. The machine gunners on the tanks following Weaver's also delivered withering fire. The Germans were falling as though some giant had pulled the parade ground from under them.

In another of the light tanks, Donald Yoerk's gunner, Technician 5th Grade George Wyatt from Rosie, Arkansas, also raked the parade ground. As the bullets dug into the blacktop, they reminded Yoerk of hailstones hitting Lake Aurora. Once again, Yoerk thought to himself, This sure isn't a secret mission any more. They were now much more likely to encounter some organized resistance, a roadblock or counterattack.

In the half-track with Allen Moses were Corporal Harley Laepple, driver; Staff Sergeant Joe Kmetz, and sergeants Redo Celli, Nick Kurelis and the radio operator, Robert Zawada. By the time their half-track passed the parade ground, some of the Germans had retrieved their weapons and opened fire. A German machine gun rattled. Laepple steeled himself to keep in line. Zawada radioed Baum that the half-track was receiving fire. Joe Kmetz manned the half-track's machine gun and began firing concentrated bursts. They were past the parade ground, but the German machine gun kept hammering away. Its bullets ripped the lid off an ammunition can and slammed it against Harley Laepple's helmet. Laepple announced loudly, "Now that pisses me off."

The lid also hit Kmetz's left arm, leaving a burn 10 inches long. "Me too," said Kmetz.

At the head of the column, Weaver was confronted by a detachment of German soldiers marching down the highway. They threw their hands in the air at the column's approach.

"Don't shoot," Vannett yelled to Malinski, "they're surrendering."

With the help of Malinski, who spoke Pidgin German, Weaver ordered the soldiers to put their rifles in the road. As was the custom, the tank ran over the weapons, crushing them beneath its treads into a mangled, useless mess. Weaver and Malinski instructed the cowed soldiers to march west and surrender to the approaching American army, trying to plant the idea in the enemy's mind that the task force was leading a major American offensive.

When these men reach the parade ground, thought Weaver, they're going to think they're the luckiest men in the world—unless the SS shoots them for surrendering.

Farther on, the light tank came upon a similar group of Germans who also surrendered.

"You don't want us to take prisoners, do you?" Weaver asked Baum.

"No, we have no place to put 'em," said the task force leader. "Run over their weapons."

This time Weaver mangled a machine gun.

As the lead tank slowed and stopped to destroy the weapons of the two contingents of Germans, Moses finished bandaging Kmetz's burned arm. The other infantrymen in the half-track were opening their breakfast K rations. Many of them were also giving themselves a treat of D rations, a thick bar of specially processed, vitamin-fortified chocolate intended to provide the nutritional equivalent of a meal. The GIs were supposed to save these for dire emergencies, but they all knew they could get extra D rations when they returned from the mission. Moses, however, saved his and only ate K rations, thinking, You never know.

Now that the Germans knew the size and location of the task force—and because the column was approaching the large population center of Lohr—Baum decided to put the more heavily armored Shermans in the lead. When Lieutenant Bill Nutto got the order for a platoon of his Shermans to take the point, he cursed.

Weaver's platoon of light tanks, Baum's and Stiller's jeeps and Hoffner's recon jeeps slowed and moved to one side to allow Nutto's mediums to take the lead. Nutto's command tank, *Cobra King,* was fourth in line.

As the column approached Lohr in the brightening morning, the men could see a roadblock ahead. The Germans had overturned a heavy truck and piled spare telephone poles in front of it. It would be impossible to go around the roadblock; to go over it meant that the front of the tank would have to point skyward, thus giving the Germans a clear shot at the vulnerable underbelly. There was a *whump*ing roar as a *Panzerfaust* let go; it hit the lead tank, which swerved, skidded and came to rest at a right angle to the road. The crew bailed out through the turret and hull hatches. Scrambling to the ground, they ran rearward in a crouch.

The second tank leveled its 75 mm gun and fired; its

machine guns blazed. The shelling, heavy and ruinous, scattered the German defenders. Then the Sherman plowed into the truck blocking the road and bumped it aside. The tank's driver put it into high gear and took to the road. The rest of the column opened fire on the Germans, who were now crawling for cover in the nearby forest. The infantry in the half-tracks hurled grenades at them.

Baum went forward and back to count the casualties. The task force had lost one man in the lead tank. The tank itself was badly damaged and abandoned after the tankers blew it up. Some infantrymen had been wounded. When the column reached cover well into the forest, it paused. The two medics, Technician 5th Grade David Zeno and Private First Class Andrew Demchak, went from half-track to half-track applying sulfa, wrapping bandages and administering morphine.

"Is this the high old time you were looking for?" Baum asked Stiller.

Stiller was silent, apparently at a loss for words.

Shortly, the column continued on through the vast pine forest, the trees along the road standing as straight and unmoving as a West Point cadet battalion awaiting inspection. There was a gentle curve in the road, and there down in the valley on their right in the early sunshine was Lohr. Baum studied the town through his field glasses. It was neat and trim and as filigreed as a wedding cake. Baum communicated with his commanders, Weaver, Nutto, Lange and Hoffner. "Don't fire unless fired upon. Let's try to slip past this town. And Weaver, I want you and your platoon back on point."

Lieutenant William Weaver was admiring the same stand of pines outside Lohr. He thought they looked like an

infinitude of Christmas trees. He began to hum "O Tannen-
baum." Vannett kept time by tapping his foot. Weaver saw a
German truck convoy, hauling 88mm antiaircraft guns and led
by two tanks, coming toward him. The crews of all the lead
tanks automatically readied their machine guns in anticipation.

As the fronts of the two columns were about to pass
each other, Weaver shouted to Malinski, "Let 'em have it."

The two tanks and dozen trucks approached the task
force in fatal innocence. When the gunners on the American tanks opened up, the Germans rose with hands
outstretched as though palms and fingers could ward off
bullets. The murderous hail cut into them and they jerked
and bounded like marionettes. The tanks and the lead truck
skittered and careened. The second truck caught fire. Some
of the German personnel began diving over the sides, but
the truck drivers could not escape. As the American tanks
rolled by, the gunners raked the screaming Germans, their
machine guns smoking from the heat.

Baum's jeep shot forward and he shouted, "Don't slow
down to mop up. Keep moving."

As *Conquering Hero* swept by, Weaver saw who they
were killing: German flak girls. At this stage of the war,
with all ablebodied men at the fronts, the Germans used
young women for their flak (antiaircraft) gun crews. The
task force was killing all of them. Weaver saw one falling
from the rear of a truck, her cap off, blond hair flying. She
landed as limply as the Straw Man in *The Wizard of Oz*.

Highway 26 followed a ridge on the outskirts of Lohr.
The town itself lay down the hill, nestled in a valley. In the
town was the command post of General Hans von
Obstfelder, who that very dawn had become the commander, or *Befehlshaber,* of all ground forces in southern

Germany. Berlin believed that the attack through Schweinheim was a probing thrust in preparation for an advance by
the United States Third Army.

By first light, Obstfelder had received several discon-
nected reports about the American column. He knew it was
proceeding east, but the reports seemed to contradict each
other. He did not know if an army was following it, because
he had also received a report that Schweinheim was still in
German hands, the Americans having ceased their attack
some hours ago. He also knew that Berlin had detached
some troops from the north to mass against the bulk of the
armor supposedly following the marauding column.

At that moment, one of his aides burst into his ground-
floor headquarters with the excited announcement that the
American panzers were on the road overlooking the town.

"Are they going to attack?" he asked anxiously.

"No, they seem to be going on past us."

Obstfelder ran from his headquarters, lower ranking
officers chasing after him. From the highway in the forest,
he could faintly hear the roar of the American vehicles as
they rolled along the highway above, about ½ mile away.
The Americans were going east, bypassing Lohr, heading
toward Gemünden.

Obstfelder finally returned to his command room. He
had troops coming down from the north. He had to know
where to deploy them. To know that, he needed more
information about the attackers. Obstfelder ordered a
squadron of reconnaissance planes to maintain constant
surveillance of the Americans. He wanted a report on the
strength and composition of the enemy force. Finally, he
called the garrison at Gemünden and ordered it to prepare
for the American armor; he ordered the bridge over the

Saale River to be prepared to be blown and the approach mined to halt the Americans' progress and deny them access to the town.

The task force passed Lohr at 0900 hours. Baum again had Weaver's platoon of light tanks in the lead and the column was keeping up a rapid pace as it headed for the town of Gemünden. Gemünden, which means "the mouthing," was so named because of its location at the confluence of the Sinn, Main and Fränkische Saale rivers.

Weaver's tank began to overtake a German train on his left. Weaver saw both freight cars and passenger cars. German soldiers at the window of the passenger cars began to wave at the American tankers. They stopped waving when they saw the main gun and the machine guns of the *Conquering Hero* turn toward them.

Driver Mabrey speeded up as though racing the train. The Germans hastily poked rifles through the windows. The doors of some of the seemingly innocent boxcars slid open to reveal small antiaircraft guns.

Soreheads, thought Weaver.

At that moment, the road dipped and the *Conquering Hero* was momentarily below the level of the train. The German guns could not fire at a low enough angle to hit the tanks.

Vannett started firing the machine gun and Malinski fired the big gun, his first shell hitting the boiler of the locomotive. The boiler hissed like Old Faithful. The two German engineers leaped from their cab.

Malinski fired again. The shell hit a boxcar that carried ammunition. There was a flash of flame, then an explosion that twisted the tracks and threw debris skyward. All that was left of the boxcar was its undercarriage, still coupled front and back with other cars.

At the tail of the column, Lieutenant Moses distributed thermite grenades, normally used to destroy damaged tanks and half-tracks, to Celli, Kurelis, Zawada, Kmetz and the others. They saw the disabled train and began hurling the grenades at it, hoping that the intense heat generated by the thermite would melt the tracks and start fires.

Joe Kmetz thought, Shit, the Germans'll kick it off the track, that's all. Nick Kurelis remembered how neighborhood kids always wanted him to ram his Lionel train engines together.

Donald Yoerk's *City of New York,* behind Weaver, also took potshots at the train, but as the tank crossed the tracks, Yoerk told his driver, Private Dominique Vallani, to stop. Yoerk saw a second train approaching them from Gemünden. He thought it could cut the column in half if it got to the crossing fast enough. Vallani moved the tank to the side of the road, and Technician 5th Grade George Wyatt turned the 75mm gun toward the oncoming train for a head-on shot, while Yoerk went to work with the .50-caliber machine gun mounted on the turret. Wyatt's first shell had no effect. The second, however, hit beneath the locomotive's chassis and wrecked the undercarriage, some of the wheels spinning dizzily, some of them simply coming off and rolling away. The crippled engine burrowed into the roadbed, the cars behind plowing into it.

"Move out," shouted Yoerk to Vallani.

As Weaver drew closer to Gemünden, the road ran parallel to a large river, the Main, which makes a huge W in southern Germany. The road overlooked the river and the series of locks used to facilitate the passage of ships. Through his field glasses, Weaver saw a tugboat with five

barges in tow waiting for a lock to open. Weaver ordered
his tank platoon to fire incendiary and high explosive shells.
The barges exploded like a string of firecrackers. The boat's
crew abandoned her and the tankers saw the men swimming
for the opposite shore. Malinski set the tug on fire with
another round.

As the column neared Gemünden, Baum realized it
had unwittingly hit upon a vital target: a huge railroad
marshaling yard. He made sure that each of the tanks
poured shells down the tracks toward the trains helplessly
stranded below. He waited until the whole of the column
had passed, and then, ignoring the returning small-arms
fire, he evaluated the devastation wreaked by his force. He
counted two destroyed trains and several more locomotives
crippled by 75mm fire. There were, perhaps, another eight
trains down the tracks. He had never seen such an invitation
to mayhem. The Army Air Forces rarely bagged this many
trains in a single raid.

He radioed his first message to headquarters of the 10th
Armored Infantry, reporting the disposition of enemy trains
at the Gemünden railroad yards and asking for an immediate air strike. Baum's message was relayed by a spotter
plane, a Piper Cub well known to the GIs of Combat
Command B.

The squadron of Piper Cub spotter planes was directed
by Captain Lewis Carpenter, who had fought as a P-47 pilot
against the Luftwaffe. In a devastating crash, both his legs
had been badly smashed. He refused evacuation and,
though unfit to continue as a fighter pilot, volunteered to fly
spotter planes for the artillery of the 4th Armored Division.
He and the men who flew with him were a familiar sight to

the 10th Armored Infantry Battalion. The men admired Carpenter's spirit and his daring. He attached bazookas under his wings and stuffed his cabin with hand grenades and makeshift charges to use in harassing the enemy.

On this day, it was Damon, one of Carpenter's pilots, who was following the task force and who relayed Baum's first message back to headquarters. When the acknowledgment came through, Damon relayed it to Baum: "Message received. Over and out."

Baum not only realized the importance of the Gemünden rail complex, he worried that if there was a rail complex jammed with trains, there were probably enemy troops, unloaded during the night to march west. It was absolutely clear that he should avoid the town itself, but he didn't know how. Gemünden had the one bridge he needed to cross to get to the highway leading to Hammelburg. The sooner he reached Hammelburg, the sooner he could start back. He caught up with Weaver's tank and halted the column.

He studied the town before him. Cobblestone streets. Trolley tracks. The ruins of an ancient walled fortress on the hill. Three church spires in the center of town. Tile roofs. Gables. Quiet. Behind him, smoke rising in black clouds from the railroad yards.

Baum drove to Hoffner's recon unit. "There's a bridge we need. Find out if it's intact."

"Why are we stopping?" asked Major Stiller.

"I'm sending out the recon platoon," Baum said.

Lieutenant Norman Hoffner drove forward, his other two jeeps following. Hoffner was near exhaustion. He had spent nine months as platoon sergeant, then as leader, drawing enemy fire, one of the jobs of a recon platoon. He had seen several officers and enlisted men blown away. Working in a reconnaissance platoon is Purple Heart work and leading one is like playing Russian roulette.

Gemünden's streets were deserted. The civilians had heard the firing at the marshaling yards. They were in their basements. Hoffner kept studying the roofs of houses on either side. They were all peaked and too steep for use by the German defenders. The men in the jeeps were on the alert, their rifles at the ready.

They ran into no roadblocks. The street eventually opened onto a wide esplanade that followed the edge of the river. Hoffner saw the stone bridge. It had four spans supported by five piers. The jeeps approached carefully, then lurched to a stop. There at the approach to the bridge were dozens of land mines which the Germans had started to bury when the platoon showed up. At the far end of the bridge, across the river, was the enemy in two matching three-story houses, one on each side of the road.

Hoffner sat for a moment. He unpinned a smoke grenade and hurled it onto the bridge. It belched and poured smoke. Hoffner threw another.

"Keep throwing these," Hoffner told the driver. Then he and the corporal dismounted. The Germans across the river started firing into the clouds of fuming smoke.

Hoffner and a corporal from each of the other jeeps ran to the land mines. These looked like pies, one put atop the other, black and shiny. Hoffner knew he could activate the mines with a machine gun, but the chances were these antivehicular bombs would also destroy the road. He and the corporals tossed the mines one by one into a nearby orchard, cowering when some of them exploded.

As the smoke began to clear, the Germans on the other side were sweeping the area with machine-gun fire. Hoffner rolled another smoke grenade to the center of the bridge where it spewed its clouds. Quickly, he and his men disposed of the last of the mines and ran crouching to their jeeps.

Hoffner raced back to Baum to report that the bridge was intact, though defended. Baum ordered the platoon to return, take cover near the bridge and begin testing the strength of the enemy. Back at the river, the platoon manned the machine guns on their jeeps and fired across it at targets becoming visible as the smoke drifted away. Hoffner crouched in an alley, aiming his carbine at the windows of the building opposite.

He had just won the Silver Star.

Baum evaluated the firing he heard and immediately made a decision. He had been told to avoid contact with the enemy, but he knew this was the only good, fast route. He would have to force the bridge. He put the medium tanks in the lead and ordered a platoon of infantry from A Company, led by Lieutenant Elmer Sutton, to go with them.

"Pin 'em down. Keep them pinned down until we're past," Baum told the perspiring Sutton. Turning around, Baum signaled "Turn 'em over" to his column. Then as his jeep jerked forward, he radioed the spotter plane, hoping he would be heard. He asked for immediate air support. He faintly heard the reply, "You'll get it. Over and out."

The column moved.

The lead tank in Nutto's force kept a steady pace, slow enough so that the infantry did not fall behind. The firing from the far bank was erratic. Hoffner's platoon with its machine guns had frightened off many of the enemy.

Nutto, in the second tank, kept up right behind the

lead tank. As they turned toward the bridge, the lieutenant saw the infantry go into their protective crouch as they ducked and darted from building to building.

From his turret, Nutto heard the *whoomp* and then the second *whoomp* of a *Panzerfaust* firing. Then there were more *whoomps*. Nutto also heard the sound of an antitank gun coming from the nearby castle ruins atop a steep cliff across the river. The Germans were firing all around. There was yet another *whoomp* and Nutto saw the lead Sherman stagger. It shuddered and stopped in the middle of the road, 5 yards in front of the bridge, blocking the tanks behind it. Nutto saw the stunned platoon leader, Lieutenant Raymond Keil, helping his badly burned crew out of the damaged vehicle.

No, *no,* he thought, they've got to move the tank. His own driver put on the brakes and stopped. Now the infantry under Sutton was proceeding alone. The platoon leader knelt at one of the abutments, waving his platoon on.

Nutto hopped from his turret and went forward. He ran into the lead tank's sergeant commander. "I'm quittin', I'm quittin'," he shouted to Nutto. Momentarily, Nutto felt sympathy for him. He knew the man had been wounded twice in the last two months. Lately, he had needed a few drinks to get into shape.

Nutto grabbed the frantic GI. "Move that tank. We've got to get by. Move it."

Baum ran up. The panic-stricken sergeant saw him and broke toward the rear of the column. He was simply unwilling to face the task force commander, who would be a lot less tolerant than Nutto of someone running away in the face of the enemy.

Nutto heard another *whoomp*. Baum heard it, too. They both turned. Nutto saw the rocketlike projectile wobbling toward them. When it hit the street to their front, it threw up tar splinters, cement and steel fragments and searing pieces of its phosphorus head. Nutto felt them pierce his arms, his chest, his neck and his legs. He was on the ground wondering if he could take another breath. Sure that he was dying, a vast disappointment washed over him: Damn it, I never screwed a girl with big tits, he thought.

Suddenly, he saw Captain Baum fall to his knees, then struggle to stand up. Baum was bleeding profusely from his right knee and his right hand.

Private First Class Solotoff ran to Baum and tried to steady him. They both stared down at Nutto, who realized that he could breathe again. He tried to take stock of his injuries. He moved his hands to his chest, seeking the feel of blood, the instinctive gesture of the wounded when physical shock obliterates pain. Nutto knew he was bleeding, bleeding badly.

Often a man wounded in combat feels a certain relief because he knows the battle is over for him. But for a man on a task force behind enemy lines that relief turns to anxiety because he knows if his wound is serious enough, he will be left behind. With that in mind, Nutto scrambled to his feet. He could feel the sliminess of his blood-soaked combat jacket.

Baum looked him over and said, "All right, back to the half-tracks. You've had enough." Zeno, the medic, was there and together he and Nutto started to the rear. Nutto was surprised he could walk.

Baum looked at his own hand. He saw that the fragment had penetrated to the bone. He leaned against the tank. Radio operator Sidles was on his knees sprinkling sulfa onto Baum's leg and wrapping a bandage around it.

Baum's pants were torn and red with blood. He knew that the fragment near his knee had cut deeply, too, probably to the bone. But he could bend the knee to aid Sidles's ministrations, so he knew it wasn't broken.

Now Baum looked toward the bridge. The abandoned tank was on fire, but Elmer Sutton, the infantry platoon leader, had made it across, two GIs were running after him and two more were set to follow.

Suddenly, the Germans blew the bridge and the two men on it vanished forever in a spume of stone and concrete. The matter was decided: there was no sense in fighting here. Baum and Sidles made their way to the jeep and Baum ordered his commanders: "Move back. Back 'em up."

With his bloody hand, he spread the map out on Major Stiller's lap and quickly searched for a route. He couldn't identify another bridge on his map; he'd have to find another one, but north was the only direction in which he could proceed.

Stiller, holding one side of the map, asked, "You want to go back?"

Baum stared at him. "We don't quit," he said. "Besides we can't go back. We created a lot of confusion. If we go back the way we came, they will hand us our ass. We gotta go ahead. The krauts don't know where we're going." Baum sent Wise, who had his own jeep, back along the column to find the road north. Baum then directed his driver to turn around and head back slowly so that Baum could look over his men and vehicles and help in directing their turn-around maneuvers.

Turning an armored column around is an intricate task and doing it under fire requires cool nerve. Baum knew also it had to be done quickly because it was only a matter of minutes before the *Panzerfäuste,* the antitank gun and the machine guns would begin zeroing in on the task force.

Basically, armored vehicles, because of their treads, need a large amount of room to reverse direction. In this situation, the tanks would need to back up until they were out of the line of sight of the antitank gun before they could begin maneuvering to change direction. The vehicles at the tail of the column were able to back up and give the tanks the room they needed. Because the alternate route that Baum had chosen for the task force was near the end of the column, the half-tracks that had not yet reached this point could simply back up and wait for the tanks to turn around, withdraw and make the turn onto the new route; then the half-tracks would follow.

When Baum reached the back of the column, the half-tracks were already inching along in reverse. Allen Moses called to Baum from the rear of a half-track and asked, "Do you want the infantry on the ground?"—pointing to his men crouched and ready to jump off the vehicle. Hearing the firefight up ahead, the infantrymen wanted to find better protection from stray bullets than the open half-tracks provided.

"No, keep them in there," Baum said. "We're not staying here. We'll be moving again in a few minutes. I don't want to look for you when we're ready. There's no time."

When the medium tanks had backed out and turned north with a rising clatter, the entire column was well out of range of the *Panzerfäuste* and the antitank gun. Baum then had Sidles radio the spotter plane his second message for the 10th Armored: "Two tanks lost. Two officers and eighteen men wounded or killed. Proceeding."

Task Force Baum was now traveling on back roads.

Lieutenant Weaver, looking to the rear from his turret, saw huge, rolling clouds of black smoke over Gemünden. He was amazed at the damage they had done.

Lieutenant Moses wished Gemünden had been their objective. It certainly represented a good morning's work.

Baum was worried. He was not following the route he had planned to take. He had to keep the column parallel with the Sinn River on his right until he found a bridge. A few miles out of the city, he came to a fork. The road to the left ran up a hill, the one to the right curved around the hill's base. Baum stopped the column, while the lead tank, Yoerk's *City of New York,* went up the hill to see which route looked better.

The left fork turned out to be a dead end. Yoerk saw only rolling hills ahead, but he searched the landscape with his field glasses. The only way for the task force to go north was the other road. He ordered Dominique Vallani to put the tank in reverse. Yoerk heard the grinding clatter as the tank began to limp. They had thrown a track.

"I'm glad we didn't lose it at the bridge," said Vallani, remembering the antitank gun.

The men climbed out of the tank and started down the hill. Yoerk stayed behind and placed an incendiary grenade inside the tank and a thermite grenade down the bore of the main gun. Back at the fork, he quickly joined his crew on one of the half-tracks.

Baum checked the wounded men again. Demchak and Zeno told him there were four badly wounded men who couldn't continue; they needed immediate medical attention.

"Put them on the road," said Baum. "Stick a rifle in the ground and a white bandage on it. The Germans will pick 'em up."

The infantrymen gingerly lifted their semiconscious buddies off the half-tracks and laid them on the greening grass.

"We'll pick you up on the way back," said one of the corpsmen.

One of the wounded men feebly waved away this bullshit.

Soon there were to be more wounded. Directly ahead was a group of Germans who had outraced Baum. They had taken advantage of the column's changing direction, sped north from Gemünden, crossed the river and now prepared to bring the task force under fire again.

In Gemünden itself at 1100 hours, terrible destruction was visited by the air strike Baum had requested. There were fires and wounded men. Snow hung like a canopy over the city.

The occupants of one more American vehicle—a jeep bearing Technician 3d Class Ernst Langendorf and two other enlisted men—took this in. Langendorf spoke fluent German. He had served for a year in Tunisia and Italy with a psychological warfare unit attached to the Allied Forces headquarters in Algiers, Tunis, Bari, and later in Naples and Rome before he was transferred to the Seventh Army for the invasion of southern France. For the past eight months, Langendorf was attached to the combat propaganda team of Seventh Army headquarters. His duties consisted of making propaganda calls over a field loudspeaker to German units opposing the Seventh Army, writing tactical leaflets in German and the interminable interviewing of prisoners.

On 26 March, Langendorf was stationed at Griesheim on the outskirts of Darmstadt. His commanding officer told him to prepare for a loudspeaker mission that had been requested by a Seventh Army unit. Langendorf, his assistant and a driver set out early on the 27th and had driven that morning over a route to the south of and roughly parallel to Baum's. Langendorf had no idea how far behind the lines he had ventured. When he saw the smoke rising from the Gemünden rail yards and the destroyed bridge, he assumed he was about to catch up to the battle.

Langendorf followed the tracks of the tanks northeast and soon came upon the tail end of the task force waiting in a clearing until Yoerk had determined which fork to take. He had seen German soldiers, undoubtedly recent participants in the battle at Gemünden, hiding in the woods. Langendorf stood erect in his jeep, loudspeaker to his lips, and demanded immediate surrender.

A German army chaplain emerged from cover and scrambled toward the Americans.

"Wer sind Sie?" he asked, using his hands as a megaphone.

Langendorf told him this was the vanguard of the approaching Seventh Army. "Surrender," said Langendorf, "before our troops have to kill you. Hitler is crazy. Germany has lost the war. You will be treated according to the Geneva Convention. It is better to surrender to the Americans than to the Russians." This was Langendorf's ace in the hole.

Retracing his path, the chaplain trotted away and disappeared. Within a minute he was back, waving a pair of white undershirts as a truce flag. The men from the woods followed him.

A German *Hauptmann* (captain), limping badly, called out to Langendorf, *"Kamerad!"*

Langendorf instructed the captain to have his men

throw their weapons into the road. The soldiers complied without reluctance, pitching rifles and *Panzerfäuste*.

"*Zigaretten?*" asked the captain.

"And white bread," promised Langendorf.

Now the Germans put their hands behind their heads. Langendorf surmised there were almost 100 soldiers surrendering. He got out of the jeep and walked toward them to throw a pack of Lucky Strikes. He walked back to the jeep and the bullhorn.

He ordered: "You will wait here until the American army arrives."

Langendorf could see the disappointment in their faces, their shoulders sag. They had thought that their war was over. If other German units arrived before the Americans, their war would go on.

Langendorf then learned from one of the tank sergeants that this was a Third Army task force. "This isn't where I'm supposed to be," he said. "You go your way and I'm going to find the Seventh Army before these jokers take *us* prisoner!"

As the column prepared to move out, Baum got back in his jeep. Again the light tanks were in the lead. Weaver's *Conquering Hero* immediately ran into a speeding German motorcyclist. The impact threw the rider to the shoulder of the road. The cycle lay crushed under one of the tank treads, its wheels still spinning. When the rider arose, Weaver saw that he was a German paratrooper. As Baum drove forward to see why the tanks had stopped, the German, who was a sergeant, came to attention and saluted Baum. Baum stared at him dourly and told Solotoff, "Find out who he is and what he knows."

The German told Solotoff his name, rank and serial number. Solotoff asked him where he was going. The

German willingly told him he was on leave from the Russian front, that he was on his way to get married, that he knew of no soldiers behind him and that he wanted to surrender.

Solotoff repeated this information and added, "I think he's a deserter, Captain."

"Give me your bayonet," Baum said to Solotoff.

When Solotoff handed it over, Baum rubbed his thumb across the bayonet's edge and glared at the German. "Ask him if he lives around here."

"He's from Hammelburg," said Solotoff a moment later.

Baum pointed the bayonet at the paratrooper's throat. "Tell him I need a bridge that will get us to Hammelburg. If he doesn't know where there's a bridge, I'll . . ."

The German quailed and quickly told Solotoff there was a bridge farther on at Burgsinn.

"Okay," said Baum, handing Solotoff his bayonet, "tell this joker he's going with us." Solotoff did and then told the paratrooper there had better be a bridge at Burgsinn—or else.

The German stood with Solotoff next to the jeep. Baum in the front seat, bandaged hand in blood-soaked wrappings, put the map on his lap. "Show me the way," he said.

The German pointed it out after Solotoff's translation.

"I'm telling you this joker wants to surrender," said Solotoff.

"Tell him if he values his ass, he'd better get us to Hammelburg."

The German studied the map again and nodded as he traced the route to Burgsinn.

Robert Vannett, standing next to the turret of the *Conquering Hero* when Baum's jeep pulled up, helped Solotoff and the German paratrooper get on the tank.

When the column had been underway for a while, the paratrooper spoke excitedly to Solotoff. Solotoff signaled Vannett to stop. The paratrooper leaped from the tank and ran ahead. Around his neck he wore a silken scarf which he took off and waved as a white flag. *"Alles kaputt,"* yelled the paratrooper to the thick woods. *"Amerikanische Panzer kommen."* Throwing down their weapons, twenty German soldiers emerged from the woods.

"What's he saying to them?" Vannett asked Solotoff.

"Everything is over. American tanks are coming," said Solotoff.

Twice more the German paratrooper repeated this process. The last time, a dozen soldiers abandoned their two camouflaged antitank guns.

"Whaddaya know?" whistled Vannett. "He's the unsung hero of the mission."

"I wish we had a million like him," said Solotoff.

At that moment, a German staff car, a Volkswagen, with three occupants drove over the rim of a hill ahead. The German driver recognized the Shermans and braked hard. The car skidded to a stop. Solotoff and the paratrooper scrambled off the tank as Vannett on the machine gun and Malinski on the main gun aimed at the now stalled German vehicle. The German noncom in the front seat brought up a machine pistol but pointed it skyward and then dropped it.

From the back seat of the car, a German staff officer with a red stripe running down each of his pants legs and red lapels on his greatcoat emerged. Haughtily Herr General Oriel Lotz walked toward the tank, his highly polished boots grinding loudly in the grit of the roadway.

Baum stalked forward. "Over here, Solotoff. Let's see what this character has to say."

Lotz gave them only his name, rank and serial number.

"Put him on the hood of one of the half-tracks," said Baum. "If there are others up ahead and they see him, maybe they won't shoot."

With bruised pride, the general was escorted to one of the half-tracks where he mounted the hood with as much dignity as he could muster. His driver and aide saluted their chief as he bounced past them. One had salvaged the general's riding crop but could not get it to him. Oriel Lotz was on his way. So was the task force. And it was much more formidable now that it had a German staff officer as a hood ornament.

The bridge at Burgsinn was intact. It was a small bridge; the tanks crossed over one at a time, each crew hoping the bridge would not buckle.

Baum gauged he was 10 or 12 miles from Hammelburg, which he could approach from the north. It was incredible he had come this far. In the distance, he could see farmers moving slowly in the fields and cows as stationary as stones. It was in the cards that the Germans would be on to him by this time, yet, he and his column had spent twelve hours and more in a devastating attack through the German rear. If the Germans intended to stop him before he reached the camp, they had to erect and man defenses pretty soon. Something told him he was going to make it to the camp. He hoped he was going to make it back. He had a half-track filled with spare gasoline, but was it enough? What kind of help would they get going back? Would they get any?

And Baum had another worry. If the Germans knew they were coming, it wouldn't be long before the Hammelburg POWs knew. With that kind of news, they might attempt a premature uprising. Baum was sure that if the prisoners tried to overwhelm their guards in advance of his arrival, many would be killed or wounded. He offered a silent prayer that the POWs would wait to see if the task force could actually reach them and take control of the camp for them.

Ahead was the town of Gräfendorf, and the landscape was blotted by hundreds of shaggy, unkempt figures, their feet wrapped in burlap, working with shovels and hoes. They were guarded by a contingent of German soldiers who were eating their rations at the side of the road. As the column roared into view, the guards threw up their hands. The German paratrooper shouted to them and they dropped their weapons, rising slowly with their hands on top of their heads.

The men in the fields began waving their arms and running toward the American column. They were Russian POWs, work slaves for the Third Reich.

The Russians surrounded Baum's jeep and the tanks ahead. They tried to kiss his hand. They shouted, *"Amerikanski, Amerikanski."* They clapped Major Stiller on the shoulder and two of them kissed Sidles. Baum saw one of the Russians take off after a German guard, knife in hand. The German turned and ran for the woods.

The German captives were sullen and cowed.

Baum managed to maintain order, despite the wild exuberance of the Russians. Solotoff found a Russian who spoke German and told him that the column was the vanguard of the American forces.

"They want to know what they can do to help," Solotoff said. "They want to know if they can take the town."

"Soon as we get through," said Baum. He knew how badly the Germans treated Russian POWs: cruel neglect, torture, summary executions. He had a vision of pillage and fire and rape that made the Spanish conquistadores look like Boy Scouts on a jamboree.

"They want the general," Solotoff said.

Baum thought a moment, then said, "Why not? Tell them the Germans are now their prisoners, except the paratrooper. Him we keep. If they're going into town, tell them the first thing to raid is the police station. They'll need weapons."

Minutes before these men had been on the point of utter exhaustion and profound despair. It was astonishing what freedom and the chance for revenge could do for a beaten man. The Russians had turned tigers. When his column had passed through Gräfendorf, Baum could hear the melee that the freed Russians were creating.

Then behind him he heard a more menacing sound. Baum searched the skies with his binoculars. It was a spotter plane, but this time it was German, a Fieseler Storch.

There it was, right on their tail. Stiller pointed it out. It was coming in low now, counting them. The men in the column knew what to do and were instantly at their machine guns. The plane was weaving and keeping its distance, a difficult target.

Every infantryman was on his feet, firing with his weapon—BAR, carbine or M-1. Even the wounded propped themselves up and were firing. Good men, thought Baum.

The single-engined plane passed by the column, waggled twice, circled and came in again from the rear. The GIs swiveled their machine guns and fired desperately. Baum could hear the ejected shells cascading on the road below.

The plane completed its sprint, turned and began to climb. Futile tracers followed it. It rocked its wings in mockery.

"Now they know who we are," said Stiller.

"They don't need a plane for that," said Baum emphatically, and added, "They want to know where we are." Stiller was beginning to annoy him.

Befehlshaber Obstfelder knew the present strength of the task force: forty-three armored vehicles (thirteen tanks, three assault guns and twenty-seven half-tracks). His three spotter planes had kept Baum's column under rough surveillance during the morning. The planes had located Baum north of Gemünden, lost him because the region was heavily forested, spotted him east of Burgsinn as he came into open country, lost him again, but now found him near Gräfendorf.

Obstfelder, through a piece of good luck, also knew where the column was headed. It wasn't to the industrial center at Schweinfurt or at Würzburg, but to Hammelburg.

Oriel Lotz whom Abe Baum had so cavalierly handed over to the Russians, had not perished. It was not difficult for the general to round up the Russians and restore order after the departure of the task force. At Gräfendorf he had availed himself of a telephone to tell Obstfelder's headquarters of his ordeal and of the fact that Hammelburg was what the Americans kept talking about; the invaders were looking for a route to Hammelburg.

Obstfelder began alerting his area commanders. By the early afternoon, he had reached General von Goeckel, the oflag commandant, as well as Oberst (Colonel) Cord von Hobe, the area commander. Obstfelder had also reached General Bernhard Weisenberger at Schweinfurt, east of

Hammelburg, and requested him to dispatch his available units to reinforce the area as soon as possible.

Then Obstfelder turned his attention to the more pressing matter of restoring order to the area through which the American task force has passed. There were panic, confusion, destroyed telephone lines, wounded and killed soldiers and civilians. He was getting reports from all over the surrounding area. Apparently there had been a small battle at Gemünden and that was why the American column had been seen crossing the bridge at Burgsinn. If, as he surmised, this column was an advance element of the American Third Army, he could expect a major offensive soon. Obstfelder knew that there was little that he could do to stem the tide. His area would be overwhelmed and he would be replaced by another commander who would be equally ineffective in stopping the Americans.

Leaving the area of Gräfendorf, Task Force Baum was still following narrow country roads. Baum was not worried about the German spotter plane that had had them under surveillance. Of far more concern to him was how he was going to reach Highway 27. If he had been able to get through Gemünden on Highway 26, he would have been able to link up with 27, which runs directly into Hammelburg. Now he was leading his column on these mountainous forest roads, hoping that somehow he would be able to find a way through to the highway.

The captured German paratrooper who had guided them this far was now lost and of no use to Baum. Along the road, working in the garden next to a cottage, was an elderly German. Standing perfectly still and gaping in disbelief at the sudden appearance of so many American tanks, the bent septuagenarian watched suspiciously as

Solotoff walked toward him and greeted him in German. Brushing ineffectively at his dusty, dark work clothes, he hesitantly returned the greeting, his long, drooping white mustache nervously quivering.

Perhaps in an effort to appease these fierce, khaki-clad panzer warriors, the tremulous peasant pulled off his cap, revealing a full head of silvery white hair, and began whining to Solotoff that he was but a poor farmer, the sexton of the Lutheran church, a harmless, God-fearing man. Besides, he added for good measure, he had a heart condition. "What could you possibly want with me?"

Solotoff turned and called back to Baum, "He says he's sick."

"Tell him he'll be a lot sicker if he doesn't get us to the highway to Hammelburg."

Reluctantly, the pitiful oldster allowed himself to be led to and put in Baum's jeep. Once the column was moving again, the old man guided Baum south past Michelau, then across a bridge over the Sinn north of the village of Weickersgrüben.

Here, however, the man said quaveringly that he had never been farther than this. He couldn't help them any more. The panic in his face was suddenly replaced by pain, and he clutched his chest. His anxiety had produced an angina attack.

"Which way?" thundered Baum.

Terror-stricken now, the man pointed desperately to a road that led up a hill. When that road shortly came to a dead end, Baum finally believed that his ancient guide was telling the truth, that he was lost. The column was stopped on a work road ending at a stone quarry. It could advance no farther.

It was a little after 1200 hours. Baum's frustration was growing as he fell further behind schedule. He had hoped to reach the prison camp soon and free the POWs so that he could start back before dark. He looked at the stretched-out, idling column. "We've got to find somebody who can get us to Hammelburg," he yelled.

Baum's driver turned around and drove at breakneck speed back to the village of Weickersgrüben. Solotoff needed no prompting and leaped out of the jeep and ran into a small inn. "We need a guide," he shouted in German. The fearful occupants directed him to a house a few doors away. He ran to it, knocked on the door and then opened it without waiting for a reply. Inside he found Bernhard Gerstenberger, whom he forced outside and took to Baum.

Gerstenberger recognized the old sexton, Anton Birsch, from the Lutheran church, who began pleading with him as Solotoff translated their conversation for Baum.

"Bernhard," he begged, "I don't know how to get to Hammelburg from here. You do. You are the best hunter and guide in the area. Go with them. Show them the way."

Gerstenberger, standing fearfully in the midst of the heavily armed tanks and half-tracks, hesitantly told Solotoff that he couldn't go, that his wife was about to give birth. But he could see that Solotoff and the grim-faced, bandaged Baum were unsympathetic. The old sexton was let out and Gerstenberger took his place in the jeep. He asked the sexton to tell his wife that he would return shortly.

When they had returned to the lead tank poised on the lip of the quarry pit, Gerstenberger realized how many Americans there were and decided he'd better cooperate. He nervously told Solotoff that the lead tanks had to back around and go back into Weickersgrüben. They had to take a different road out of the village. That road, Gerstenberger assured Baum, would take them to Highway 27, the route to Hammelburg.

Along the way, the column met two German soldiers

who immediately ran when the tankers yelled at them. Gerstenberger was surprised that no effort was made to kill the two soldiers. He was also relieved—the Americans were probably going to let him live.

"That is the way to Hammelburg," Gerstenberger said, pointing down toward the valley. "Please let me go back to my wife."

The column had reached the crest of a large hill. There was a highway crossing the valley below. Baum saw other hills, more gradual, stretching to the south as far as the horizon. God damn it, he thought. Almost there. He kept studying the road below, not hearing Gerstenberger pleading to be set free.

Before giving the command to proceed, Baum finally heard Solotoff ask, "What about the guide?"

"Let him go," said Baum, who then turned to Gerstenberger as he walked away and said, *"Mazel tov."*

Gerstenberger, as he passed by the full length of the armored column, worried about the fact that he had aided the enemy, had saved his life by guiding them. Sneaking back to his home, Gerstenberger heard the sound of gunfire coming from the direction of Hammelburg. He rejoined his wife as she went into labor, and helped her deliver their son.

After making them comfortable, he said, "Dearest, I'm afraid I must go into hiding for a while. The Americans forced me to show them the way to the Hammelburg highway. If the SS finds out what I did, they will come and shoot me."

After a tearful farewell, the proud new father left, not to return for ten days, when the war in that part of Germany had ended.

:: 6 ::

Back at the Camp . . .

Every morning after breakfast the POWs in Oflag XIIIB walked through the camp looking for friends, seeking solace and comfort with buddies, hoping for news and words of hope.

The morning of Tuesday, 27 March brought unexpected events. When Richard Baron stopped to talk to John Ernest Floyd, he was told that von Goeckel had issued an order for the POWs to start packing up, that they were due to march to another camp that day. It was only one of many rumors, so Baron and Floyd didn't dwell on it.

In the barracks-lined company street, Baron rejoiced in the first nice day that had dawned since he came to the camp. A bright March sun warmed him. Despite the war and his deprivation, now the earth was greening, Baron felt hope, hope that soon he would escape this dreary, comfortless existence.

He lengthened his stride along the street and took off his combat jacket. As he folded it neatly over his arm, he recognized an old school friend, First Lieutenant Joe Geer, standing against the corner of a barracks, staring soulfully at the bright sky.

Joe's younger brother, Jim, had been one of Baron's closest friends at Manlius. The Geer boys' father had been a

Regular Army colonel. Joe had been the oldest cadet at
Manlius, staying on three years past his class while he
lackadaisically made up subjects. Joe was a loner, at odds
somehow with his background and his present. Quiet and
reserved, he kept his own counsel at school, closeting
himself in his room to listen to jazz records: Ella Fitzgerald
singing with Chick Webb, Fats Waller and Bunny Berrigan
improvising. Joe Geer drummed on the dome of his cobra
lamp with toothbrushes, a talent that Baron at the time
thought extraordinary.

In Hammelburg, Joe Geer and Richard Baron happily
renewed their friendship and in hurried strands of conversation tried to catch up on each other.

"How did you get here?" asked Baron.

"I was in the 28th Division. They got me on December
18. They cut off our whole regiment."

"What other camps have you been in?" POWs always
wanted to know what a permanent oflag was like. But
Geer's experience paralleled Baron's.

Baron then asked about Joe's brother Jim and learned
that, as far as Joe knew, he was okay.

They talked about the food at Manlius, the notorious
prune whip, which when stirred usually collapsed into a
small amount of liquid; the pot roast simmered in grease;
the pitchers of milk which both longed for now.

Together the two walked up the hill overlooking the
camp. Baron felt Joe was extremely depressed. For a
minute, he was distracted by explosions in the distance.

"What do you think that was?" asked Baron, hoping it
might be the Allies approaching.

"I don't know," came the reply. Although Geer's hope
was the same as Baron's, neither of them wanted to tempt
fate by uttering it.

"It sounds like a battle," Baron said.

From the hillside, the two men saw the company streets below filled with POWs milling around. The other kriegies had heard the noise, too.

Baron and Geer heard the whistles of the guards summoning the prisoners to lunch.

"If they're coming for us," said Joe, "the Germans will shoot us first or move us."

Baron, too, had considered this possibility. "No," he said. "Colonel Waters knows how to stall. He'll handle them. And our side will get here fast enough to save us." As they parted in the compound he added, "Look, Joe, meet me over there at my barracks after lunch." If the POWs were to be moved, Baron the veteran wanted Geer to be with him so he could help him out.

"I'll try," Geer replied.

Not many German generals commanded POW camps. But then not many German generals had served *das Vaterland* as long and as loyally as Gunther von Goeckel, Hammelburg's commandant. Von Goeckel had taken a bad chest wound in the trenches in 1916, which cost him his left lung. Thereafter he was a staff man, an administrator, serving Germany for the next thirty-seven years. He had seen a great many governments come and go in that time and he had outlived all of them.

Gunther von Goeckel was lean, clean shaven, aristocratic, competent and a model of military bearing. He was also vigorous despite his disability. He had married a young woman at the beginning of World War II and she and several members of her family, forced to flee the Russians, had come to live with him in his substantial house outside the main gate of the *Lager*.

Von Goeckel was none too sanguine about either his nation's or his own prospects. Lately, there were evenings when the air was still when he could hear the dull thuds and muffled explosions of the guns many miles away. He could certainly count the airplanes that dotted the sky on their daily raids. Von Goeckel knew the war was drawing to an end. He had, however, spent a lifetime doing his duty, one way or the other, and he continued to do so. He ran the oflag consonant with the directives from headquarters and the Geneva Convention in so far as he understood them.

To feed the American officers which Berlin dumped on him without warning, von Goeckel often had to depend upon certain arrangements with the Serbs. He had to borrow from their supplies and recruit their medical and dental personnel.

If only the war had been waged against the Serbs, running a POW camp would have allowed him uninterrupted time for solving military problems and chess problems by mail. The Serbs behaved themselves. It was almost as though they were professional prisoners of war. The "Amis," as he called the Americans, for the most part never realized that a prisoner of war camp is one of the many conditions of war, that inhabiting one demanded as much discipline and obedience as taking a well-defended position or conducting an orderly retreat. Von Goeckel had been surprised to see that the first group of Amis interned in his camp became lackluster soldiers, sullen and disrespectful even to their ranking comrades in arms. They talked endlessly about their bad luck as though they thought luck should be as evenly distributed as the turnip soup at their lunch. Later groups of Amis were much better soldiers and prisoners.

On 23 March, von Goeckel had requested permission to evacuate the prisoners before the Allied armies to the west liberated them. Anticipating that Berlin would approve his request, von Goeckel had alerted Goode to prepare the POWs for the move. But before noon on Tuesday, 27 March, Berlin ordered him to hold. The Americans had broken through at Schweinheim and the roads were to be kept open for support troops; Berlin didn't want the roads clogged with thousands of marching POWs.

The command of the Hammelburg *Lager* was in the hands of Oberst Hoepple and, though von Goeckel outranked him, Hoepple nevertheless commanded the Hammelburg area. When Hoepple learned from Obstfelder that an American tank column might attack his command, he summoned von Goeckel and asked how many men he had for the defense of the oflag.

"I have two hundred men," said von Goeckel, "all of them old. They are armed with rifles salvaged from the Belgians five years ago. They have thirty rounds per man."

"Tell them to keep the POWs in their barracks," said Hoepple. "If the Americans do attack here, order your men to pull back from the oflag to the stalag on the other side of the hill. I want your guards to stay out of the way of my regular units. Have them get the Russians ready to evacuate."

Von Goeckel asked what units Hoepple had.

In the *Lager* itself, Hoepple said he had a small cadre and a company of combat engineers undergoing training in antitank defenses. In the small town of Bonnland, 3 miles to the south on the Hammelburg range, he had 100 combat-hardened commissioned and noncommissioned officers learning techniques of antitank and house-to-house fighting. With this group were five panzers. At Ansbach, some miles south of the *Lager,* was an officer candidate school that had assigned a company of eighty cadets to Hoepple's command. Though young, each of the cadets had had at least one year of combat. Lastly, the command at Schweinfurt was dispatching for his relief a company of *Panzerjäger* (tank destroyers). Hoepple had decided to position his defenders to the north to repel the attack if possible and to the south and west to contain it if it broke through.

Henceforth, Hoepple said he could be reached at his command post (CP), which was in a building outside the oflag but within the *Lager.* On the second floor was a large window running the length of the room from which complete surveillance of the *Lager* was possible. This command post was indeed the ideal area commander's war room. It was connected by telephone to dozens of other points as far away as Höllrich and Hessdorf to the west, Bonnland and Hundsfelt to the south, and the two hills to the north. There were, as well, at least 100 bunkers, with telephone, on the antitank range itself. Throughout any battle in the area, Hoepple would be able to talk directly to his subordinate officers. He also had the tactical advantage of knowing the exact distances, calibrated precisely, between points on the range.

Goode and Waters's headquarters in Oflag XIIIB was in a separate building. Every noon the "canaries" from each barracks met there to take back "the bird." The bird was the news and the canaries sang it to their barracks mates.

At noon on 27 March, Waters greeted the canaries. He

told them the Serbs had learned by their radio that an American column was on its way eastward, that it might pass close by Hammelburg.

Several of the canaries volunteered as "stooges," who would keep their eye out for German guards while others packed up contraband. The cry "Goon up" meant that those inside had to hide the contraband immediately. Most of all they feared Feldwebel Knorr, a sergeant the POWs called "the ferret," who prowled the barracks constantly with a long stick he stuck into the ground to discover tunnels. But Knorr didn't appear and the men were not interrupted until one of the stooges came in and announced, "The guards in the towers are coming down. They're bringing their machine guns with them."

Colonel Paul Goode saw that General von Goeckel had his steel helmet on the desk and that he was wearing his holstered Luger. Goode saluted and sat beside his Serbian counterpart, Colonel General Brastich, who had also been summoned to the commandant's headquarters.

Hauptmann Hans Fuchs, who spoke English with a clipped British accent and, in peacetime, manufactured violins and cellos, was the German interpreter.

Von Goeckel informed Goode and Brastchic that an American column was headed for the camp, probably to liberate it. Goode winked at the Serbian general who repressed a smile.

Von Goeckel continued, "We must naturally keep order in the camp. You are still my prisoners and I am still responsible for your detention and safety. My men can bear no interruption in their duties. I expect the prisoners of war to take refuge in their barracks and in the air raid trenches.

Gentlemen, it is late in the war. I beg you to remember that the Americans will be firing in your direction when they fire at us."

Then the commandant dismissed them. Alone, he left his sandbag-girdled headquarters. Raising his field glasses, he stared north. Momentarily he thought he spied the outline of an American Sherman tank on a ridge 1,000 yards away.

On the way back to *his* headquarters, Goode heard gunfire. So did Fuchs, who was accompanying him. Both recognized the sound of American 105s and German 88s. Because the Germans often confiscated watches when they took prisoners, Goode didn't have one. But he knew it was early afternoon and that a battle was in progress.

West Pointer Donald Stewart lived in the same barracks with Curtis Scott Jones who operated the secret radio. Jones had picked up German news accounts which warned of the attack, and Goode's orders for the men to remain in their barracks confirmed it. The sound of firing brought Stewart to the window. Suddenly he forgot entirely about the gunfire.

"My God," said Stewart in wonderment, "they're raiding the mess. They're throwing the food out."

The mess personnel, also ordered to prepare for evacuation, had begun to dump food supplies. Canned goods, Red Cross parcels, loaves of bread, vegetables and small casks of margarine began piling up in the street outside the mess. Cheering men streamed from the barracks, Stewart among them. Men were clustered around the cornucopia in a thick, impenetrable semicircle, the tallest among them leaping high like basketball players to snare the food sailing through the air. When Stewart saw a friend, Bob Thompson, he thought they could help each other.

"Let me boost myself on you," yelled Stewart. "I'll catch something for us."

But Thompson never heard Stewart. He dropped to his hands and knees and began wending his way through the legs of his high-springing fellow prisoners. Stewart saw Thompson emerge on the other side shaking his hand, which had probably been stomped several times. Thompson was cradling several cans in his other arm.

Stewart thought to himself, I am an officer and a gentleman—but of medium height. There must be a way to get some of this. He ran around to the entrance of the mess and saw to his dismay that several other gentlemen of medium height had hit upon the same idea.

By the time Stewart had pushed into the commissary, it was barren. The rousing cheers of the fortunate faded as they sped back to their barracks to gorge themselves. Stewart stood rooted in disappointment as other men butted by him to see if friends would share.

There was nothing left. The pantry was stripped. All Stewart saw was a gunnysack lying atop a scuttle of coal. Desultorily he opened it. His eyes widened. Inside the gunnysack was a bag. Flour? Salt? What? Stewart stuck a wetted finger in. Confectioner's sugar!

He gripped the sack as though he had swiped it and hurried back to his barracks. He and Jones took turns with a spoon, ladling the powder into their mouths. Stewart remembered seeing Harpo Marx eat a bowl of sugar in a movie. And now Jones looked like Harpo Marx, licking his lips, his eyes two orbiting moons.

Stewart sealed what was left in the sack and sat down

with his back to the chimney and wrote a letter to a girl in Chicago, intending to mail it when he was freed. Thirty-two years later he still had the letter and the girl in Chicago was somebody else's wife and a grandmother to boot, living in a trailer camp outside of Gary, Indiana.

:: 7 ::

The Battle for

the Hammelburg Oflag

Before the war, Hauptmann Richard Koehl had been a Catholic priest and he still considered himself bound by his vows, although he now commanded a veteran company of *Panzerjäger*. He and his men had fought on the Russian front until two months ago, when they had been moved west to help counter the Allied advance into Germany. On 27 March, Koehl and his unit were in Schweinfurt, a vast military depot about 20 miles east of Hammelburg, to be refitted and resupplied.

That morning he received orders to proceed to Hammelburg to intercept an American tank column approaching from the Main River in the west. Koehl and his column of eight *Panzerjäger* entrained for Hammelburg immediately, arriving there by noon. (Trains run faster than armor, and transportation by rail would enable the *Panzerjäger* to reach their destination with full tanks of gasoline.) Koehl would be resupplied by a small six-truck convoy that would proceed by road.

An hour after his arrival, Koehl received a communiqué that the Americans were probably heading for the prison camp located about two miles south of Hammelburg.

Studying his maps, he observed that the most direct route from the Main to the oflag was eastward on Highway 26, then Highway 27. He therefore chose to wait for the Americans at the railway station, which lay on the western edge of the town and was only 1,000 yards from the highway. This spot afforded the greatest visibility: He would ambush the enemy column as it came around the curve of the highway at Untereschenbach, and if the column turned off the highway on its way to the POW camp, it would follow a road that would bring it within even closer range.

Koehl's tank destroyers were 88mm antitank guns mounted on the chassis of Panther tanks, the vehicles commonly called "Ferdinands." The heavy armor of the panzer chassis could generally deflect American shells. The 88mm gun was supposed to be accurate to a range of 1,500 yards, and its shells were designed to pierce the armor of Sherman tanks. The one drawback was that the Ferdinand's gun's traverse (its horizontal turning radius) was small, only 30°.

As Baum approached Hammelburg, he knew only that the camp lay somewhere to the south of the town. When he came around the curve near Untereschenbach he saw an intersecting road that led south and over the Reussenberg hills and decided to take it in search of the camp. At that moment Koehl's Ferdinands fired. Baum's column was traveling at top speed and entirely escaped injury. In response to the German fire, the Americans shot off everything they could and the Ferdinands went silent. Two had been destroyed and the six remaining momentarily gave up the attack in the face of overwhelmingly superior numbers.

Baum ordered his column to turn right at the intersection which was 1,500 yards closer to the enemy guns. It was a difficult maneuver for the mediums that would probably force the stretched-out column to slow down behind the lead tanks. Assault guns had been included in the task force specifically to meet antitank fire with their high explosive antitank (HEAT), larger HE rounds and their white phosphorous (WP) smoke rounds. Baum now ordered these guns to position themselves about 500 yards up the hill where the road widened into one of the tourist observation lookouts ubiquitous throughout Europe. From there they could protect the column from the enemy 88s.

When the American tank column was halfway up the hill, moving away from the German antitank forces, Koehl's Ferdinands fired again. This time their targets were barely crawling. The first salvo disabled the lead Sherman. The second hit another, but the crew managed to get it off the road and into a field.

The assault gun platoon was commanded by twenty-four-year-old Technical Sergeant Charles Orlando Graham from Thurmond, West Virginia. He had enlisted in the army in 1940 when he realized that working as a short-order cook in the Hotel Lexington was the road to nowhere. He had assumed command of the platoon only two days before when his lieutenant was killed in the battle for Aschaffenburg.

Graham watched the muzzles of the Ferdinands flash down by the railway station as they directed their fire on the turning column. The Germans, taking advantage of the awkward position of the American tanks, maintained an accurate aim and hit yet another Sherman and several half-tracks as they strained up the hill.

While Graham was setting up his three big guns at the tourist lookout, Baum was speeding up and down the hill in his jeep. He had to keep the tanks at the front of the column moving so that the half-tracks behind them weren't forced to stop. Some that had stopped had been hit already. He shouted orders to the tanks to shove aside the lead tank, which was now on fire and blocking the road. He then raced back down the hill.

Graham's guns were readied facing the town of Hammelburg and the flashing Ferdinands. "Range 1,000 yards. Fire at will," he screamed over the noise. Two of the 105s began firing. One of Graham's gunners, Private First Class Herbert Reynolds, delayed firing on the enemy in order to let off several smoke shells to shield Baum and the fleeing column.

When Baum reached the lower part of the hill, he found that men were abandoning even the undamaged vehicles. Standing up in his jeep, unmindful of the whistling shell fragments and explosions, he yelled angrily at the half-track drivers to get moving again, to drive off the road and around those vehicles that had been disabled. Baum needed as many of the men and the vehicles as he could keep intact for the attack on the POW camp. If the men dismounted and began dispersing for cover, it could take the rest of the afternoon to get them all back together again.

First Sergeant William Mackin of Company A, a brewer from Milwaukee, was in the back of Captain Lange's half-track when a shell exploded near the driver. Instinctively, all the men crouched down with their hands over their helmets. Mackin leaped out, pulling some of the others from the vehicle. He grabbed them by their arms and yanked them toward him the way he had yanked cases of bottled beer off the shipping dock to load onto the waiting trucks. Several of the men leaped over the sides to escape.

Mackin expected to see pools of blood, but apparently no one was wounded. It hadn't taken twenty seconds for the shocked and frightened men to flee the half-track, most of them amazed that they were still alive. In the front seat, however, Lange was slumped unconscious, seriously wounded. Mackin and two others carried their captain to another half-track. All around them, men spilled out from other half-tracks to climb up the hill on foot.

"Let's haul ass," said Mackin to his men. "We'll be safe over the hill."

Donald Yoerk and his gunner, George Wyatt, had also been riding in Lange's half-track since their tank *City of New York* had thrown a tread. Going up the hill on foot, they came upon a disabled tank and saw two tankers struggling to extricate a body from the interior. Yoerk jumped into the tank and helped hoist the dead gunner through one of the hatches. The interior of the tank was splashed with fresh red blood. Yoerk and Wyatt helped the wounded crew members limp to a half-track and left the dead gunner where he lay. (A retired German pensioner buried him on the spot the next day.) Then the two of them, along with Vallani and the two uninjured tankers, started up the damaged tank with the help of a maintenance sergeant and followed the road over the crest of the hill.

As the column slowly came to a halt on its way up the hill, Allen Moses and his men waited impatiently in their half-track. When a vehicle near them was hit, they began to climb off their half-track in order to run after the column—despite the exhortations from Captain Baum who rushed by in his jeep.

Robert Zawada threw down his M-1 and jumped after it. Zawada, from "Little Warsaw" in Cleveland, had spent a year at the University of Indiana in the Army Specialized Training Program. He was a shy nineteen-year-old with big ears, and because he had the highest IQ in the company, had been made the radioman.

When he hit the ground, Zawada couldn't find his rifle. He was defenseless. Panicking, he remembered that there was a "grease gun" (M-3 submachine gun) strapped above the front seat of the half-track. Clambering back onto the vehicle, he found that the straps of the grease gun were tangled around its hooks, and it took him several minutes to free the weapon. When he looked up, he saw that the half-tracks ahead of him had moved on and were disappearing over the top of the hill.

Suddenly realizing that he was sitting at the wheel of a perfectly good half-track, Zawada threw it in gear and drove on. He soon caught up with Lieutenant Moses, Kurelis, Kmetz, Laepple and the rest of his platoon. They had thought Zawada was dead.

Graham's assault guns down the hill were beginning to turn the tide of battle. His short-barreled 105s were fitted with direct sights. Because the ammunition was conveniently stored in racks around the sides and floor of the vehicle, the gunners were able to fire eight to ten rounds per minute. A good gunner slammed the shell in so hard and so fast that he usually whacked his elbow on the return motion. An experienced observer could tell how hard and how long the gun had been in action by noting how sore the loader's arm was.

After only a minute of firing, the assault gun commanded by Technician 4th Grade Alfonso Casanova from San Antonio, Texas, scored a direct hit on one of the Ferdinands and watched it lumber from its camouflaged position toward the shelter of Hammelburg. Casanova ordered his gunner, Private First Class Jack Stanley, to redirect his gun on another of the Ferdinands. Stanley and his loader, Private First Class Lawrence White, were working with exquisite precision and got off thirty rounds in the next few minutes. The fire from the five remaining enemy guns began to slacken.

Suddenly Graham spied a convoy of six trucks moving toward the Ferdinands on the highway from Schweinfurt. He ordered Private First Class Reynolds to elevate his gun in order to gain greater range. This was the convoy sent after Koehl with his spare ammunition and gasoline. Its vehicles were traveling in a tight bunch so that when Reynolds found the range and his 105 blew up one truck, the explosion started a chain reaction, blowing up the other five. The assault gun crew could feel the force of the massive explosion of gasoline and shells as well as see the billowing fireball and rising clouds of black smoke.

Under the deadly fire of the American guns, and with the task force now disappearing over the hill, Koehl decided to break off the fight. He had failed to halt the American column, but he had damaged it: two medium tanks, one light tank, five half-tracks and two jeeps were disabled.

Ironically, both forces had destroyed the reserve supplies of the other side. The Americans had obliterated Koehl's supply convoy. Koehl had wrecked the half-tracks carrying the extra gasoline for the task force. The only gasoline Baum had now was a few jerricans on each vehicle and what remained in the fuel tanks.

Once the Americans had turned south, Koehl was certain they were headed for the oflag. He decided to follow them there on a road parallel to their route but down in a valley hidden from sight, so that he could intercept or attack the Americans at some other advantageous location. He ordered his men to pull out of the railway station and head towards Fuchsstadt, two miles east of Hammelburg. There he would pick up the valley road south to the POW camp and meet a new supply convoy.

After watching the Ferdinands withdraw, Graham and his exuberant crews turned and rumbled up the hill to catch up with the rest of the task force.

At the top of the hill was the French Cross, an enormous crucifix surrounded by a white fence, which had been erected in 1919 by the French government to commemorate the soldiers who had perished in Hammelburg during World War I. From this vantage point, Baum could see for miles. Amidst the checkerboard of open fields and stands of trees, about 1,700 yards down a gentle slope, lay the prisoner of war camp. Baum felt relief, elation, pride—he had made it. He had reached his objective.

Quelling these emotions, Baum attended to the next part of his mission. Scanning the POW camp through his field glasses, he could see that it was not heavily defended; he had enough men and vehicles to take it. His heart lifted.

Baum led the column across the crest of the hill to a large grassy plateau. Here he halted the vehicles and waited for some trudging infantry to catch up. When he went to brief his officers, he was surprised to see among them the badly limping Nutto, his leg wrapped in bloody bandages, ready to receive his orders.

Catching Baum's somewhat skeptical gaze, Nutto growled, "I can manage."

Baum arranged the tanks across the edge of the meadow, side by side about 50 to a 100 feet apart, the so-called "desert formation," used when the tanks were no longer confined to a narrow road. When the line advanced, the infantry would be bunched behind each tank; once the enemy began to fire, the infantry moved up between the tanks to retaliate. Baum placed the five light tanks on the right, the six mediums on the left. The jeeps were placed behind the crest of the hill, as were the assault guns, which rejoined the column as it moved into place. From this protected spot, they could fire over the tanks at the German defenses and guard the rear and left of the task force.

After briefing Weaver and Nutto, Baum went to Lieutenants Allen Moses and George Casteel, the two remaining infantry officers. Because Lange had been wounded, Casteel, who had been the executive officer, was now A Company's commanding officer. Baum ordered them to break the second and third platoons into separate squads of six or seven men to follow behind and between the tanks. The first platoon was to wait in reserve near the assault guns. The infantry was to secure and mop up when the tanks overran the enemy positions. The captain watched the two officers signaling the men, who had congregated in small groups. The noncoms responded to their orders and led the men to their positions behind the tanks. Then Baum ordered the drivers to bring the half-tracks up as soon as the firing from the defensive points ceased. They were to carry the liberated POWs back to the American lines.

As the line was forming, Baum returned to his jeep and found Stiller awaiting him. "Now that we're here, what are you going to do?" he asked the major.

"I'll take one of the squads, if that's okay with you," Stiller replied. He acknowledged Baum's nod by drawing his .45 from its holster and walking over to a group of men waiting behind a Sherman.

Baum stood up in his jeep, briefly scanned his massed forces poised to attack, and then waved his arm—go!

The tanks ground forward slowly at 5 miles an hour, the infantrymen trotting crouched behind them, warily eyeing the barbed wire perimeter of the camp. Baum's jeep followed behind the line.

One of Graham's assault guns fired a shot over the advancing line. It hit a haystack, which burst into flames. The storm of smoke and dirt momentarily obscured their objective. Not knowing what they had actually hit, the gun's crew were cheered by this evidence of visible damage to the Germans.

When the line of tanks was 500 yards from the camp, Baum tensed up, knowing that the last 500 yards of open ground is within small-arms range of the defenders.

The as yet unseen defenders were a company of combat engineers under the command of Oberst Hoepple, who had planned their placement himself.

At 200 yards, the line was hit with small-arms and *Panzerfaust* fire. The tanks and assault guns retaliated.

Inside the camp, General von Goeckel realized that the American machine guns were hitting the Serbian compound. He thought perhaps the Amis had mistaken the dark gray Serbian uniforms for those of the Germans. Tracer bullets had set the roof of one of the barracks on fire. He hurried off to find Colonel Goode.

Bill Dennis, the pharmacist captured at Bastogne, was in the American infirmary when the fire started, and from its second-story window he could see much of the camp and the battle in progress.

Dr. Marc DeMarco warned him away from the window. "Let's get these sick guys on the floor," he ordered.

As quickly as they could, Dennis and the doctor lay the wounded and sick on the floor next to their bunks.

"If they've come for us, some of these Joes are going to be disappointed," said DeMarco. "They're too sick to go." As an afterthought, he added, "You're not going either, Dennis."

"That an order?" asked Dennis.

"That's an order," said the doctor.

Dennis went back to the window. In the distance he could see the Serbs trying to put out the fires in their compound. He hoped the Americans had brought medical personnel with them but he couldn't spot an ambulance with a red cross. An ambulance might be lying low behind the hill, but Dennis knew that was no place for a combat medical detachment.

Once the shooting began, Baum could pinpoint most of the enemy positions. There was a line of foxholes just outside the barbed wire from which enemy riflemen and one or two machine guns were firing. The heaviest concentration, however, was coming from a group of nondescript outbuildings—several sheds, a stone house, a stable. There seemed to be a number of machine guns there plus one or more *Panzerfäust*. Baum shouted into his radio, "Nutto, enemy fire at ten o'clock. Move on 'em. Weaver, hold up and wait where you are."

The infantrymen were bunching more and more tightly together behind the tanks as the line got closer to the barbed wire. As Nutto's Shermans swiveled on their treads slightly to the left, the foot soldiers tried to swing with them. But at this angle they found themselves exposed to small-arms fire, and so they spread out alongside the tanks to begin shooting at the enemy. Major Stiller was yelling and leading a squad of men forward. From the tanks, the machine gunners poured out a concentrated chatter. The battle seemed to be taking place in slow motion and Baum had to look closely to see that the tanks were moving. They were.

Donald Yoerk, still in the tank he had salvaged earlier on the hill, caught sight of the water tower at one end of the camp. When he pointed it out to them, his gunners leveled their big gun and punched a hole in it near the top.

General von Goeckel walked brusquely into Colonel Goode's office and shouted, "Your army is killing Serbs. You must tell them to stop. The Geneva Convention forbids fighting in a POW camp."

"That's true," said Goode. "But I have no way of communicating with those tanks."

"I am now your prisoner," von Goeckel announced to the flabbergasted Goode. "Now it's your responsibility."

Berlin had issued standing orders to all stalag commandants to evacuate all Russian POWs as soon as liberation threatened. The Germans knew well what they could expect from liberated Russians. Von Goeckel had 3,000 Russian POWs in the enlisted men's stalag on the other side of the hill, and he was to march them eastward, away from the encroaching American forces. Surrendering to Goode freed the oflag guards to replace the stalag guards who would accompany the Russians. Von Goeckel ordered his elderly oflag guards to leave their posts and machine-gun towers and take positions in the stalag, and ordered the stalag commandant, Oberst Hans Westmann, to start the Russians marching as soon as the new guards arrived.

Von Goeckel had surrendered the entire oflag, includ-

ing the Serbian compound, which was now also left un-
guarded. The Serbian prisoners included both Communists
and Royalists. The Germans preferred anyone to Communists, and so before retreating from the camp, Hauptmann
Fuchs, the liaison officer, approached Captain Dragon
Yosefovitch, the Royalist Serb adjutant with whom he had
become friendly. He showed him where the remaining
German rifles were stored and where the key to the
ammunition was kept. When the Germans departed, fifty of
the most trusted Royalists, headed by their commanding
officer, Colonel General Brastich, immediately armed themselves and manned the deserted German posts to keep
order in their compound. They all knew the Americans had
come to rescue Americans, not Serbs, and that they would
have to take care of themselves and not allow the Communists to take over.

As the battle continued, John Waters volunteered to
contact the Americans. He went to the barracks to retrieve
the American flag that had been carried from Szubin.
Captain Emil Stutter, Lieutenant George Meskall and
Lieutenant Jim Mills volunteered to accompany him.
Hauptmann Fuchs, the liaison officer, said he would go
along with them to interpret and help secure safe passage
through the German line. He would carry a white flag made
from a sheet.

With Waters and Fuchs in the lead and the junior
officers behind, the five made their way through the camp to
the front gate where the fighting was in progress. The camp
itself was in an uproar: the news that von Goeckel had
surrendered spread among the kriegies, electrifying them.

The flag bearers proceeded through the gate and
turned left on the road passing in front of the commandant's

stone house. From behind the house, a German soldier in camouflaged fatigues suddenly appeared.

When he saw the raised rifle, Waters shouted, *"Amerikaner!"*

The soldier fired.

Waters thought he had been felled by a flailing chain. The bullet hit him below the right hip, smashed the bone and was deflected off at a right angle, chipping his coccyx and exiting from his left buttock.

On the ground Waters thought, You son of a bitch, you've ruined my fishing. Later he learned that had the bullet been 1/16 of an inch higher, he would have been killed, or at best, paralyzed for the rest of his life.

Deliberately and menacingly, the soldier advanced on the stunned party. He forced Fuchs to stand against the wall of a nearby guard shed.

My God, thought Waters on the ground, he wants to shoot one of his own officers. He heard Fuchs explaining desperately. The soldier jabbed with his rifle. Fuchs kept talking.

Numb from the waist down, Waters could see sweat bathing the faces of his three companions. Fuchs explained that Von Goeckel had surrendered the camp and the American POWs were trying to reach the attackers in order to prevent further injuries to the prisoners. At last, the soldier lowered his rifle and ordered them to return to the camp. Stutter, Meskall and Mills sagged with relief that their own little Armageddon had ended. All three ran to Waters, and Mills and Stutter rolled him into a blanket retrieved from von Goeckel's house. Each man clutching one end, they first carried Waters to the German hospital outside the camp gates. There the German attendants insisted they had no room for this wounded American officer and suggested he be taken to the POW hospital within the compound. Disgusted and dismayed, the two Americans struggled back into the camp with what they believed to be a dying man.

As they staggered through the main gate, they were met by Dragon Yosefovitch. Yosefovitch, who spoke exemplary English and had served as liaison between the Serbian and American commanding officers, had observed the progress of the flag bearers and became alarmed when he saw his close friend Waters wounded.

Despite the fires in the Serbian compound, there had been no casualties there, and thus Yosefovitch was able to summon quickly two Serbs with a stretcher to carry the injured Waters to the POW hospital.

Yosefovitch shepherded the stretcher to its destination and insisted to the surgeon, Colonel Radovan Danich, and his assistant, Giry Georgevitch, a dentist, "This officer must live."

Outside, Nutto's Shermans had silenced the German defenders and Baum saw the enemy retreat in military order. He made a mental note that not only were there *Panzerjäger* opposing him in the north, but also that the retreating infantrymen were experienced soldiers. He then called up Weaver's reserve platoon from their station behind the line.

When Weaver received the order for his light tanks to resume their advance, he saw two POWs in the compound at the flagpole, struggling with the halyard. Jerkily, the Nazi flag came down and a crude American flag went up. He ordered Mabrey to take his tank at high speed over the last 200 yards and smash straight into the wire fence near the flagpole. The other light tanks followed his lead.

Hitting the wire was like charging a cargo net, but somehow the tank broke through. Donald Yoerk brought his tank in beside Weaver's, turned at a right angle and began running along the length of the wire fence, which sang as it snapped and was crushed under the tank treads.

Vallani was the first man out of the tank. He saw hundreds of prisoners charging toward him, waving their hands on high. The first kriegie to reach him leaped onto the front of the tank and asked, "Got a cigarette, buddy?"

:: 8 ::

Fifteen Hundred,
Eager for Freedom

During the battle for the Hammelburg oflag on 27 March, two POWs took advantage of the departure of the German guards and climbed up a ridge so they could watch the tanks below them.

One was an Australian lieutenant, L. Y. Lyall, who had served with the 6th Australian Division in Palestine, Egypt, the Western Desert and Greece, until he was captured on the island of Crete in May 1941. As a professional tanker, Lyall noted that Baum's attack should have come out of the east so that the ascent would have been more gradual and would have forced the Germans to retreat downhill.

The other POW, an English captain named Edward Jode who had served with the 133d Field Ambulance Battalion until he was captured in Belgium in 1940, listened to Lyall's comments and added, "Doesn't seem like very many of them, does it?"

"No matter how many, the tankers still need high ground," replied Lyall.

They watched the battle peak and end, and watched the Germans pull back and heard the firing cease.

"Looks as though the Yanks knew what they were doing after all," said Lyall, noting the empty guard towers.

"What say, old chap?" said Jode. "Shall we have a go at it?"

With a nod, Lyall and Jode ran across the compound. They climbed the ladder to one of the towers, dropped from its platform to the ground below, outside the wire, and ran for the woods. They were the first POWs liberated from Hammelburg.

Two miles away near Fuchsstadt, Hauptmann Koehl halted his column of Ferdinands. On this mission, his CO was Oberst Hoepple, who was coordinating the defense of Hammelburg. He reported to Hoepple the strength of the enemy force and informed his superior officer exactly what damage his tank destroyers had inflicted and what damage they had sustained.

Hoepple ordered Koehl to wait where he was until resupplied, then asked Schweinfurt to send additional *Panzerjäger,* fuel and ammunition.

Hoepple was furious. He scolded von Goeckel for his premature surrender of the camp. There was no question that defending the camp against such superior numbers was hopeless, but since they were expecting reinforcements, they should not have surrendered. Now the new troops would have to retake the camp.

Breaching the wire fence had ended the battle, and this was the moment the men of Task Force Baum would remember. For some it was a precious moment—they had brought freedom to their comrades in arms.

First Sergeant William Mackin saw three POWs run up, eager to join in the fight, and ask for any available weapons. But there were no extra rifles. There had been no time in the height of battle to do any more than pick up the wounded and care for them. Some of the POWs were lucky enough to find rifles on the battlefield. Mackin wrote out his casualty report.

Joe Kmetz began counting the prisoners who surged through the broken wire, but he soon gave up. The brass had screwed up again. There were a lot more prisoners here than the task force could possibly transport, even if the original group had arrived intact.

Harley Laepple climbed into the front seat of a parked half-track when he heard the medics, Zeno and Demchak, ask for help with the wounded. He drove behind the medics as they checked the bodies sprawled grotesquely on the landscape. Zeno and Demchak rolled them over. Sometimes they began life-saving procedures; sometimes they simply moved on. Other infantrymen came to help lay the wounded into Laepple's half-track.

Technical Sergeant Charles Graham was greeted by a lieutenant colonel who scrambled onto his assault gun. Shaking Graham's hand, the POW said, "Am I glad to meet you. Things have been pretty rough here. I never thought I'd see anybody so hungry that they would have to fight over a little garbage."

In the command half-track, radioman Sidles was aghast at the number of prisoners. He could see that Baum was equally upset. The captain sat there for a moment staring at the mass of men, all eager to rejoin their compatriots, all begging for weapons. Then he motioned Sidles over and told him to radio a message: "Mission accomplished. Request air cover." It was not really true, Sidles thought; Baum had not accomplished his mission, he had only reached his objective.

Private First Class Solotoff had leaped out of the command jeep at the end of the battle and was now trying to make his way back to it through the herd of POWs. As he searched and pushed, he was stopped by Major Stiller, who said, "Tell Baum I'm going to find Johnny Waters. I'll be back."

Richard Baron and John Ernest Floyd and William Meiggs were among the masses of men who clustered around each of the tanks. One tanker threw out a carton of rations and in the rush for the food, Baron shouldered his way closer to the turret. "Where's the infantry?" he called to the tanker.

"Sixty miles back," the man answered grinning.

"They're not with you?" asked Baron in disbelief.

"Nope," said the tanker, "we're just a task force."

"Oh, shit," said Floyd. Both he and Baron knew well enough what that meant. During the battle, they had assumed that the Allied armies had moved up. Now they knew it was just a combat patrol that was going to try to return to the American lines.

"You got any DDT?" asked Baron.

The tanker, pleased that he had what a POW wanted, produced a GI olive drab can. Baron, Floyd and Meiggs pushed their way back to an open space and doused themselves from head to foot with the powder. This brought immediate relief to their lice-infested bodies for the first time in several months. Although their morale had improved, they were still anxious to get the hell away from this prisoner of war camp and its terribly debilitating memories.

"Let's find one of their officers," said Baron. They agreed that they had better get going soon while the enemy was still disorganized.

The trio proceeded from tank to tank, as though they were moving from one evangelical pulpit to another. The tankers, bestowing food and cigarettes on the kriegies, excitedly described the mayhem they had wrought at Gemünden. In fact, the tankers could not stop talking about the trains they had disabled and wrecked.

"Sure wish they'd brought more infantry with them," said Floyd. "Tanks are good to get to a place but it's the infantry that's got to hold it."

"I sure wish I could find the CO of this outfit," said Baron. "I want to know why he's waiting to get out."

The task force commander, Abe Baum, was inundated by prisoners. His thrill at actually liberating the camp was short-lived. The prisoners were stampeding and now were virtually overrunning him. He could think only of New Year's Eve in Times Square. He had come to carry home 300 or 400 men and found instead 1,500 eager for freedom. The sheer numbers staggered him and he was momentarily bewildered.

Even more staggering was Baum's realization that these POWs were without discipline. In fact, no one seemed even to be trying to control them. The liberation had become a melee.

Quickly he came to himself. These men should be in formation, their commanding officers maintaining order, readying them for whatever action they would have to take. But he couldn't even get out of his jeep because of the press of prisoners around it. He was about to punch his way out when a POW colonel forced his way through and shook hands with him. It was Colonel Paul Goode. Baum and Goode wrestled their way through the crowd and stood on its outskirts.

"We only expected to find three hundred American officers here," said Baum.

"Five times that," said Goode.

"I don't have room for that many."

"You mean you're not staying to hold the camp?"

"Hell, no. The front is sixty miles from here. My orders are to come in here and get out as many POWs as I can."

"You'd better tell them that," Goode remarked matter-of-factly.

"Me? You tell 'em. They're not under my command. And you decide who's going and who's staying. I have to regroup my own men."

Baum left Goode and picked his way through the milling crowd. Eventually he found Nutto and Weaver, Hoffner, Moses and Graham, and gave them orders to determine their casualties preparatory to reorganizing the force into a column. That done, Baum began looking for Colonel Goode again. He was disappointed to find him exactly where he had left him. He was beginning to realize that Goode would probably be no help at all.

"What's the story?" he asked the colonel.

"We haven't decided yet what to do."

Baum, his knee stiff and sore, his hand throbbing with pain, angrily climbed onto the hood of his jeep. Hands on his hips, he shouted for quiet. The word "quiet" spread in murmurs and whispers like the waves created by a stone thrown into a pond. Cluster by cluster, circle by circle, the anxious kriegies heard and came running to form one big, silently expectant crowd around Baum.

"We came to bring you back to American lines but there are far more of you than we expected. We don't have enough vehicles to take all of you. Those of you who want to go will have to go on your own." Pointing west, he said,

"When I left, the lines were about sixty miles back in that direction at the River Main. That's all I can tell you. The Seventh Army should be moving up closer by now. Some of you who want to go may be able to walk along with the column, but remember, we'll probably have to fight our way out of here."

He could hear the groans and feel the resentment and bitter disappointment of the POWs. He didn't have to articulate the fact that some of them would have to stay in the camp. They clearly understood that. It was also obvious that many of them were in no shape for a grueling cross-country march or for whatever fighting would have to be done along the way.

Baum fought back the tears welling in his eyes. His elation at having reached the camp had been transformed to despair when he recognized the futility of the situation. He had been sent behind enemy lines to do a job that was impossible. He would have to abandon these POWs.

The gaping POWs stood before him, paralyzed. Even now he might be able to save some of them if only someone would take charge of them and restore order. At this point a good senior ranking officer should order the men into formation, take them back into the compound and decide who, if any, were to go out with the task force. Baum felt that he could not do this himself because they weren't his men, and he was supposed to bring them out, not return them to the barracks. Rage and frustration overwhelmed him.

Major Stiller had fought his way through the onrush of POWs coming out of the camp. Stopping several of the men to ask the whereabouts of Colonel Waters, he finally heard, with great distress, that Waters had been seriously wounded and had been taken to the hospital. Inside the nearly deserted compound, Stiller scouted around until he found the hospital.

Once he was there, Yosefovitch explained to him how Waters had been shot. The doctors, surgeon Danich and dentist Georgevitch, explained the extent of the injury and how the bullet could have killed Waters. There was still a chance, they said, that he would be paralyzed from the waist down for the rest of his life. They had operated to repair what damage they could and had found, fortunately, that no major artery or vital organ had been hit. Their main concern now was with preventing infection.

The quick action of Yosefovitch in getting Waters to the hospital and the skill of the two Serbian physicians had saved his life. Stiller spent some time with Patton's critically injured son-in-law before returning alone to the task force.

While at the hospital, Stiller also learned that Major Albert Berndt and his two medical aides, upon realizing that Waters had failed in his attempt to contact the American invaders, had recovered the improvised American flag and run it up the flagpole. This was the flag that Weaver had seen as the task force approached the camp.

Captain Benny Lemer analyzed Baum's announcement the way he would a poker hand. Baum had put the cards on the table: there wasn't room for everyone. And the danger would be great for those who did follow the column. There were no maps for the POWs, no weapons, no food. There was little hope of getting the entire operation back to the American lines without heavy fighting and casualties.

Lemer, who had been captured during the Bulge with the 106th, knew what stumbling around a forest meant for men without combat experience. He hated being a POW, but in the camp, he had a hope of getting out of the war alive.

Slowly, he walked back into the compound, and several hundred men walked with him. He went into his barracks and found that others had already preceded him. They were discussing the prospect of escape.

"We're better off here. At least nobody is shooting at us. Besides, the war is almost over. Didn't Baum say the Seventh Army would be here soon?"

Then the men in Lemer's barracks took some of the cigarettes they'd cadged and began cutting each into four parts, sticking the truncated sections in homemade reed holders.

One individual at the scene knew early that he would not return with Task Force Baum—the German paratrooper who had guided the column to the bridge at Burgsinn. In the mass confusion of the break-in, he had stolen away and crept as inconspicuously as possible into the camp. Like Stiller, he was looking for the hospital, the place where German guards were least likely to be and where he might find a sympathetic ear. At the hospital he found Yosefovitch and begged for help, explaining that he could not remain with the task force, but that if he stayed with the Germans, the SS would shoot him as a traitor. Yosefovitch found him a Serbian uniform and kept him secreted in the Serbian compound until the camp was finally liberated.

Jim Mills was late in joining the POWs milling around outside the wire because he had waited in the hospital to hear about John Waters's condition. When he ran out to the gates, he saw men already walking back into the camp. He couldn't believe the men would return willingly.

"They're not staying and they can't take all of us with

them," one of the kriegies said. Mills hadn't seen how few
vehicles were available and hadn't heard Baum's announcement. He was overwhelmed by wonder and gratitude that
his fellow soldiers had come to free him. He knew that men
had died today so that he could go home, and he meant to
take advantage of this opportunity, even if he couldn't go
with the task force.

He knew this was the time for him to take off on his
own. It would be dangerous, but he could make his way
west by the North Star and once he got near the lines, he
would be able to hear the sound of guns. He started toward
the woods. When he turned back for a last look, he saw
men climbing like ants on the tanks. And as he reached the
woods, he saw other kriegies following his example.

When Baum finished his announcement, stunned silence ensued. Finally Goode asked for a show of hands of
those men who wanted to go with the task force. Baron was
one of those determined to go. He would fight as hard to go
as he would in the going. He knew they ought to move
soon, so he didn't even bother raising his hand. Instead, he,
Floyd and Meiggs ran immediately to the tanks to find a
place for themselves.

As they neared one of the half-tracks, they saw
Demchak and Zeno inside tending the wounded. Ten to
twelve men had climbed on each tank. The trio of Thunderbirds found a place on the fourth Sherman, near the center
of the column. They had been in combat a long time and
knew better than to choose the front or back of the line.
Then Baron told them to hold his place for him.

"Where're you going?" asked Floyd.

"I want to find my friend Joe Geer. I want to make

sure he's got a place." Baron walked along the tanks, which were now swarming with men. He kept asking for Joe Geer.

He climbed aboard one tank and peered down inside the turret. In the interior of the tank, which was lit by a small red light, he saw a lieutenant with a bandaged knee sitting stiff-legged over a map. "When are we going to move?" he asked.

The lieutenant—it was Nutto—answered, "We're figuring it out now."

Finally a voice called back to him, "Geer's on the second tank." That would have to do, even though that was a dangerous spot. Baron ran back to his place. He would have felt more comfortable if Joe were with him and his friends so they could watch out for him.

A sergeant came up through the turret of Baron's tank. "Some of you have to get off the front. We can't see and we won't be able to fire our guns. There's room on the half-tracks."

Men dropped off and began running to the half-tracks which were backing around, lining themselves up at the rear of the column. The three Thunderbirds stayed on the tank.

•

Approximately 200 kriegies were finally mounted on the tanks and in the half-tracks, far too many. Captain Paul A. Kunkle of the 44th Division, captured in Rauwiller, France, sat waiting on one of the tanks with a pillowcase tied over his shoulder. It was stuffed with toilet paper, a towel, old socks and some food. An earlier arrival shouted that Kunkle and the pillowcase wouldn't both fit. Kunkle dropped the pillowcase.

Minutes later, however, he had to abandon his place altogether when a tanker told them they had to get away from the main gun. Kunkle, who thought this escape the crowning adventure of his war in Europe, dropped off and ran to the rear of the tank. He found a last small space and clambered up. One of the tankers called, "Stick the aerial up your ass and hang on."

When Lieutenant John Slack got on a half-track, it was almost filled to overflowing. He was carrying a beautifully woven Italian blanket that he had kept throughout the war and had hung onto even when he was captured. But space was scarce and Slack sadly dumped the blanket. Someone in the half-track had found a container of C rations and passed them out. Slack forced the blanket out of mind.

Donald Stewart, the sack of sugar secured in his bedroll with several packs of cigarettes, also decided to go with the column. Like all the POWs, he was bewildered and angry when he found out that the task force was an isolated unit on a raid and not the advance of a strong force. In his opinion, risking the lives of both the POWs and the rescuers by sending an unsupported task force was a waste of valuable resources.

He was making his way to a half-track when he saw a wounded soldier lying behind a tank that was backing up. Stewart yelled at the soldier to move, and several other kriegies tried to stop the tank, but it ran over the man's head. When Stewart ran to the spot he saw only the legs and trunk of the body. Where the head should have been was now a tank tread. Stewart had been captured at Sidi Bou Zid in Africa and had survived the march from Szubin to Hammelburg. The most vivid memory he would retain of the war, however, would be the sight of that headless soldier.

There was room only on the hood of the half-track.

Stewart climbed aboard and was frightened by the look of utter fatigue on the face of the driver. The man could barely raise his hand to signal Stewart to move to the other side of the hood and not block his vision.

Lieutenant Robert Thompson had been captured in Europe in September 1944, interned at Szubin, and hospitalized at Hammelburg with malaria. He decided that despite his fever, he would go, too. By the time he made his way from the hospital, ignoring the protests of the doctors, there wasn't room for him on any of the tanks.

He hid in a clump of bushes while the task force readied itself. When it started moving, he ran out toward a half-track where a helping hand hoisted him aboard and he went forward to where he could hold onto the machine-gun mount for balance.

Dentist Robert Walborn wanted to go out with the task force, but he wanted his friend, Dr. John Linguiddy, who ran the aid station, to go with him. Linguiddy, however, didn't think much of their chances.

"It's something to think about," said Walborn, and then he persuaded his friend to walk over to the tanks. "At least it's something from America. Let's just go over to one and put our hand on it. Just to feel something from America."

When they reached a tank, Walborn pushed through men standing to its rear and found space beside the turret. Sitting there he stared down at the reluctant Linguiddy.

"Linguiddy," said Walborn in mock amazement, "I do believe there is room up here for you." He stretched out his hand. Linguiddy took it and was pulled up. Now that he was actually on the tank, he was happy to wait with Walborn for their trip to freedom.

*   *   *

Driving his half-track, Harley Laepple had to crane his neck to see past the two POWs on the hood. It was hard enough maneuvering a half-track in the dark without the added problem of impeded vision. Laepple wished Baum had chased the POWs away. He had heard the captain say the task force couldn't take this many, but that was not the same as ordering the kriegies off. Laepple knew that Captain Baum had given the "school" solution to the problem: tell the men they can't go, but take anyone who wants to go anyway.

One of the men on Laepple's hood was Lieutenant Colonel Joe Matthews. Matthews knew it was an officer's duty to escape from a prison camp.

He had had to reconsider that injunction tonight. He came to the conclusion that risky and dangerous as the escape might prove, the injunction still held for him. He was surprised and disappointed when his partner on the hood tapped him and shouted, "I'm going back," before the column even started. But Matthews hardened his resolve. If they got in to get us, he thought, I'm going out all the way with them.

Abe Baum was frantic to move, to get going. He knew that an armored column was an effective force only when it was moving from one point to another, overcoming obstacles along the way. Standing here on the hill, they were easy targets. He knew he should have been out of here by noon. Now he could see the evening stars emerging. He hoped the cover of darkness would offer the vehicles some protection until the column could get moving.

Nutto, Weaver, Moses, Casteel and Hoffner formed a

semicircle in front of Baum. Lieutenant Walter Wrolson, the maintenance officer, joined them, followed shortly by Technical Sergeant Charles Graham, commander of the assault guns.

Taking the map from Nutto, Baum spread it out on the hood of his jeep. His commanders crowded in close. "We're going to try to move south along this route. Our first objective is to reach Highway 27 over here in the west. Then we'll follow that until we find a bridge back across the Main River. The Seventh Army is over here in the southwest somewhere.

"Nutto, I want you to take your medium tanks and three half-tracks with infantry, and probe down this way. See if the road is open. Keep me informed. Any questions?"

"What about roadblocks?"

"We avoid them. We can't afford a firefight at night. Look at those half-tracks and tanks. They're covered with prisoners. We'd lose every one of them. We dodge roadblocks. We back up. We run around them. That's why I want Nutto to go out first—to find a clear route to the highway. Once he's found it, then we barrel-ass out of here."

Suddenly Major Stiller appeared and tapped Baum insistently on the back. As Baum turned, he heard Stiller saying, "Colonel Waters was wounded during the attack on the camp. They just operated on him. He's going to be okay, but he can't be moved now. We'll have to go without him."

Baum nodded as if to say "So what?" and then very quickly reiterated the plan for Stiller.

"Why can't we head north and pick up the highway?" asked Stiller. "It's closer that way."

"Because we fought antitank guns there," said Baum impatiently. "We can't go back the way we came. The enemy who defended this area when we came in have had a chance to dig in. Why fight an entrenched enemy? I'm going around them. I'm going south to find the Seventh Army."

"But we don't know where the Seventh Army is," Stiller countered.

Although inwardly, Baum sympathized with Stiller—a good soldier with nothing to do on the mission—he fired back, "I said we're moving south. For God's sake, stop challenging me. I have enough on my mind. And I'm still running this show. Nutto, get going. Find me a clear route." Nutto left the small group and began ordering his tank commanders to mount up and move out.

"What about gasoline?" Stiller asked. "They got our main reserve when we came in."

"We have enough for a good run tonight," Baum replied. "The half-tracks and tanks have some of their own spare jerricans. We'll see what we need in the morning and try to find some more."

Baum stepped back from the little group and announced to all, "Okay, men, let's get this mess straightened out. Form up a column so we're ready to move out as soon as we get the word from Nutto." All eyes turned to watch the six medium tanks roar to life and begin chugging away from the camp, followed by the three half-tracks.

"I want the five light tanks at the front, then five half-tracks, the assault guns, the recon jeep and the rest of the half-tracks bringing up the rear." As Baum announced the order of march, each commander nodded as his vehicles were mentioned.

All of a sudden, the medium tank at the tail end of the column blew up. One of Hoepple's combat engineers had sneaked into the area as dusk fell and gotten off one good shot with his *Panzerfaust.*

The explosion ended Baum's dream of a miracle that would somehow enable him to bring back the POWs in an orderly way. He immediately gave the command for the column to spread out and set up a defensive formation while they were waiting to move out.

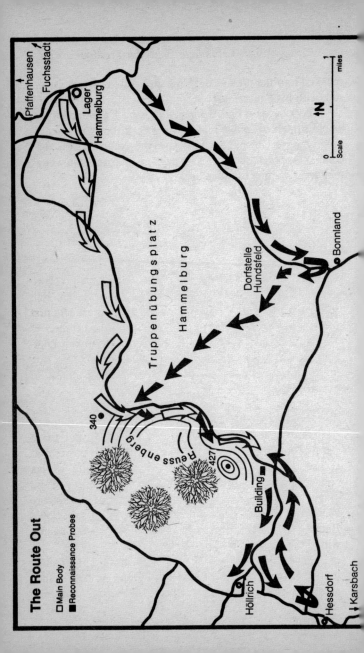

:: 9 ::

Like a Blind Worm

Over the Countryside

Oberst Hoepple, the commanding officer of the Hammelburg area, took advantage of the time while the task force assembled to reorganize his own defenses. His first priority was to block the way the Americans had come.

He now had more time to entrench his combat engineers and weapons effectively. Once the engineers were dug in, he knew this escape route was blocked. These men were expert in the use of the deadly *Panzerfaust*.

Nutto's reconnaissance group followed a southbound secondary road leading away from the camp and for a distance running parallel with the main road that passes east of the Hammelburg *Lager*. Connected directly to his communications network in his CP 300 yards north of the oflag, Hoepple watched the slow progress of the enemy vehicles. Now he began tightening the screws on Task Force Baum. His primary objective was to bottle up the enemy within the *Lager*.

Since the probe was headed south toward Bonnland, the German commander alerted the group he had in that area. He ordered these 100 officers and senior noncoms, who had been undergoing rigorous training in antitank combat techniques, to set up a series of roadblocks in the Bonnland and nearby Hundsfeld area. This sealed up the task force's exit to the south.

To the west at Höllrich, on Highway 27 roughly 5 miles from the oflag, Hoepple had deployed a company of infantry officer candidates who had just arrived from their school in Ansbach about 30 miles away to the southwest. By coincidence, this group had recently completed antitank training in the *Lager* and were therefore familiar with the terrain. To bolster the roadblock manned by these formidable cadets, Hoepple ordered his five Tiger tanks to Höllrich. This closed up the western exit from the area.

To the east, Hoepple wanted to place Koehl and the remainder of his platoon of Ferdinand tank destroyers with their 88s. Although this force was stranded for the moment in Fuchsstadt, Hoepple had arranged for it to be resupplied from Schweinfurt. When the supply convoy reached Koehl, Hoepple would decide whether or not the platoon would be moved, depending upon the location of the enemy. It was a powerful mobile reserve.

The road that the probe was following was little more than a narrow trail. Nutto was using Sergeant Kenneth Smith's Sherman, his own tank having been destroyed coming into the *Lager*. To avoid ditches, ravines, roadblocks, tank traps and ambushes in the inky darkness, Nutto decided that whenever the terrain ahead was shielded from view, he would stop, get out of his tank, and reconnoiter on foot. As a result the probe would go forward for a few minutes, stop while the injured Nutto painfully scouted ahead, wait until he returned to his tank, start again, stop, and so on.

*   *   *

Richard Baron was one of those with Nutto. When the probe first started out, he was exhilarated and optimistic. He was happy to be back in action as part of an American fighting unit again. He was overjoyed to find a place on the Sherman. As an infantry officer, he felt secure there; no matter how uncomfortable, hanging onto a tank was preferable to walking. Besides, most infantrymen were not accustomed to the luxury of a metal shield offering protection from small-arms fire.

However, as the tanks ground forward slowly and stopped and ground forward even more slowly only to stop again, Baron's exhilaration turned to consternation.

Once when they were stopped, the drivers cut their engines and from the front came the frantically whispered order, "Quiet! Quiet!" Baron, scarcely breathing, leaned even closer against the cold steel skin of the tank. From the other side of a rise, he heard the faint sound of a squad of German soldiers singing. He wondered what the drunken soldiers were celebrating. He didn't know it but they were returning to Bonnland to report to their unit, ordered there to repel an enemy attack force.

Baron's group sat wordlessly, filled with apprehension. They knew now what it was like in a submarine waiting for a destroyer to pass overhead. The Germans passed by and the noise of their singing trailed off. At that point, the twenty or so men on the tank with Baron—five on each side of the turret and another ten or so on the back of the tank—sighed with relief. They moved forward again. Riding on the Sherman it was impossible to talk or hear over the sound of the big engine and clanking treads.

The first recognizable landmark reached by Nutto's group was the tiny hamlet of Hundsfeld on the road to Bonnland. This was a group of about eight houses standing at an intersection, one of whose arms led northwest to

Obereschenbach. Nutto looked at the dark, quiet homes and thought that the residents were hiding in their cellars. Actually, the houses were deserted; the hamlet was an infantry training area for house-to-house combat.

Slowly the column clanked along the narrow roadway. The houses and yards along the road were connected by a stone wall about 6 feet high. About 200 yards beyond the intersection, Nutto spotted a pile of logs stacked skillfully across the road. By radio, Nutto informed Baum about the roadblock.

"Hold up," came the reply, "I'll be right there."

Baum sped in his jeep away from the main task force waiting with the bulk of the POWs. Since he knew the way was clear, it took only a few minutes for Baum to cover the distance it had taken the probe an hour to negotiate.

"What have they got down there?" asked Baum.

"Trees across the road. Want to look?"

Baum limped forward with Nutto until he could see the roadblock. "They're down there," said Baum with finality. "They're waiting." He knew it was suicidal to attack a roadblock at night because it was too difficult to plot the enemy's position.

He turned and started back, saying to Nutto, "Go back to that intersection in Hundsfeld and try that road. If it's open we can probably hit the highway from there." He looked at his watch. It was 2130 hours.

"We'll have to back up these tanks," said Nutto, resigning himself to another delay, another intricate set of maneuvers.

"Back 'em up," said Baum. "While you're doing that, I'll send the recon platoon up that road. You follow as soon as you can."

The three half-tracks waited while the gyrating tanks

backed up or spun around on their treads to resume the search for an escape route.

Baum sped back to the anxiously waiting main body of the task force. He noticed that about half of the POWs had reentered the barbed wire enclosure. Well, he thought, that solves part of our problem.

Turned around and underway again, Nutto's group left Hundsfeld on the new road and immediately began curving almost due north. Nutto observed the unplanned change of direction dispassionately. After all, he mused, it was the only choice and besides, it might turn out to be a smart move at that. The road was now headed into a hillier area where the probe was much less likely to be spotted.

The Americans did not know that Hoepple had both the probe and the column under constant surveillance. When the Bonnland defenders had informed him that the Americans had changed their direction at Hundsfeld, Hoepple wasted no time. He ordered a platoon of combat engineers to proceed directly to Hill 340, which overlooked the road Nutto was on and which the column would have to pass if it were to reach the main highway.

Within the hour, Hoepple could see the tanks through his field glasses, the shapes taking on distinction. He heard their engines and the clank of their treads. Hoepple told the engineers to get ready for the American armor heading toward them.

Although this was a secondary road and was unpaved, Nutto had no trouble finding his way. As a result, there was less concern about unexpected natural hazards and the probe was able to make better time. Up ahead, Hoffner, in the last remaining reconnaissance jeep, was checking out the road. Too soon there was firing. Every head in the probe turned in the direction of the sound, but all were then frozen, motionless, everyone fearing—knowing—that the way was blocked. Nutto called Baum and told him it was the recon platoon taking the fire. Baum told Nutto to wait. Once again, Baum left the column and drove to the probe.

When the recon jeep came speeding back, braking hard as it reached the lead tank where Baum was waiting, the driver suddenly began weeping.

"Is he hit?" Baum asked Hoffner.

"No," came the sad reply. "He's had too much. He'll be okay. I'll drive for a while."

"What happened up there?"

"The krauts have a roadblock and they're dug in on a hill above, covering the roadblock. If we go that way, they'll kick our teeth in."

"Okay, I guess we'll have to turn off here. This trail on the map heads west and will probably take us to the main highway at Höllrich." He ordered Hoffner and his men back to the column waiting at the oflag.

The new trail seemed to have the advantage of going through heavily forested terrain. Nutto figured that Höllrich was about 4½ miles away and located right on the highway.

"Go, go, go," Baum shouted hoarsely to Nutto, and then followed Hoffner back to the oflag.

When Baum arrived back with his main force, he could sense the mounting anxiety of his men. He could hear the bitching and criticism from the worried, impatient and tired POWs. He knew they thought he had fucked up the mission by staying in the vicinity of the POW camp, but he had more important things on his mind than soothing POWs. He didn't have time to explain his plans to a wildly dispersed audience, nor did he deem it necessary. The main column was spread out over an area of at least 1 mile.

* * *

The trail to Höllrich curved around the base of Hill 340 and headed to the southwest. Because the forest blocked the moonlight, the night seemed even darker than it had before. The probe was making little better time than when it had first set out. Once out of the forest, and when Nutto figured that he was nearing Höllrich, he halted the probe and called Baum on the radio. Checking the map against the surrounding terrain, Baum and Nutto were able to orient the probe near the base of the Reussenberg, Hill 427 on the map, the tallest hill in the area.

"When you get into Höllrich," Baum said. "On the other side of Höllrich—see it on the map?—you should be able to find Highway 27. When you do, and if it's clear, let me know. Okay? Get going."

Baum hated to send the exhausted, badly wounded Nutto out on the probe. But Nutto was the CO of C company, the medium tanks, and Baum knew he needed them up front if a fight developed. And Nutto was the only experienced medium tank officer he had left.

The slow pace, the starting and stopping, the back-tracking and regrouping of the probe, and the cold were beginning to have an adverse effect on some of the already physically weakened kriegies. Those riding on the tanks found it more and more difficult to hold on. Whenever the vehicles stopped, they would climb down to stretch their legs and to escape the frigid steel upon which they had to sit. Many began to realize that their rescue was not going to be a fast ride to the American lines. So far, the probe had been stopped in every direction it had tried to move. Sustaining all the POWs was their hope that some place up ahead was a gate to freedom, a route not blocked by the enemy, and that they would find it.

Back with the waiting column, the members of the task force took advantage of the delay, to catch some much needed sleep. For the kriegies, however, the interminable waiting, following the wondrous expectation of being rescued, of being whisked out of their imprisonment and carried swiftly to freedom, was getting them down. Few knew about the probe that had been trying for several hours to find a clear, safe route away from the camp and back to the American lines. Pacing and resting alternately, the kriegies speculated endlessly about their chances and told each other they were ready to fight. As the night wore on, as they became more fatigued, more frustrated, they complained loudly to each other: Why had the task force not yet begun to move? What officers were leading it? Did they know what they were doing? During the night, more than 1,000 POWs slipped away to walk dejectedly back into the camp.

Nutto proceeded more than a thousand yards before coming to a fork. He wasn't sure where he was exactly, but he could make out houses nearby.

After getting down from his tank again and walking, Nutto decided to take the road to the right, because he saw that it eventually led onto a cobblestone road. It is axiomatic among tankers to take the better road.

Slowly the tanks and half-tracks inched along. Now there were more houses, more intersections and side streets. At each, Nutto walked a short way to look for any activity, any sign of defenders. He didn't want to be surrounded and cut off from the rest of the column. And everywhere was silence, always the oppressive silence.

German civilians cowered within the houses, not daring to make a sound. The task force had wandered into a town posing as a graveyard.

Richard Baron was on the fourth tank in Nutto's probe. His tank waited beside a stone wall for half an hour while Nutto was making his forays. Baron's eyes were accustomed to the darkness, although there wasn't much to see. Then suddenly, he could make out the shapes of people creeping along the other side of the wall. In whispered Pidgin English, they identified themselves as "French," or "Russian," or "Farm workers." They wanted to know if the column was American.

Baron was uneasy. The noisy, milling shapes would help the enemy to locate his position. In French, he whispered to them, "Get away from here or we'll all be killed." The warning was effective and they dispersed.

Nutto made it through the town of Höllrich, and sure enough, there was the highway. This was it. He hurried back to Casteel's half-track to radio Baum.

He heard Sidles respond and then Baum got on. "We're in Höllrich and we found the highway," said Nutto.

Baum was elated. "We're moving up. Move onto the highway in ten minutes. We should be there in twenty minutes."

When Nutto, back in his tank, swung onto the highway, two bright flashes of *Panzerfaust* fire were seen by everyone in the group. In the flash, Baron could see the outline of a Tiger as it fired its 88mm gun at the second Sherman.

The concussion doubled Nutto over. He was numb.

At first he could not react. His mind registered but his

reflexes didn't respond. Someone from below shoved him up out of his perch in the turret and he fell, bouncing down the side of the tank. He saw machine-gun fire felling men, and dimly he knew his vehicles were backing up, trying to turn and retreat. His pain was intense. As he crawled over a dead body, he noticed that the Sherman behind him was under fire from the Tiger. He saw it hit. Bodies flew from it, as though catapulted.

Baron felt anxious. He feared the worst, knowing that his good friend Joe Geer had been riding on the second tank and could not have survived the fire.

Nutto didn't lie in the road long before he heard German soldiers climb into his damaged and now un-manned tank. The Germans started it up. They make them good in the old US of A, Nutto thought.

The enemy soldiers satisfied themselves that the tank was operable. An officer came over and prodded Nutto with a booted toe. Nutto groaned. The officer pointed a pistol in his greasy, dirt-caked face and asked in English, "Are you a Negro?"

Nutto said, "No, I'm not," vaguely aware that if he had been and had admitted it, he might have been shot on the spot. Many Germans had been frightened by "atrocity" stories, tales they had heard about the "ferocity" of American Negroes. He tried to pull up his sleeve to reveal his white wrist, but the officer simply pulled the pistol away and walked on to the next body.

Walborn and Linguiddy, hanging onto the turret of the third tank, had the best view of the German ambush. They saw an enemy tank, camouflaged with debris and tree branches, swivel its 88mm gun and fire at Nutto's Sherman. Walborn felt the shell tear into the tank the way his dentist's drill cut into a tooth. The Germans fired again. Again a shell burst into the armor. Nutto's tank returned one round, but the shell simply bounced off the heavy armor of the Tiger.

When the Sherman directly behind Nutto's crashed into the suddenly halted lead tank, Walborn saw men fall off from the impact. Then the German 88mm fired again.

Walborn and Linguiddy leaped from their tank, Walborn landing badly, tearing the ligaments and muscles of his left knee, an injury that would trouble him for years. Linguiddy felt something hit him in the face, blinding him in one eye.

Despite their serious wounds, both men got quickly to their feet and dashed to the sidewalk for cover. The tank they had abandoned got off a round and started backing up. Ignoring their pain, Walborn and Linguiddy scrambled onto the tank again as it pivoted on its treads. Ahead of him and to the left, Walborn saw a dug-in German soldier level a *Panzerfaust* at one of the half-tracks and fire. But then the German was buffeted from one side of his foxhole to the other as a burst from the Sherman's machine gun killed him.

Captain Paul Kunkle was riding on the very back edge of one of the Shermans. In turning around, the driver backed up so savagely he hit a stone wall, the tank's treads biting loudly into the stone. Luckily, Kunkle had seen the wall and had pulled his feet up in time to prevent them from being crushed between it and the tank.

During all the maneuvering by the probe, many of the kriegies wondered if they should be there. A few of them had climbed off the vehicles and either started back to the oflag or to take off on their own. No one tried to stop them, because when a man left his place, it made more room for the others.

When the second Sherman rammed into the disabled first one, Kunkle heard moaning in the road. The tank commander yelled, "Get off. Run for it." Kunkle and the other men on the tank jumped as the driver threw it into reverse and tried to disengage the Sherman from the one in front.

Almost as soon as he hit the ground, Kunkle heard a *Panzerfaust* shell cutting cleanly through the Sherman's armor. He ran into a doorway. When he saw the other tanks backing up and beyond them, the half-tracks doing the same, Kunkle sprinted, machine-gun fire closing in behind him. Though the half-tracks never slowed once they turned around, Kunkle got a grip on the rear door and someone helped pull him in.

The tank on which Baron was riding had not even begun to follow the lead tanks when the Germans unleashed their ambush. Escaping damage, the tank backed up immediately into the shelter of a side street. Baron saw the other undamaged tanks banging forward and back as they strove to turn around. Eighty-eight millimeter shells crashed about them—the enemy had more than one tank manning the roadblock. At last, the four surviving tanks and the half-tracks took off, hurrying as fast as they could back toward the task force.

At midnight, when Baum had received Nutto's message about finding Highway 27, he felt immense relief and a new sense of hope. He ordered Lieutenant Hoffner, the leader of the recon platoon, to lead the task force to Höllrich directly, and as Baum did so, he thanked his lucky stars that Nutto had been assigned to the mission.

Baum's jeep sped along well ahead of the column to reach the probe. He leaned forward in anticipation when he heard gunfire ahead. The anticipation turned to bitter disappointment when he heard a shell ricocheting off armor plate. That meant at least one enemy tank, probably a Tiger, was attacking Nutto.

As Baum approached the outskirts of Höllrich, he encountered the returning probe vehicles. They stopped at his command. Climbing up to the turret of the lead tank, Baum asked for a report and swore in stunned disbelief when he heard the losses—two tanks and the irreplaceable Nutto.

Once again, Baum's combat instincts helped him recover from the shock and he began evaluating the situation. He quickly decided that he had one more chance to reach the highway under cover of darkness. There was a back road that bypassed Höllrich and led to Hessdorf, a little more than a mile farther south and, like Höllrich, situated alongside Highway 27.

This time he would send out just two tanks and no infantry. Going to two of the Shermans that had just returned from Höllrich, he ordered the POWs off and told them to wait with the half-tracks.

He ordered Weaver and Hoffner to disperse the main column in a clearing on the side of a hill on their right—he described a clearing he had just passed—and await his orders. Baum would follow the two-tank probe in his jeep, and if he reached the highway through Hessdorf, he would order the column forward to join him.

Skirting along the forest as it climbed the mountain, the road passed the edge of a relatively flat, good-sized semicircular clearing, described by Baum to Hoffner and Weaver. To the south and east, there was a clear view of the valley that sloped gently down from the plateau. The west and north sides were heavily forested, with the north side rising steeply up the Reussenberg. Near where the road passed the clearing stood a stone building, apparently a barn or storage building erected originally to shelter live-stock grazing in this high pasture.

When the task force arrived, the vehicles circled around the barn and then fanned out facing the two open sides of the clearing to form a defensive perimeter. The tanks were in the center, the assault guns to the left and the half-tracks on the right and near the barn.

The kriegies who had been riding on the probe tanks watched as the two Shermans started down the road with Baum following in his jeep. Every now and then, some of the survivors of the tanks lost in Höllrich came trudging down the road to rejoin the group of POWs who had been on the tanks that were now exploring the road to Hessdorf with Baum.

Baron had been on the fourth tank, but along with the other POWs, had dismounted when Baum had told them to. The POWs knew, as did Baum, there was a strong possibility of another fight and they were quick to oblige.

The two medium tanks and Baum were on a narrow trail. It was so narrow that Baum could not pull up beside the lead tank. He leaned over and stared at the odometer, trying to gauge how far he had come—52 miles. The three vehicles passed through rolling land, the sides of the road sometimes rising up beside them, sometimes dropping away.

It was 0230 hours. Baum had about four hours before daylight to get to Hessdorf and, he hoped, find Highway 27 so the column could proceed. It was at this point that he thought he saw movement ahead to his right.

Suddenly a *Panzerfaust* let go and hit the first tank. The second tank and Baum's jeep skidded to a halt.

Quickly the jeep edged off the road so that the second tank could back up. The surviving tankers spilled out of the first Sherman and ran for Baum's jeep and the other tank, which made it back to the road. Soldiers jumped on. With a soldier on his back, others pressing against them, Baum took off, the tank following. They made it out of range of enemy fire and to the group of half-tracks and POWs at the intersection.

Baum looked over his shoulder at the receding road. Nobody was following them. Now what? he asked himself. He had to face the answer: he couldn't get out tonight. There were simply no more roads to try. He would move the column to the high ground back on Hill 427. There he could consolidate, tend to the wounded and drain the gasoline from some of the vehicles to resupply the others. In the morning, they would set out again; this time they'd have the option of going cross-country to avoid roadblocks. And, if they had to, they'd stop and fight. That meant he'd have to leave most of the POWs behind.

Baum turned to the members of the probe force and the waiting POWs.

"Let's get back to the assembly area on 427, back in that clearing. We'll reorganize so we can attack out of here in the morning," he explained.

The Shermans labored as they started the climb. Baron, Floyd and the other kriegies ran for the half-tracks and crawled in. The one Baron picked, however, wouldn't roll. The engine raced in neutral, the driver trying again and again to get it into gear. Finally, giving up, he jumped down and yelled to his passengers, "The differential's gone. We'll have to walk."

The napping infantrymen woke up and hopped out. Some of Baum's infantry had been on the go for over 100 hours and were so tired they were falling asleep in the half-tracks at every opportunity.

Baron and his buddies looked at the ascent and then at each other. "Another hell of a hike," Floyd offered dejectedly.

"Let's push it," said Baron. "C'mon you guys, push!" He didn't want to be on foot behind the departing half-tracks and prayed that somehow the gears would eventually take hold again.

Baron and the others strung along the sides of the half-track began pushing, cursing at the weight despite their loss of breath. "Together now: one, two, three." Shoulders, backs, legs tensed. Slowly they made headway until, at last, the gears found purchase and the half-track took off. Several of the men fell down as the vehicle shot forward. They ran to catch up with it. Sputtering and whining, the half-track followed the dirt road up the mountain.

On the road, below the clearing where the task force was regrouping, a crowd of approximately 75 milling kriegies began to congregate. When Baron noticed it, it consisted of virtually all the POWs. In a flash, Baron realized what was happening, the truth of his intuition not needing proof or explanation.

"They're deciding to go back," he said, nudging Floyd and Meiggs and nodding in the direction of the group.

"I can't really blame them," came Floyd's laconic reply. "It's been a long night. Personally, I think that captain who's running this here show is lost. Seems to me we're like a wounded rabbit crawling through the brush with a hunter getting closer all the time."

"That's no way to talk, Ernie," Baron shot back. "Pretty soon you'll be over there with them getting ready to walk back into that camp."

"No, you know I ain't aimin' to quit. You and me been in tougher spots than this and come through. I'd rather die than go back to that place."

"I think we'd be better off if we just broke through one of the roadblocks. We'd take casualties, but I think this armor could force its way through."

"Yeah, I know what you mean. Even trying to avoid a fight the way they're doing, they're still losing people and vehicles."

A kriegie came over to Baron, Floyd and Meiggs and asked in a whisper, "Are you guys going back?"

"Hell no, we're sticking with the task force," said Baron.

"They'll probably get us all," said the kriegie.

"Look, if you want to go back, go. It's no good your hanging around here frightening people." Baron wished his answer hadn't been so biting, but he knew that keeping up morale was essential. He and his friends walked even farther away from the group.

Many members of the task force were napping again as the main column sat and waited for orders, the vehicles' engines growling in neutral.

Vannett turned to Weaver and said, "Maybe we shouldn't sit and idle the engine while we're waiting."

Weaver ordered the engines stopped on all the vehicles to conserve gas.

"We'll be rolling, really rolling, as soon as we find a clear route to that highway."

"If we wait much longer, the *Conquering Hero*'s gonna say, 'That's all she wrote,'" said Malinski, thinking that the tank's fuel supply must be low.

Weaver knew this crew was experienced and he didn't have to worry about them doing anything stupid. They were aware of the danger. It also occurred to Weaver that he himself was now an experienced tanker.

Malinski, however, continued to ponder the situation. This was an impossible mission. In fact, to him, it seemed a suicidal one. True, they had gotten in all right—suicidal missions usually did. He just wished that they'd be able to do as well getting back. "What this task force needs," he said enigmatically to Vannett, "is an authority on retreats."

Just then Baum, leading the survivors of the probe, could be seen coming up the hill.

When Baum got back to the task force, he summoned Moses, Weaver, Graham, Wrolson and Stiller. He told them his plan.

"Some of the POWs don't want to go on. They want to go back," said Stiller.

"I'll take those who want to fight," said Baum. "Tell that to Goode."

Colonel Goode was with the group of approximately 75 kriegies observed earlier by Baron. When the colonel learned of Baum's decision, he climbed onto a tank. In no time at all, the POWs moved closer to hear him.

"We have to face it," said Goode as loudly as he dared. "Most of us can't keep going. We should go back to the camp. We have tried our best. If we stick with the task force now, we'll weigh them down. We'll follow the road back toward the oflag. Those of you who are able to go on and are prepared to fight can stay with the column."

There were only a dozen kriegies who wanted to fight. Among them were Richard Baron, John Ernest Floyd, William Meiggs, Joseph Matthews and Bob Thompson.

At the first glimmer of dawn (about 0500), more than 200 kriegies began lining up two by two, ready to march. Colonel Goode, carrying a white flag, led the column. Donald Stewart, still carrying his sack of sugar, fell in at the rear. As the line tramped up the first rise, Stewart turned back for a last look. He saw the flurry of activity around the tanks and half-tracks.

The kriegies picked up the step. Stewart was marching beside Dr. Robert Walborn. After fifteen minutes, Walborn stopped Stewart and asked, "What's that? That noise?"

"Sounds like tanks."

"Is it the task force?" asked Walborn.

"No," said Stewart. "The noise is coming from over there." He pointed north.

"It sounds like men digging in, too," said the dentist. "Who could be digging in?"

"Only the Germans," said Stewart.

Others heard it too, faintly to be sure, but the experienced among them knew what it was. The enemy was closing in on the task force. And the POWs were so exhausted, dispirited and incapable of independent thought, that it didn't occur to even one of them that Baum should be told about this.

The tanks Walborn and Stewart heard were in reality the Ferdinands, the tank destroyers, of Hauptmann Richard Koehl.

Oberst Hoepple had asked Oberst Messmacher to guide the refueled and resupplied platoon into the *Lager*.

Messmacher knew every ravine and gulley of the Hammelburg *Lager* because he had served as an adjutant in the area many times.

Messmacher found a disconsolate Koehl; he had been waiting nearly ten hours for fuel, ammo and replacements. When he finally received his orders, Koehl was amazed. Panzers, let alone *Panzerjäger,* have trouble fighting at night. But Messmacher assured the Hauptmann that he could lead the five Ferdinands through familiar territory without incident.

Koehl and Messmacher plotted the route. At 0300, they would start across the open terrain of the southern part of the *Lager* to a point behind a hill 1,500 yards east of the Reussenberg. While Baum had to work his way over the countryside like a blind worm, Messmacher acted as radar for Koehl, easily guiding him to his position before dawn. Once in position, Koehl learned that he would be supported by infantry. Then this priest began preparing a witches' Sabbath.

Hoepple also had an excellent officer commanding the forces blocking the western exits from the *Lager.* Hauptmann Diefenbach, who had lost a leg on the day the Germans invaded Poland, had been an efficient, highly respected training officer for the last five years. When the American task force had entered the Hammelburg area, Hoepple had ordered Diefenbach to bring a company of his officer candidates to the *Lager,* to the Höllrich-Hessdorf area, and set up roadblocks. Hoepple had also supplied them with five Tiger tanks.

Diefenbach's eighty eager, young cadets were armed with rifles, machine guns and a large number of *Panzerfäuste.* While an American infantry company carried one or at best two bazookas, a German infantry company carried at least ten and sometimes as many as twenty. The German *Panzerfaust* was not only much superior to the American bazooka—firing a larger projectile and having a better sighting system—but the infantrymen were also far better trained in its use. German infantrymen received extensive training, drill and field practice, which, coupled with the army's wide experience in the use of *Panzerfäuste* in the campaigns in North Africa and on all the European fronts, made them truly formidable weapons in the hands of every infantry company. The heavily armored Tiger tank, when accompanied by *Panzerfaust*-bearing infantry, was a terrifying force capable of knocking out the more lightly armored Sherman tank and routing its infantry support with its few bazookas.

In the defense of Höllrich and Hessdorf, Diefenbach's real advantage was the constant flow of information about the enemy armor he received from Hoepple. When he arrived at Höllrich, Diefenbach carefully briefed his cadets on his plan—turning his orders into a lesson for them—and then had his officers personally position each of the cadet combat squads. The eighty cadets had forty *Panzerfäuste* and they settled in and waited anxiously, hoping the Americans would come their way so they would have a chance to demonstrate their skill and courage. Their orders were very specific: in both Höllrich and Hessdorf, they were to wait until they had a clear shot on at least several enemy vehicles. Even then, they were not to begin firing until they were given a signal.

The cadets, hidden in the darkness around the intersection of Highway 27 and the road coming into Höllrich from the *Lager,* watched breathlessly as Nutto, the lone American tanker, limped slowly down the street, checking out the side streets. Soon after he retraced his steps, they could hear the roar of the enemy tanks begin to grow louder as they clanked noisily forward. One of the Tigers fired the opening shot, the cadets' signal to begin the attack. The cadets, thrilled by the roar of the battle, were exhilarated by their own skill in halting the enemy in its tracks. They took a few casualties from the doughty American tankers, but they held, and forced the enemy to retreat back into the *Lager*.

Even before Hauptmann Diefenbach left his command post to check on casualties and to inspect the captured and destroyed American vehicles, he dispatched a squad of cadets on bicycles, their *Panzerfäuste* strapped to their backs, to support the roadblock at Hessdorf and to inform its defenders that the enemy was likely coming their way next. The young men pedaled off madly, spoiling for another chance to fight and to relate their success to their comrades. When Baum and his two-tank probe reached Hessdorf, the cadets were ready. They hit the lead tank with the first *Panzerfaust* shot. Cheering wildly as the other tank and the jeep sped away in full retreat, the cadets fired again and again.

Diefenbach, briefed on the action at Hessdorf, contacted Hoepple and reported that the American armor was retreating, apparently toward the Reussenberg. Indeed it was. Hoepple had received other reports confirming this. Before he issued new orders, Hoepple felt great confidence. Not only had he successfully bottled up the Americans within the *Lager,* but he had forced them to take up a position exactly where he wanted them—on a target range commonly used for antitank problems by panzers and *Panzerjäger* in training. Once he knew where they stopped, he would know their exact range and could destroy them from virtually any spot in the *Lager,* even in the dark. He would wait until daybreak, but as far as Hoepple was concerned, the fate of the intruders was now sealed.

Hoepple's orders to Diefenbach were to send twenty of his cadets and their *Panzerfäuste* to track the Americans up the Reussenberg and position themselves farther up the slope, covering the trail leading north over the mountain. Immediately upon receiving their orders, the cadets started after Baum. Following silently behind their officers, they stole through the forest and set up a firing line on the steep terrain, looking down at the enemy force in the clearing. This time, the signal to begin firing would be a salvo from the *Panzerjäger* which Hoepple had positioned behind a hill 1,000 yards east of Baum's position.

Hoepple also sent the contingent of officers and senior noncoms from Bonnland into the same area and positioned them to provide support for the *Panzerjäger.*

:: 10 ::

Apocalypse on

the Reussenberg

After Goode led most of the kriegies away to regroup and prepare for their return march to the camp, Baum turned to the members of his task force and the six remaining POWs. It was 0400 hours. Baum told his remaining platoon leaders—Graham, Moses, Weaver—to organize their groups and to refuel as soon as it was light. Then he asked to see the POWs together.

Many of the POWs were wearing the Thunderbird shoulder patch which Baum recognized as belonging to the 45th Division, an experienced combat group. He knew he could recruit some of these officers to replace those he had lost.

"How many of you POWs are in good enough shape to fight your way out?" he asked.

All were.

"I want you officers of the 45th to take command of the infantry in the half-tracks. The rest of you will fight along with my infantry. There are plenty of weapons around that our wounded don't need anymore. Once we're rolling again, any time we hit a roadblock, I want you out of those half-tracks. This time we're going to fight our way through."

The men nodded.

"We're going to consolidate the vehicles. As soon as it's light, go help drain the gasoline from some of the half-tracks for the Shermans. Cannibalize any vehicle we're leaving behind for food and ammunition. We should be able to leave by 8:30."

"How many half-tracks are we taking?" asked Baron.

"Eight," answered Baum. "That leaves eight to destroy."

"How far can we go?" Floyd asked.

"We ought to get twenty-five, maybe thirty miles out of them," said Lieutenant Wrolson, the maintenance officer.

"That can probably get us south to Karlstadt and across the Main," said Baum. "Then, if we haven't found any more gas, we'll proceed on foot. I guess you guys are used to that.

"Finally, we're going to have to leave the wounded here in that barn. In the tanks you'll find some red cloth that we use to mark targets for the artillery. Make it into a red cross and put it on the roof.

"Now get your asses moving. Keep after the men siphoning the gas. That's our main priority."

Baum went to the half-tracks parked near the barn. These had been carrying the wounded, some his task force people, some POWs. Two of the POWs had died. A number of GIs were helping medics Zeno and Demchak lift the wounded out and carry them into the barn. Baum and a corporal carried the very seriously wounded Lange, who was in deep shock and mumbling incoherently. Settling the wounded in the dark was difficult, delicate work. The barn had a dirt floor, but using some bales of hay stacked there, it was possible to make crude pallets for them.

Working with the few supplies they had—sulfa powder,

bandages, tourniquets and disposable Syrettes of morphine—the medics did their best. Despite their ministrations, the air was filled with moans. Some of the wounded were sweating profusely while others shivered with cold. All the remaining blankets from the tanks and half-tracks were brought inside for them.

At 0530 there was enough light to begin the work of refueling. First the few jerricans of spare gasoline were emptied into the vehicles that would be continuing on. Then all empty jerricans were collected around the half-tracks that would be left behind. Some men used pumps to siphon the gas from the gas tanks into the cans. A few enterprising tankers crawled underneath, cut the fuel lines and filled the jerricans directly. This process was faster than pumping, but it was also wasteful since a certain amount of gasoline was spilled, both on the ground and on the men doing the work.

Baron, Meiggs and Floyd each took charge of a half-track. The men recognized their shoulder patches and accepted their authority and their first orders readily: "As soon as we've refueled, eat what you can; do your pissing and shitting now and get some sleep while you have the chance. You'll need all your strength. We'll be fighting later."

Lieutenant Allen Moses pondered the plight of the task force as he oversaw his men draining gasoline from a half-track. As an officer, he was usually told only what he needed to know in order to accomplish a specific mission—taking a bridge, occupying a building, crossing a stream, holding a particular piece of real estate. He was never told what the overall strategy of the war was and never knew what was going on in the rest of the world. He knew about only his immediate area, which he evaluated in terms of immediate position, strength and orders. Moses looked around at the scurry of activity: consolidating the gas into a few vehicles meant that in the morning Task Force Baum would be much smaller than when it started out, but each vehicle would have its full capability when it moved out.

Captain Abe Baum briefed his officers and checked on the wounded. Then he walked from vehicle to vehicle answering any questions and encouraging his men. There were about 240 of them and now that they were all together in a compact group, most of them felt confident and optimistic about fighting their way to the American lines.

On the morning of 27 March, first light was at 0730 hours. At that time, an orderly awakened Oberst Hoepple, who was dozing in his command post in the *Lager*. From this room, with its panoramic view, he could see the entire valley. Hoepple was up in an instant, field glasses at his eyes, searching the Reussenberg in the imperceptibly growing light.

"American tanks on the Reussenberg," he telephoned to Koehl, who was on the mountain below Baum. "Most of them are still under cover of trees."

"I can see some of them," said Koehl.

"When the Americans start their engines, get ready to commence firing," said Hoepple. "Don't fire until they move into full target view." Hoepple then gave Koehl the precise range from his position to the clearing so that his 88s would be on target from the first shot. Then he called Diefenbach.

Diefenbach reported that a *Panzerfaust* platoon was in position just inside the forest within 50 yards of the American armor. The officers and noncoms from Bonnland were dug in below the clearing. Hoepple told him, "The attack is to commence as soon as you hear Hauptmann Koehl's *Panzerjäger* start firing."

*　　*　　*

The morning light gave the men of Task Force Baum new strength and hope. They had almost finished siphoning the gasoline. Baum held a final briefing with his officers. "We're not stopping for any roadblocks this time. We take them out. If we hit a defensive position, we overrun it. If we meet Tigers, we fight them. If we hit a wide stream, I want a half-track to go in as a bridge for the tanks."

He asked the officers about the men each had in his half-track. "I want you to give them a pep talk," he said. "We go like a straight arrow until we run out of gas. Then we may be able to get some air support if we're far enough south. Sidles is trying to reach the Seventh Army on the radio right now.

"Remember, we've got to bowl over the krauts. Mount up."

It was 0810 hours. The officers ran to their half-tracks; their men, seeing them coming, began to climb aboard. Baum went to his jeep and drove it to the lip of the plateau facing south to survey the scene. He glanced back at his battered force and saw that nearly everyone was ready. A few individuals were still on the ground heading for their vehicles. "Turn 'em over," he shouted. The tanks roared to life and began to edge forward. The half-tracks growled and began jockeying to fall in behind the tanks. Baum's jeep moved into the column.

A sheet of hell engulfed the clearing. This little piece of the Reussenberg range boiled with fire and noise. The ground shook with concussion after concussion. Geysers of dirt and steel were thrown up. Here and there tree branches fluttered to the ground. Several whole trees, cut cleanly through the trunk, tumbled over.

To Baum, it seemed that a single enemy salvo had utterly destroyed his task force. Tanks were ablaze. Half-tracks careened or stopped suddenly, the infantrymen spilling out and running for cover. The enemy's attack was so well coordinated that Baum had difficulty isolating the sources of fire. From his jeep, using his field glasses, he was able to pick out a group of five *Panzerjäger* slowly advancing up the slope toward him. They were firing faster than Baum had ever seen *Panzerjäger* fire. They were, he thought, like semiautomatic rifles. Behind the Ferdinands he could see infantry advancing as well. Scanning across the slope, he next picked out a group of five Tiger tanks firing their main guns and their machine guns. Infantry was also following the tanks. The attack on the front of the column was so intense that Baum never had a moment to deal with the *Panzerfaust* fire coming from the forest at his rear.

On his side, Baum was proud to see that, despite the enemy's completely unexpected attack, many of his tankers were returning the fire. Graham's assault guns boomed their reply, as did several tanks. The German attack, however, was overwhelming and most of the American infantry were either running for cover or pinned down. As the tanks were hit, their crews were forced to abandon them. The enemy's fire was unremitting and, it seemed to Baum, uncommonly accurate.

Within three minutes of Baum's order to move, the entire clearing seemed to be one single sheet of flame, every vehicle hit. The abrupt onslaught, the accuracy, the destruction wreaked in such a short period of time was beyond comprehension. It was then, almost as suddenly as the attack had begun, that it occurred to Baum that he had lost control of the situation, that he had lost the task force.

Baum looked around and saw Sidles sitting in his half-track, concentrating so intently on his radio that he was oblivious to the inferno raging around him. He was tapping out his last message in Morse code: "Task Force Baum surrounded. Under heavy fire. Request air support."

"Every man for himself," Baum shouted, leaping from his jeep and running for the cover of the woods. Solotoff, Stiller and Sidles followed, and easily caught up with their commander. Baum's knee hampered him and soon he was skipping rather than sprinting.

Donald Yoerk was stepping back from a half-track with a jerrican he had emptied into it when the incoming shells began their devastation. He dropped the can and raced for his tank which was standing beside the stone barn. Before he reached it, he saw 88mm shells hit the barn, penetrate and explode within. Shells also hit the roof, and the stone walls suddenly and quickly collapsed, falling in as efficiently as if a demolition crew had dynamited them. Stones rained on the tank. Yoerk simultaneously realized that his tank had been badly damaged and that the wounded had been crushed by their makeshift shelter. He could hear no cries, no screams. He hoped the armor-piercing shells had killed them instantly upon exploding. If anyone was alive under the rubble, he had no chance to be rescued. (In fact they were all dead.)

Task Force Baum was now taking small-arms fire from the east and south.

The antitank guns hit Technician 4th Grade Casanova's assault gun, wounding him, Jack Stanley and Lawrence White. Nevertheless, they were able to fire three smoke shells in the hope of screening the task force.* Then they

---

*Tankers were trained in the use of tactical WP smoke which had three purposes: screening friendly movement, preventing enemy observation and accurate fire, and causing casualties.

began pumping shells to their left. Casanova heard the German fire intensify as his 105 banged away. A second shell hit them. Blood gushed from Stanley's chest. White crawled out through his hatch but was able to struggle only a few yards before he fainted.

Casanova loaded and fired the gun single-handedly. Three times he slammed shells into the breach. Another 88mm shell hit the gun and Casanova was nearly knocked unconscious. He saw his assault gun steaming like a piece of dry ice. Climbing out, he started to crawl away.

Technical Sergeant Charles Graham's assault gun was the first to return the German shelling. Graham kept it firing although German shells pocked the ground around him and two glanced off the gun itself.

Some nearby infantrymen tried to signal Graham. They were covered with dirt from cascading geysers and one of them had a dent in his helmet. He ran to Graham's gun and screamed through his cupped hands, "For Christ's sake, stop shooting. You're drawing their fire. You'll get us all killed."

Graham, ignoring this plea, urged his crew to continue. Soon enough he saw German infantry moving across the range and heard machine guns spraying his vehicle.

"Cease firing!" Graham yelled. Quickly, he and his crew climbed out and made for the woods.

William Weaver was in the open turret of the *Conquering Hero*, pointed south. Mabrey had just started the light tank's engine when Weaver suddenly felt as though he were an infant being rocked in a savage cradle. As he turned, he saw the tank nearest him engulfed in flames, burning like a Viking pyre. Inside the *Conquering Hero*,

Malinski, Vannett and Mabrey were badly shaken. Their weapons were no match for 88s.

"Out," Weaver ordered his crew. "Head for cover."

Harley Laepple was turning his half-track to get in the column. As he backed down into the valley, his line of sight was filled by flaming bursts from *Panzerjäger,* the last thing he had expected to see.

Allen Moses was pushed from this half-track by one of the men behind him and landed flat on the ground. Kurelis, Celli and Kmetz were already there. Moses drew himself up to a kneeling position to search out some cover. More men leaped from the half-track, one of them landing on top of him.

There was another wave of shells, and Moses thought that he and his men had somehow staggered onto an artillery range. If they were to find cover, they would have to find it in the woods.

"Follow me," he called. He made his way on elbows and toes, cradling his carbine across his arms.

Harley Laepple sat glued to the steering wheel. Then he felt a *Panzerfaust* shell from his left hit the tread. The half-track waggled as though it were skidding and Laepple dropped from the driver's seat and ran to the rear of the track for cover. He collided with one of the men who was jumping from the rear. Laepple picked himself up, bruised and breathless. He knew he had to get out of there.

Robert Zawada, who had been sitting beside Laepple, dropped to the ground on the other side. As he landed, a *Panzerfaust* shell tore his leg off below the knee.

Zawada, lying on his back, knew the leg was gone. He had seen it fly. In shock, he didn't feel the pain, but he was afraid to look, afraid he would faint or sicken or incapacitate himself so that he couldn't do what had to be done.

Blood was spurting from the stump. Zawada steeled himself to stanch it. He took off his necktie. Maybe George S. Patton knew what he was doing when he insisted that combat troops wear neckties. Without looking down, Zawada tied the necktie above the knee. He unsheathed his bayonet and stuck it between the loop and his flesh and twisted it twice. He felt the flow lessen. He twisted it again and the flow stopped.

Now to pass out, to rid his consciousness of the nightmare. But he didn't. He lay where he was, watching the battle. Panzers east and south, almost upon them. One of the assault guns sent off its last shell, then there was silence.

The Germans were here. Zawada saw the steady, grim-faced German infantrymen following the panzers. One of the Tigers pulled up and Zawada was afraid its machine gunner would kill him. He crawled to the shelter of a nearby tree felled by the 88s' fire.

German infantrymen stepped in front of the tanks and began rounding up Americans. An older German bent over Zawada and removed the bayonet from the tourniquet, substituting the handle from an entrenching tool and using it to tighten the binding. He left but soon returned with two Germans carrying a stretcher. Zawada wriggled from behind the tree and, pushing with his arms and good leg, maneuvered himself onto it. The Germans lifted him and carried him to one of the half-tracks. Zawada wished he'd stayed in his half-track because some of them obviously had not been destroyed. Then, finally, he passed out.

Baum found cover in the woods with Sidles and Stiller. He guessed that fewer than a hundred men had made it to the woods, many of them without weapons because of their hasty retreat. The Germans had surprised the task force at the moment of greatest vulnerability and the result was immediate demoralization.

Baum crouched and looked behind him constantly. He shouted out his last order to the task force. "Fan out. Don't follow me. Break up into groups of twos and threes and go your own way so we won't be so visible. Make your way west. Get as much distance as you can between them and you before they get here. Get going."

He saw that despite his command, ahead of him the sergeants were following the officers and the men were following the sergeants. They were moving in bunches. Baum knew this was a natural instinct in a combat infantry-man and now it was too late in the game to ask the men to rethink the rules they had been trained to obey.

In charge of a half-track, Richard Baron had counted twelve men ready to climb aboard. "Let's get ready to move out," he said. They pulled themselves into the vehicle, Baron the last in, taking the last seat on the right-hand side.

He saw Baum swing his arm to signal the start-up and he heard the motors roar. The lead tanks moved. Baron felt confident. So did the men. They held their rifles as men do when they feel they can weather the battle ahead.

Suddenly every vehicle ahead of Baron's was aflame. He thought the task force had come under point-blank artillery fire. When a gasoline-laden vehicle is hit, the fire burns around it in a 10-yard perimeter. And Baron's half-track was feeling the heat. Flames were coming toward them.

"Let's go," Baron yelled and he jumped out. He and his men ran up the hill for the woods. Despite the shelling and the crackle of small arms, Baron heard Baum shout, "Every man for himself."

As Baron, Floyd and Meiggs reached cover, they realized the task force had been destroyed; they turned to view the scene. Most of the vehicles were burning. Men were running, crazed with fear and panic. No one tried to help or care for the wounded. Baron's little group tried to get as far away as they could to avoid being hit. It would have been impossible to remain alive in that blazing inferno.

POW Bob Thompson had faced the decision of going back to the camp with Colonel Goode or staying with the task force. He told his friend John Slack he was staying. At least with the task force he wasn't a prisoner, and being free was worth whatever the risks might be.

Once he had decided, Thompson was resolute. On the bluff of the Reussenberg, he had listened carefully to Baum's orders to the kriegies and armed himself with an M-1 and two bandoliers of ammunition. He had barely finished helping siphon gasoline when the Germans commenced their attack. Thompson was mounting a half-track when German armor-piercing shells blew it away from him.

He took off at a dead run for the rear of the stone building just as its walls and roof collapsed, annihilating the wounded inside. Thompson hit the dirt and crawled to a demolished corner of the structure. From this position, he saw Zawada leap from a half-track and his leg fly off. Behind the rubble, several men crouched next to him. They were unable to move because machine guns were raking the area. An enlisted man crawled over and huddled beside him. "We're whipped," the man said, "we just don't know how to give up."

Thompson unbuttoned his jacket and shirt. He was

wearing two T-shirts, his prized possessions, even though they were gray with dirt. One of them, however, could serve passably as a white flag. Thompson stripped it off and tied it to the muzzle of his M-1.

Bullets knocked the rifle out of his hands, but the German fire soon ceased. Thompson heard the crunch of hobnailed boots and saw a German soldier approaching them. Many of the American soldiers were hastily throwing away the Lugers and German compasses they had, fearing reprisals for the souvenirs they had taken from fallen German soldiers.

"*Raus, raus,*" the German shouted. Cautiously, Thompson raised himself. The enlisted men, watching his example, slowly stood up too. The German motioned them to their feet. Thompson stayed with this group, wanting the Germans to think he was a task force officer. He had the notion that if a kriegie fought, the Germans had the right to execute him.

A squad of German infantry came up. They motioned with their rifles and Thompson and twenty enlisted men moved out, holding their hands clasped atop their helmets. They walked into the blackened and smoking clearing. Thompson winced at the smell of burning flesh. Some of the tanks and half-tracks looked like old prairie schooners scorched by a forest fire. Others, undamaged, were being driven by the Germans.

A German officer who spoke a clipped English told them to collect the wounded and dead. When they had finished—and there were more wounded than dead— Thompson and the men were ordered aboard one of the operable half-tracks that had been refueled by the Germans and was to be used to shuttle survivors back to the oflag.

Sad, bone weary, Thompson took his seat. When the

half-track got under way, he began rummaging under the seat for any food left aboard. He came upon a small metal box about the size of a pack of Camels. He opened it—diamonds!

He closed the box quickly and stuffed it in his shirt. He guessed at what it was: someone on the task force had invested black market profits in valuable stones.

At Hammelburg, Thompson was herded with the other captured men into the huge horseback riding ring at the northeast end of the camp. Quickly, Thompson bent and with his hands dug through the sawdust covering the floor and then down into the dirt. He put the box into the hole, kicked back the dirt and tamped the mound with his feet. He then moved over to where the German soldiers could search him.

Twenty-two years later, Bob Thompson went back to Germany determined to claim the diamonds from their hiding place. American Embassy officials in Bonn secured permission from the Federal Republic for Thompson to go to Hammelburg in this quest. The riding ring was still standing and the windows still had bullet holes. But the building had sometime before been converted for coal storage. Thompson had to hire laborers to move twenty tons of coal before he could dig.

The shoveling took four days. Thompson dug. No box. Thompson thanked the laborers for their efforts and went home.

Four weeks later, in April 1967, he received a letter from the American Embassy at Bonn informing him that a civilian living in Hammelburg heard about the American's excavation. The civilian volunteered that a friend of his, hired by the American Occupation Forces in 1945, worked at cleaning out the riding ring and found the metal box with the diamonds. However, that man had long since emigrated to Chicago, a city to which Thompson repaired hoping at least to look at the treasure trove.

He had no better luck in Chicago than he had at Hammelburg.

:: 11 ::

Every Man for Himself

Baum, Sidles and Stiller ran as best they could through the woods. Solotoff had not followed them. As they went farther, they heard the small-arms and tank fire cease. The krauts are rounding them up, thought Baum about his task force.

Taking a compass heading, the three men turned due west. Shortly they heard the baying of dogs behind them. Baum redoubled his efforts to keep up with Stiller and Sidles.

Before beginning their descent down the other side of the Reussenberg, they dropped to the ground, the three of them breathing in desperate gasps. Some distance away, they saw six of their fellows burst from the forest and start downhill. A line of German soldiers materialized suddenly in front of these men. Five threw up their hands, but the sixth turned to retreat into the forest, thought better of it, and turned back, hands high.

Good thinking, thought Baum. The GI had turned just in time, because a German had a rifle leveled at his back.

Sidles, Baum and Stiller forgot their tortured breathing and backed up into the forest. The Germans had apparently not seen them.

"We'll wait for night," said Baum. "Maybe they'll walk by us. Cover up with leaves." They burrowed into the forest floor.

Sidles saw the German first. He was approaching with a rifle, making straight toward them. This German had seen movement. "He's going to shoot us, Captain," said Sidles, who then snaked up a small incline to the cover of a cedar tree.

The soldier looked at the motionless Baum and Stiller. Stiller rolled over. Supine, he raised his hands. Baum got to his knees and fumbled for his .45 under his heavy coat. His hand was too heavily bandaged, however, and he was unsuccessful.

The German laid his rifle down and unholstered a pistol. With his free hand on his hip, as if posing, he slowly took aim and shot Baum. The bullet tore away Baum's fly, burned the side of his scrotum and cut through his inner thigh.

"You son of a bitch, you shot my ball off," Baum shouted, remembering his close encounter with the land mine. Why are these guys always trying to castrate me? he thought. I don't look that Jewish.

The German laughed and came closer. "I speak English," he said. "I used to live in Bridgeport, Connecticut. I came over here to fight for the Fatherland in 1939. Move it."

From his hiding place, Sidles leveled his carbine at the smirking German. But he debated with himself. Six GIs were caught only minutes before on the hillside. If he shot this man, the Germans might kill all of them. Sidles lowered the carbine and removed the bolt, throwing it into the forest. He took a chance, dropped the weapon and stood up, his hands on his helmet. It worked. The German saw him and motioned him forward.

Baum took advantage of the German's momentary distraction to throw away his dog tags that identified him as Jewish. The German holstered his P-38 pistol and picked up the .45 automatics Baum and Stiller had discarded. He ordered the three men to march to the edge of the forest and then, oddly, remarked that not enough good German-American boys had come back to help Hitler.

Even though he was in great pain, Baum realized he still had his compass concealed in his jacket. He thought, Maybe I'll come out of this yet. But his wounds and his exhaustion were taking their toll. He stumbled, almost falling, and Stiller and Sidles had to half-carry him.

They came almost immediately to a clearing populated by several dozen cowering GIs, dogs nipping at them while a platoon of German infantry laughed.

Now there was no doubt that the war was finished for the three of them—for Sidles, remembering the five campaigns through Europe; for Stiller, knowing no sensible man would have posted odds on their chances; and for Baum, finally realizing that every fight ends in defeat for someone.

They marched back through the forest to the site of the final battle, where they joined the growing group of Americans who had been captured.

A sergeant from the task force said to Sidles, "Too bad we haven't got two lives. One to give up in Germany and one to use to go back to the States."

A German officer separated the surprised and protesting Stiller from the rest of the group. Because he was a major, they thought he was the task force leader. A sergeant and two enlisted men confiscated valuables from the task force members one by one. When Sidles dropped a spoon from his pocket while being searched, he was told, "Pick it up. You'll need it—if you find anything to eat."

After the search, the captured men were marched back toward the oflag. Sidles supported Baum as the captain struggled to keep up. There were German civilians along the road that led to Hundsfeld, and the young cadets armed with *Panzerfäuste,* who had come to see the new prisoners and pick up American souvenirs. As they passed a farm-house fronted by a stone wall, Baum gave out. His wounds had begun to bleed again. He lay down on the wall.

"I can't make it any farther," he told Sidles.

Sidles tried to convince him to go on, but he knew that when a man's strength is gone, it's gone; no words can restore it. Sidles saw that one of the guards did not like the delay.

"Leave me," said Baum. "I'll make out somehow from here."

Sidles shook his hand and turned and ran up the road to join the tail end of the marching column. He was sure that was the last he would ever see of Abe Baum.

When Lieutenant William Weaver was separated from his men, he also ran into the woods to escape the ambush. First he saw German soldiers ahead of him, then he heard others calling to each other. Weaver sought a hiding place, but it was futile. He waited. A young German approached and stuck a Schmeisser submachine gun into his belly. "For *you,* Lieutenant, the war is over," said the soldier, empha-sizing his point by jamming the muzzle even harder into Weaver.

And a short war it was, too, remarked Weaver to himself.

*   *   *

Robert Vannett had taken refuge behind the ruins of the stone barn with the others. When he saw Bob Thompson wave the white flag, he, too, surrendered to the advancing Germans.

One of the German noncoms recognized Vannett's 4th Armored patch and led him directly to the *Conquering Hero,* which had taken some hits but was not disabled. The German, using hand signals, indicated that he wanted Vannett to get in and point the tank west.

Vannett realized the Germans were salvaging the tanks for their own use, that his tank would attack any Americans following the task force from the west. He was about to protest, but he then considered that these were seasoned, tough soldiers "who didn't take any bullshit."

Vannett stayed in the light tank until noon, when a German officer climbed aboard and told him to drive it back to the oflag. This was Vannett's second trip to Hammelburg, both made in the same tank; the second time, he would stay. He had no choice. Asking one of the kriegies for a cigarette, he was shocked when the answer was no.

"For Christ's sake," he said, "we gave you those cigarettes yesterday. They were ours."

"Tough shit," said a kriegie who was of a more philosophical turn of mind.

Vannett wondered why he and the rest of Task Force Baum had gone through hell to rescue people like this.

When Baum, Sidles and Stiller took off at a run for the woods, Private First Class Irving Solotoff did not get far. Shell fragments sprayed the backs of his legs, so that even if he had had the strength and disposition to run, he would have left a trail of blood behind him. He went over to the medics, who had remained to treat the wounded, and they bandaged him.

When the Germans herded them together, a burly *Unteroffizier* (sergeant) searched each man. In Solotoff's wallet, he found the mezuzah.

"Jude?" he asked menacingly.

"I'm the interpreter," said Solotoff, fearing for his life.

The *Unteroffizier* thought it over and then said in German, "Very well. Tell all the Americans to empty their pockets. Put everything on the ground." He thought another moment, then asked, "What made you do this?" His arm swept the field.

"I don't know," said Solotoff.

The German *tsk*ed sadly several times.

Lieutenant Allen Moses fled with his comrades— Kurelis, Celli, Kmetz, Laepple and Sergeant Frank Boston. Once safe, Moses ordered his men to split up. He would stick with Celli and Kurelis; and Kmetz, Laepple and Boston would try it together.

Celli, Kurelis and Moses slipped by the German perimeter in the west and then went northwest to the Saale River, where they took refuge in a barn. When they saw that the farm was inhabited by a lone woman, Celli said, "Maybe we can get some food from her."

Moses felt his pockets. He still had two D ration bars. Such rations had bought them many things in France; perhaps they would buy something in Germany.

The three sneaked across the barnyard and knocked on the kitchen door. When the woman answered, Moses produced the bars. She waved the three in. They stood uncomfortably in a clean kitchen heated by a black stove. Yellow curtains hung around the window and there were sturdy chairs at the table. The woman made them an omelette as big as a saddle and poured them glasses of milk from an earthenware pitcher.

The four did not exchange a word. Moses wondered if the woman thought they were Germans. When they finished, the three men dodged their way back to the barn where they covered themselves with hay and fell asleep.

When Moses awakened, he was looking straight into the bore of a machine pistol. The two German soldiers kicked Celli and Kurelis, who awoke with a start. The Germans stood over them and laughed at their dismay.

Kmetz, Laepple and Boston had a longer run. It took the Germans five days to find them. They walked past an antiaircraft battery where the crew sat singing around an accordion player. When a sentry challenged them, Kmetz hurled his last grenade and the three took off as Germans shrieked in pain. Crossing a field toward the Main River, however, they were captured by a German platoon and interned with Australian POWs near Frankfurt.

Baron, Floyd and Meiggs had taken off into the woods together. "Fight or get killed," said Floyd as he ran. "Looks like gettin' killed, that's whut."

After an hour of running, and near collapse, the three arrived at the edge of the forest at the base of the Reussenberg.

A gradual slope led to a small valley. Behind them, farther up the mountain, German soldiers with automatic weapons and dogs were methodically sweeping the area. "We can't stay here or they gonna get us with the dogs, just like rabbits," Floyd said. "There's a wheat field down there. We gonna run into it and lie low. C'mon. Keep down."

The men kept 30 yards apart and spent the morning

and afternoon in the field. Baron, lying prone, his arm
across his forehead, fell asleep. In the late afternoon, Floyd
awakened him. "We can really cover some ground at
night," he said.

Together they found and awakened Meiggs and the
three were soon out of the wheat field, across a road to
fallow, rolling land. Once again Floyd led. Spaced 30 yards
apart, Floyd, Baron and Meiggs headed roughly southwest,
avoiding the roads until nightfall. As the darkness deep-
ened, they risked following a country road and were able to
increase their pace considerably.

They had one bad scare. Coming to a wooded area,
Floyd abruptly came face to face with a lone German soldier
who was evidently lost. He and Floyd stared at each other,
then Floyd darted, like a basketball player leading a fast
break, off the road and into the woods. The confused young
German darted off in the opposite direction. When Baron
and then Meiggs reached this point, Floyd told them what
had happened and commented, "I reckon I scared him as
bad as he scared me."

The rest of the night was uneventful as they followed
along the road even more cautiously than before. At
daybreak, they decided to keep walking rather than taking
the safe approach of hiding and getting some rest. Nevertheless, they passed an uneventful day trudging along,
they hoped, to freedom.

At dusk, they came to a small bridge. As Floyd reached
the other side and Meiggs started across, three German
sentries appeared around a bend in the road. Two of them
were walking, one carrying a *Panzerfaust,* and the third was
riding a bicycle. The cyclist was so surprised to encounter
armed American soldiers that he ran his bike off the road
and fell. The other two, however, were alert enough to

draw their pistols. Floyd and Meiggs slowly put their hands over their heads. Baron, still some 20 yards behind Meiggs, saw the capture and ducked for cover. One of the Germans glimpsed him and shouted after him, but didn't bother to follow. Baron would have to go it alone now and decided that he would begin to work his way south, keeping close to the river. After two hours of wading and ducking in and out of the reeds growing along the bank, he was spotted by a squad of German soldiers on patrol. Squatting in the rushes, Baron could see two of them raise their rifles and take aim at him. He stood up slowly and formally surrendered. The *Leutnant* (lieutenant) commanding the squad walked up to Baron, searched him and said, "Aha, you're one of those who were at the party at Hammelburg."

The Germans kept him in their bivouac that night, and in the morning marched him to the road where he met Floyd and Meiggs. Two young, arrogant German boys marched the three back toward Höllrich, taunting their prisoners with cocked rifles. Along the way they rendezvoused with other small groups of new prisoners.

At Höllrich the three were housed in a barn with a few other kriegies, the last to be rounded up. The next day, Baron was detailed to one of the nearby fields where he found wagons arriving with the bodies of dead American soldiers for burial. The corpses were dark, muddy, frozen in terrible contortions, unrecognizable. German civilians had dug a row of separate graves along the hillside.

Handling the dog tags of the dead as gracefully as a cardinal handles a rosary, a German officer passed them to Baron. Baron thanked him and started to go through them. When he found the one he was sure was there—JOSEPH GEER—he shuddered and put the tags in his pocket.

A group of enlisted men, recruited for this duty from

the stalag, put the bodies in the graves one by one. Baron
and the others stood by motionless.

That afternoon the last group of fifty to sixty kriegies
and task force members was delivered to the oflag and
herded into the riding ring. The setting reminded Baron of a
horse show he'd seen at Madison Square Garden. There
were stables to one side, bleachers and boxes on the other.
In one of the boxes sat General von Goeckel with several
German officers near him and a number of Allied POW
officers, including a Canadian who was checking names
against a list.

Baron waved the dog tags in the air and one of von
Goeckel's aides summoned him to the box. Baron handed
the dog tags to the Canadian, saying, "These men are dead.
Verifiably dead. I saw their corpses."

He wanted the news to go home accurately. He wanted
no false hopes on the part of Geer's or anyone else's family.

From the riding ring at the *Lager,* Baron and approximately 100 other POWs were marched to the railway
station in the town of Hammelburg. Here they boarded a
train that proved to be more comfortable than expected.
Although the boxcars were mostly forty-and-eights, there
were only twenty officers in each, with three guards
accompanying each group.

Like most of the other escaped POWs, Baron was
concerned for his life. He wasn't sure how the Germans
would react to recapturing them as part of the task force.
He was not that familiar with the rules of the Geneva
Convention and thought that the Germans might have the
right to summarily execute them.

As it turned out, they had no real cause for alarm. The
pragmatic Germans recognized the demise of the Third

Reich and tried their best to make the Americans comfortable. Every day brought the Eastern Front and the hated and feared Russians closer to Berlin. The accommodating guards told the Americans that their destination was Nuremberg.

After traveling for a few hours, they were attacked by American fighter-bombers. The train stopped quickly, and everybody fled for the neighboring woods to escape the air attack. The guards tried to stay close to their captives for their own protection. Several of the POWs immediately turned blankets into an identifying panel and laid it on the ground. Others waved their arms desperately at the planes. The pilots recognized that their targets were American POWs and signaled them with a friendly waggling of wings and circled the group. One of the pilots jettisoned his under-the-wing drop tanks. So the POWs had gasoline for cooking.

The rest of the train trip was uneventful because Allied intelligence spread the word that American prisoners of war were going by train to Nuremberg. When the train arrived there, the prisoners were unloaded on the northern outskirts of the city. They were immediately moved to a highway that was several hundred feet higher than the railroad elevation.

The group was shepherded toward the celebrated Olympic stadium grounds, but before they had gone very far, the sky was filled with Allied four-engined bombers, Flying Fortresses. The bombing of the city and the railroad yards commenced. The earth shook as if an earthquake were in progress. It seemed the whole city was in flames.

Everyone hit the dirt. From Baron's high vantage point, even while prone he could see everything. He witnessed the most frightening evidence of mass destruction any of the POWs had ever seen, even though many of them had been bombed by the Germans.

It was all over in thirty minutes. The city was deathly quiet. Not a citizen was visible in the rubbled streets. The shaken group of prisoners was led through the stadium which was familiar to all of them from the magazine photographs and movie newsreels showing Hitler addressing the German populace. It was awesome to be there in person. They slept that night on the very track that Jesse Owens had raced over.

From Nuremberg they were shipped to Moosburg, 40 miles north of Munich. Moosburg was the largest POW camp any of them had ever seen. It housed approximately 40,000 Allied prisoners—English, Australian, French and American. There were even a few American naval officers. This was a permanent camp, not the temporary sort that most of the kriegies were accustomed to. It was well organized. There were frequent inspections. The Americans kept their quarters neat and clean. Each week, the kriegies received one Red Cross parcel for every four men, a welcome sight since of course there was little food. At this final stage of the war, the German communication and supply lines were so disrupted that they had insufficient food even for themselves.

The Germans called one important *Appell* at which they announced the death of Franklin D. Roosevelt. Since Roosevelt had demanded unconditional surrender, the Germans seemed to believe that his death would improve their bargaining position and hoped this news would intimidate the prisoners. The prisoners, while saddened by the President's death, observed for themselves that the war was in its final days.

*   *   *

One of the men from the task force who made it to the American lines was Technical Sergeant Charles O. Graham, commander of the assault-gun platoon.

He had filled his pockets with rations before abandoning his assault gun. When he heard Baum's last orders, he told the wounded Casanova, "The krauts are not going to take me prisoner."

He took off with four men, running and double-timing for two hours until they came to a hill. There were two ways to continue: through a ravine or along a footpath. The other three opted for the footpath. No sooner had they started than Germans with dogs confronted them and captured them on the spot.

Graham, having chosen to go up the hill by the ravine, escaped the Germans' notice. Once he got to the top of the hill, he was surprised by an enemy soldier. Each of them was armed with a pistol and each took aim at the other. But nothing happened. Simultaneously, each man nodded and warily holstered his weapon.

In Pidgin English and in Pidgin German, Graham learned that his antagonist was a deserter who wanted to hide out. The deserter wanted Graham to shoot him in the arm, a wound that would get him out of the fighting and shipped home to his wife and three children.

But Graham refused. He was afraid the German would bleed to death before help came. Shots might also bring the enemy with their dogs.

The German warned Graham not to go through towns on his journey because civilians would kill a lone American. If Graham faced capture, he was to make sure he surrendered to soldiers. It was safer. Each man then went his own way.

Graham pushed on through the next day and exhausted

his rations the second night. On the third night, after another day of walking, he decided to approach a farmhouse and take food at the point of a gun. As he neared the front steps, several German soldiers exited. Fortunately, they didn't see him as he ducked behind a wall. When they disappeared, Graham thought, Suddenly, I don't feel so hungry any more.

The next afternoon, he came across an American POW working on a farm. The soldier told him the entire area was filled with German troops, so the Allies must be moving toward it. He hid Graham in a barn. Later that night, the POW produced a loaf of bread he had stolen, and Graham wolfed it down. After a rest, Graham set out again on his journey, now going due south.

He was six days from the Reussenberg when he heard the sound of artillery. He speeded up, sticking to the roads, hoping to reach the lines ahead more quickly.

At a crossroads, he ran into three German officers. They were confused at meeting an American. Did this mean the Americans had outflanked them? Were they surrounded? A quick inspection of Graham's tatterdemalion figure told them that he was not part of a normal combat unit. Nevertheless, Graham had his .45 leveled at them. He took their weapons, maps, dispatch case and compasses and waved them away.

As he jogged along, he saw a tank. He thought at first it was a Sherman and almost waved, only to stop suddenly when he realized it was a Tiger. He took off in the opposite direction with the Tiger and its accompanying infantry platoon after him. Graham did not think he could outrun them and was beginning to lose heart when mortar fire rained down between him and his pursuers.

"You pick 'em up, Lord, and I'll lay 'em down," he prayed as he turned on the last of his speed.

His legs moved of their own accord, no longer under his control. He felt alien in his own body. His heart felt as though it would burst. But he kept running.

Ahead of him was a skirmish line. Behind it—GIs. At least they looked like GIs. Graham put his hands on his head and began shouting, "I'm Technical Sergeant Charles O. Graham, assault-gun platoon leader, 10th Armored Infantry Battalion."

One of the GIs looked at him and spat. "He's probably a kraut in an American uniform. We ought to shoot him."

"Where're your dog tags?" asked another.

Graham produced them.

"How about your pay card?"

Graham dug it out.

"He could have taken that from any American soldier," said the first GI. "Who's your division commander?"

"General Hoge," said Graham.

"What Army are you in?"

"Third Army," said the exasperated Graham, "and Blood and Guts Patton runs it. Ever hear of him?"

These GIs from the 45th Division believed him, finally, and sent him to the rear where a doctor advised Graham to eat only some slices of pineapple. A captain came by and told him he was charged with desertion.

The long-suffering Graham lost his patience, spat out his pineapple and said, "Somewhere in Germany there's a Third Army headquarters. You ask them about Task Force Baum. When they say they've heard of it—and they will— you tell 'em you found somebody who knows what happened to it."

The captain did call Third Army and the brass responded.

Three days later, in a fresh uniform, Graham went up to Third Army headquarters and made a complete report to General Hoge and later to Colonel Creighton Abrams.

(Graham stayed on in the army for another nineteen years. He was discharged a Master Sergeant, a six-striper with three Silver and two Bronze Stars and a Purple Heart.)

:: 12 ::

Good Luck/Bad Luck

In the early afternoon, the last contingent of Germans returning from the Reussenberg to the *Lager* bivouac area found Abe Baum. The semiconscious captain was still lying on the stone wall. They put him into a horse-drawn wagon and delivered him to the oflag.

The oflag was nearly deserted now. Von Goeckel, following his orders from Berlin, had evacuated all of the kriegies who were not seriously sick or wounded, sending them off on foot toward Nuremberg. As soon as Hoepple's soldiers returned with others they had rounded up, von Goeckel sent them off, too.

But the hospital remained crowded. Two POWs brought Baum in and eased him as gently as they could onto a wooden bench. Baum sat exhausted, taut with pain, shivering from the cold, his clothes torn and caked with blood, pine needles from the forest still stuck to his face.

Bill Dennis saw him and hurried over. The wounded and the near-dead had been coming into the hospital all morning, and Dr. Berndt had been operating on them ceaselessly. Dennis carefully began taking off Baum's coat and then his combat jacket and heavy belt. On the belt hung Baum's empty holster and a compass case.

"That's my compass," Baum whispered hoarsely. "They didn't find it. Hold onto it for me, please. I'm getting out of here the first chance I get, and I'll need it."

Dennis examined the GI-issue compass. Baum, whose eyeballs stared in absolute fatigue, fell asleep before Dennis could reply to his request. Dennis thought Baum was lucky to make it into a hospital, let alone try to get out of one. He pocketed the compass and inspected, then cleaned the wounds. The smart of alcohol roused Baum.

Dennis whispered, "Who are you?"

"Task force commander," said Baum between clenched teeth.

Dennis nodded and went for Berndt, who had finished another operation. "You've got one more," said Dennis, "the commander."

"The one the Germans are looking for?" asked Berndt.

Dennis nodded. The two men came back to Baum, and Berndt started ripping the 4th Armored patches off Baum's jacket and shirt. "I'm putting him down as a returned kriegie. There's a room at the end of the hall, the one where we store medications. Put a cot in it."

When Dennis returned, Berndt was digging bits of metal from Baum's hand. "Into the bone," muttered the doctor.

"What about the bullet wound in the thigh?" asked Dennis.

"Do I still have nuts?" asked the grimacing Baum.

"The bullet exited," said Berndt. "But one of them looks damaged."

Baum hoped it was the same one that had been injured in France, so he'd be left with one good one. Then he went to sleep.

When he awoke the next morning, he hobbled to the

hallway where Dennis urgently reminded him to get back into his room, to stay in hiding for the next few days. Baum sat on his cot lost in the sights and memories of war. He knew he was too badly wounded to escape right now. But when would he be able? When would he have a chance?

When Robert Zawada regained consciousness after the battle on the Reussenberg, he was lying in bed in the Hammelburg hospital. He saw a cannister of ether at his head. He also saw a doctor with a saw. The doctor said they would have to amputate what remained of his leg above the knee.

Zawada thought about that as he lay in terrible pain and discomfort. His mattress ticking was filled with straw, and his pillow was two blankets rolled beneath his head. He had to lie perfectly still. The doctor had warned him, had begged him to discipline himself. Any writhing, any movement, would stimulate his circulation, and the partially healed stump of his leg could begin hemorrhaging.

Zawada tried to think of his girl, of how she and his parents would take his handicap, of his future, but he kept coming back to his past and the more he thought about his past, the more he thought about luck.

One of Zawada's friends was a sea-going marine who had survived a ship's sinking without getting wet. The ship was in dock on one of the Pacific islands when a Zero unloaded a bomb on the bow. The ship went down nose first. Zawada's friend, stationed in the stern, kept to his post and as the ship began its inexorable dive, stepped onto the dock, dry, ready for duty. That was luck. Thirty sailors had perished.

Zawada, too, had had his share of combat, but he had actually "seen" little of it. The other men, the GIs in the back of the half-track, can see what is happening, can duck or run or fight. But a radioman sticks with the radio, crouching over it, unable to shield himself from the shells and bullets and fragments, closing his eyes to disaster because he cannot leave his radio. So Zawada realized he had had his share of luck to have survived this long. His luck had simply run out at Hammelburg. Then again, he thought, maybe not. After all, he hadn't been killed, or blinded, or lost a hand or arm. He figured he wouldn't have much cause for complaint—if he could survive this POW hospital.

Sometimes Zawada wanted to cry. Sometimes he clenched his teeth and steeled himself to the interminable passage of time. Bill Dennis came over and wiped his brow and helped him with the bedpan, saying, "One or two more days, fella. You're healing just fine. Hold on." Zawada wondered whether "Hold on, fella" was more comforting than "Tough shit, buddy." Both expressions meant "sweat it out." Zawada wished someone would help him.

Across the aisle from Zawada lay John Waters. Waters now knew he was probably going to live, but he didn't know yet whether the wound would incapacitate him. He knew he was woefully weak. When he tried flexing his arm, he found he couldn't tighten the muscle. If he was incapacitated, he was out of the army, a thought that was truly disturbing to him. The army was his whole life. A West Point graduate, he sincerely believed in the academy's ideal of duty, honor, country. He was trained to command men and to serve his nation. The possibility that his career might end after only fourteen years had never occurred to him before. He was utterly unable to conceive of himself as a civilian, pursuing a life outside the army.

*   *   *

When Dr. Berndt and Bill Dennis finally let Abe Baum leave his windowless hiding place, he immediately went to check on the survivors of his task force and to find Lieutenant Colonel John K. Waters. Stiff and sore, but ambulatory, Baum made the rounds up and down the two long rows of beds lining each side of the ward. The terrible plight of the sick and wounded devastated him. He spent a lot of time with Zawada, the most seriously wounded of his men. Then Baum talked with a young black soldier who had been captured in the Battle of the Bulge after losing one of his legs. Chatting for a while, Baum commented on what bad luck the man had suffered. The GI's response surprised him.

"When I get back," he said, "nobody can say that no Negroes were ever in combat."

Baum crossed the aisle and sat on the empty bed next to Waters. In the bed on the other side of Waters lay Lieutenant Hugh Johnson, 36th Infantry Division, sick for some time with pneumonia. Both were eager for details of the war, for news from the States. POWs get little news and they know that most of the rumors and gossip they get from other POWs and from the guards are pure bullshit.

Baum summarized the progress of the war for them as best he could: the campaigns in Sicily and Italy, D Day, and so on. When he got to the achievements of Patton's Third Army from the invasion of France to the crossing of the Main, however, Baum, as a participant, could recreate the most significant battles in some detail. Waters and Johnson were especially interested in his description of the role Patton's tank force had played at Troyes, a textbook illustration of an armored attack on a city. And, of course, they were thrilled by the courage and endurance of the trapped men at Bastogne and the heroism and daring of those who relieved them.

Finally the three men discussed Task Force Baum, how well it had done, and why it had ultimately failed. They agreed that it had been far too small a force to do the job of liberating the Hammelburg POW camp. Baum did not mention his suspicion that the real goal of his task force had been to rescue Waters. And Waters, if he suspected that this was its goal, did not mention it either. Baum thought it ironic, if Waters's rescue was Patton's reason for sending the task force, that the general's son-in-law should be injured as a direct result of the attempt. For a while he even wondered if Waters might have been wounded by a stray bullet from his task force. But Waters alleviated this fear by explaining what had happened.

At Third Army headquarters, one of the staff officers in the operations room went to a large wall map. On it were arrows, each representing an element of the Third Army and showing its deployment along the front. Isolated from the others, 60 miles behind enemy lines, was a single red arrow pointing from Aschaffenburg to Hammelburg. The staff officer removed it unceremoniously.

A reporter who happened to be in the room at the time asked, "What was that arrow doing all the way down there? Was that a part of the Third Army? Why did you just take it off the map?"

He never received an answer.

During the night of Thursday, 5 April, Baum and many of the POWs in the hospital heard the rumble of gunfire. It didn't seem very far away; by morning, it seemed much nearer.

Baum stopped by to visit Zawada. He asked, "What happened to your buddy?" and pointed to the empty bed beside the radioman.

"He died last night," said Zawada. "Pneumonia."

"Shit," said Baum, looking down the ward, thinking that every empty bed represented a GI who hadn't made it.

"Do you think I'll ever get out of here?" asked Zawada. "Before I die of pneumonia?"

"Don't talk like that," said Baum with sudden emotion. "Can't you hear that gunfire?"

Zawada lifted his head and listened. A weak smile crossed his face.

Baum went to the window. "Hey, you guys, come here. Look, the krauts are taking down the swastika. One of them's holding a white flag."

Wounded and sick kriegies helped each other hobble to the windows. Zawada supported himself on one elbow.

"Yes, it *is* a white flag," shouted Baum.

The men whooped.

"Somebody's got to be near. The Germans are surrendering. They've come, all right, they've come to liberate us."

One of the POWs dropped to his knees and started praying.

"Whaddya see? What's going on?" implored Zawada, echoing the calls of the other bedridden POWs.

"They're getting ready to surrender the camp, sure as hell," said Baum. "The Germans are stacking up their weapons. The American army can't be far away. Listen! Listen!"

The men quieted. They heard the unmistakable clank of tank treads.

"They're here!"

The tanks rolled into view, entering the gate, humping and bumping into the camp. In the center of the oflag stood a stiff, impassive General von Goeckel.

The POWs were hanging out of the hospital windows, waving and cheering the tanks on.

There was a multitude of tanks and Baum knew this was no task force. This was at least a division, with thousands of dogfaces coming up behind. Ironically, the commander in the lead tank entering the camp, Baum noticed, was a former OCS weapons instructor who had tried to flunk him out because he was thought to be a troublemaker in class.

By noon, the armor had also taken the town of Hammelburg and had surrounded the prison camp. Von Goeckel and his small cadre still waited uncomfortably for the appearance of an American commanding officer.

At 1300 hours, an armored car drove up and two GIs pushed open the main gates. The car sped in. An officer stepped out and spoke to von Goeckel, who pointed toward the hospital. The officer took off at the double.

He entered the hospital building. A few minutes later, when the officer appeared in Baum's ward, he was met at the head of the stairs by Abe Baum.

"Who liberated the camp?" Baum asked.

"The 14th Armored Division, Seventh Army," came the reply. "Listen, I'm Major Charles Odom, chief surgeon, Third Army. Where's Colonel Waters?"

"Over there," Baum nodded his head toward Waters's cot. The doctor, who was also General Patton's personal physician, brushed past Baum quickly. Baum eyed the clean-shaven, cleanly-dressed officer suspiciously.

"Funny meeting you here, Howard," said Waters wanly.

"We've been worried about you, Johnny." Odom pulled down Waters's dirty blanket and made a thorough examination of his wound.

When he finished, he straightened up and said, "They did a damn good job on you, but we want to get you to a better facility and give you a thorough going over. I'll be right back."

Abruptly, Odom was gone. From the window, Baum watched him walk swiftly to his car and issue orders into a radio. Baum waited for the doctor to return. So did Zawada.

Within a half hour, Baum saw two Piper Cubs appear over the horizon. They glided down to land at a small airfield near the oflag.

Odom reappeared in the ward followed by two GIs who carried a stretcher.

As the two GIs lifted Waters from his bed and placed him on the stretcher, Zawada asked Baum, "Where they taking him?"

Baum went over to Odom and asked.

"Thirty-fourth Evac Hospital in Gotha," Odom replied.

When Baum relayed this information, Zawada asked bitterly, incredulously, "They got something against guys who lost their legs?"

The speedy evacuation of Waters did not sit well with Zawada or any of the other patients.*

---

*For the next three long days, the only American medical personnel the POWs saw was an orderly. Major Berndt and the other doctors, for some reason, were evacuated on the first day of the camp's liberation. The conscientious medical orderly, a corporal, is well remembered by everyone who was in the POW

For Baum, watching at the window, the pieces all fell into place. George Patton had sent Odom for Waters. He cared about his son-in-law. Fine. But Odom did not even ask about Major Stiller. He did not ask about Abe Baum. Apparently Patton didn't care about them at all.

When Baum had first seen the tanks, he had been exhilarated by the idea of liberation. He had thought about going out and talking to the tankers of the 14th. Now he walked slowly to the little room in which he had been hidden for almost two weeks. Sitting on his cot, he held his head in his hands and thought about the 294 men who had set out in Task Force Baum, all of them killed, wounded or captured. Fifty-three vehicles—all destroyed or captured.

Trying to liberate a POW camp, even if it seemed impossible, was a noble objective. Sacrificing so many good men on an impossible mission to rescue one man was far less noble; it was criminal. This was the first time that members of the 4th Armored Division had failed so utterly. Even so, the task force had gotten further than it had a right to, solely by the heroic efforts of its men. Baum remembered Patton's promise of a Congressional Medal of Honor. He believed that several task force members deserved such recognition. Baum's depression was turning to anger. Why would he do that to us? he thought. *How* could he do that

---

hospital. He had stayed up with Waters for several nights after the colonel had been wounded. After Odom left, the corporal was the POWs, only source of medical attention, and the only food the patients got was whatever he could scrounge from the 14th Armored Division. The snafu that caused the ward in which Baum and the others were housed to be overlooked for three full days by the evacuation personnel has never been fully explained.

to us? Why didn't he give us any air support? And now, how can he forget about us, ignore us?

Baum made a decision. He had to have the answers. And to get them, he would have to see Patton.

He arose from his cot, emerged from his hiding place and returned to his observation window. He watched as Waters was loaded into one Piper Cub and Odom climbed into the second.

Then he watched the two Piper Cubs fly off through the blue sky to safety behind the American lines.

:: 13 ::

Paris in the Spring

Over the next few weeks the POW compound at Moosburg began to fill up with all the Hammelburg survivors.

Some had walked. Others had been driven. Many arrived by train.

Of course, there were many who never made it. A few had escaped. Lucky enough to be in the vicinity of Nuremberg while the 45th Division was taking the city, they fled. The guards were lax and friendly to their prisoners now, because they, too, sensed the Götterdämmerung to come.

Other POWs were not so lucky. Some were killed or wounded by Allied air raids. Others were shot because they wandered, usually at night, near a nervous enemy sentry or outpost.

Rumors of liberation, the end of the war and an American victory kept the prisoners hopeful. When Baron heard from some of the arriving POWs that the 45th was in the area he, of course, felt even more confident than most that salvation was close at hand.

One day a German antiaircraft battery knocked out an American bomber in the vicinity of the camp. Baron saw two parachuted figures floating down under the sunny skies. Ironically, the two American airmen landed directly within the barbed wire of Baron's compound. A German guard appeared instantly and led them unceremoniously into an adjacent barracks which was to be their home for the duration. This was probably the quickest capture and processing of prisoners in history.

Two days after the airmen had landed in the POW compound, the sounds of battle approached, then bypassed the whole camp. There was no fighting in the vicinity. The battle was over in the area.

At 1400 hours, sirens could be heard approaching the main gate. Six white-helmeted American MPs on motorcycles escorted a jeep into the compound.

This was the grand entrance of General George S. Patton, Jr., commanding general of the Third Army.

His posture resembled that of a victorious Roman emperor. The prisoners were thrilled at this display by a three-star general. He made them feel important.

Patton dismounted in front of Baron's quarters and questioned the surrounding group of officers about their treatment. Baron joined the group and observed Patton's anger after the general inspected several of the barracks. Baron knew that Patton's outrage at the conditions was well founded but wondered what effect Limburg, Hammelburg, Bad Orb and Nuremberg would have had on the general since these camps were so much worse.

Raising his hand for silence, Patton announced loudly, "Now you goddamned men, listen. I'm going to get you home just as soon as goddamned possible."

The men returned to their barracks and within half an hour the word was out. The 14th Armored Division's mobile kitchens had arrived with hot food. A medical detachment had arrived at the same time to tend to the sick and wounded. Patton had ordered that the men at Moosburg be fed with the best American steaks available. Ironically, the German prison kitchens had no equipment suitable for grilling or broiling steak, and the prime meat ended up being chopped into hamburgers for the Americans.

The doctors advised the now liberated prisoners not to overeat because most were suffering from malnutrition. Inevitably, everybody did overeat, and consequently most sought refuge at the barbed wire where they could retch in what little privacy they could find.

Because he was fluent in French, Baron was appointed to the position of liaison officer with the French POWs, giving him an exit pass from the camp. After making sure that they were well provided with food, medical and general supplies, he transmitted a complete roster to the Allied staff. There wasn't much more he could do without taking on the job permanently. And Baron wanted to go home. When he heard that Father Barry, his regimental Catholic chaplain, had sent several trucks to bring back any Thunderbird POWs, he decided to join the reunion in Munich, which was now headquarters for the 45th Division. Resigning his liaison job, he requisitioned a BMW convertible from the neighboring town, took advantage of his pass identifying him as a staff member of the Moosburg camp and drove to Munich in time for the fun.

Arriving in Munich, he quickly located Floyd and Meiggs at 1st Battalion headquarters and joked with Colonel Krieger about Floyd's prediction that they would not get back from Krieger's last assignment. The ex-prisoners were regaled with the battalion's exploits after their capture. They were wined, dined, clothed and really given a warm welcome. After visiting with their comrades, they realized they had to return to Moosburg or be declared AWOL.

Baron, Floyd and Meiggs drove back in a style to which they were not accustomed. As they approached the main gate, they noticed the obvious attention of the MPs. They drove around the camp, losing the MPs who had given chase, and hid the car in the woods. Then the three dove through the holes in the barbed wire just in time to join their formation which was being loaded into trucks to be taken to nearby Landshut. From there C-47s flew them to Rheims. Then they were trucked to Camp Lucky Strike, a large muddy area that had been hastily converted into an installation to house the immense numbers of RAMPS (recovered Allied military personnel). The streets were duckboards, the housing tents, but there were several permanent buildings that served vital functions: The mess hall was open all night for all orders (the RAMPS enjoyed being served by the German POWs who worked in the mess); the quartermaster supply issued new clothing; and the finance office gave the men a partial payment of $25 against back pay. Not knowing exactly what was due these RAMPS because their financial records were in St. Louis, Missouri, the army was taking no chances on the possibility of overpaying anyone.

On Baron's second day at Lucky Strike, General Dwight D. Eisenhower, Supreme Commander of the Allied Expeditionary Forces, arrived to address the newly arrived RAMPS. Although it was drizzling slightly, everybody attended. After appropriate words of welcome, and praise for their exploits, Eisenhower went on to say in his whimsical manner, "I don't know why you are all still here. If I were in your place, I'd be in Paris. I want to assure each and every one of you that you will never be court-martialed for anything short of murder or rape."

Within two minutes, the General was standing alone.

This speech by itself probably won him 50,000 votes in the 1952 presidential election.

Later that day, on an avenue in Paris, Baron was approached by the famous *New York Times* war correspondent Drew Middleton, probably because the young lieutenant was not attired in the dress uniform that was usually seen in Paris. Middleton liked to interview combat soldiers, from whom he felt he could get the flavor of war for his stories. After learning that Baron had been liberated recently from a prisoner of war camp, Middleton invited him back to the Hôtel Scribe, the gathering place for newsmen for many years.

They were seated at a table in the dining room. After introducing Baron to the other correspondents in the room Middleton ordered a large steak dinner for him. The newsman asked Baron for his home address and telephone number and his parents' names; then he excused himself from the table.

No sooner had Baron finished his draft beer than the correspondent returned with a Teletype message that he handed to the astonished and moved young officer. It read:

FAMILY NOTIFIED BARON OK. PARENTS ELATED. BERNSTEIN—CITY DESK.

:: 14 ::

Baum vs. the Brass

Baum, typically, had no patience for the evacuation procedures of the 14th Armored Division. Having recovered, at least in his own opinion, from his injuries, he wanted out of Hammelburg as quickly as possible. First, he wanted to get to the 34th Evac Hospital in Gotha where he knew Colonel Waters had been taken and where General Patton would eventually show up. Second, he wanted to get back to the fighting, especially he wanted to be with his unit when the war ended. So when he saw an ambulance pulling away, he jumped on the running board, the first of several hitchhiking rides that would take him to the Gotha hospital.

In Gotha, the examining physician announced that Baum's wounds were healing quite nicely. The two officers from G-2 (intelligence) of the 4th Armored Division—Major D. G. Dayton and Lieutenant S. J. Tobin—who visited Baum in his room for debriefing, were amazed by his story. They confirmed his suspicion that it was the first total loss of such a large task force from the 4th Armored.

At the end of the session, Tobin announced, "Patton has classified this mission Top Secret. Speak to no one about it until it has been declassified. Now, Captain, get some rest. God knows you've earned it."

"Rest?" Baum shot back, utterly surprising the two officers. "I'm ready to leave. I want to get back to my unit." The shrug of their shoulders said that that was not for them to decide.

Patton came to see his seriously wounded son-in-law as soon as he learned of Waters's whereabouts. With two of his aides, he hurried through the hospital corridors to Waters's room.

Waters heard him coming. He recognized the tread of a general and the pat-pat of two aides. Though weak, Waters rolled onto his side and extended his hand. Feebly he supported himself on one elbow, as the beaming general entered the room. Patton took Waters's hand in both of his and his grin broadened.

Waters's first question was, "Did you know I was there?" Without missing a beat, Patton said "No."

Waters never again brought up the question. Patton gave him news of his family and told him about the progress of the war, that it was nearly ended.

Then Patton stepped back and one of the aides stepped forward and read the commendation for the Distinguished Service Cross, awarded Waters for his heroism in North Africa.

Patton took the medal from its white-satin lined case, and draped it about his son-in-law's neck. There was another warm handshake. Patton left.

Early in the afternoon, Baum got word in his room that the brass was touring the floor. The brass, it turned out, was General George S. Patton. Baum was sitting up in bed when the general came in. His roommate, more seriously wounded than Baum, struggled to his feet and came to attention; Baum did not.

"Get back in bed," Patton said after returning the man's salute.

Patton's aide stepped to the bottom of Baum's bed and read aloud a citation:

> For extraordinary heroism in connection with military operations against an armed enemy in GERMANY. On 26 March 1945, Captain BAUM led an armored task force in daring action into enemy territory to liberate Allied prisoners held by the Germans near HAMMELBURG, GERMANY. Enroute, as the column entered the town of GERMUNDEN [sic], Captain BAUM was wounded by enemy rocket fire. Despite his wounds he continued to lead the force throughout the day and the following night until he was again wounded during action on the outskirts of HAMMELBURG. Captain BAUM's fearless determination, and his inspiring leadership and loyal, courageous devotion to duty are in keeping with the highest traditions of the military service.

When the aide had finished, he opened a small case, from which General Patton removed the medal. Stepping to the head of the bed, he pinned the Distinguished Service Cross to Baum's hospital gown. This formality completed, Patton signaled for the aide to leave the room.

"How do you feel, Captain?"

"I'm okay, General," Baum replied, "How's Colonel Waters?"

"It appears he'll be okay."

"Have you heard any news about Major Stiller?"

"No," Patton replied, "nothing." Patton seemed uncharacteristically ill at ease.

"I hear that the Germans thought we were the whole

Third Army and came after us. Is it true that the 4th Armored was able to advance without opposition?"

"Yes," Patton answered, smiling slightly, "that's true. You really did one helluva job. I always knew you were one of the best."

"You know, sir, it's difficult for me to believe that you would have sent us on that mission just to rescue one man."

"That's right, Abe, I wouldn't."

In the days since he had watched Colonel Waters evacuated from Hammelburg by Dr. Odom, Baum had had a lot of time to think about Task Force Baum and about General Patton. Baum greatly admired Patton and felt that the general, especially when compared to other generals, was one of a kind. The army needed him, the Allies needed him, even though the war was ending. Baum therefore finally decided that there was no point now in making trouble. The reason he had raised the matter with Patton in the form of a statement, an assertion that invited confirmation by the general, was to let him know that Baum was not going to make an issue of it. He wanted the general to realize that despite Task Force Baum, he could trust his subordinate's loyalty; Abe Baum posed no threat. And that is exactly how Patton interpreted the exchange. He was immediately more relaxed, no longer physically tense. His mood and the tenor of their conversation also lightened noticeably.

Baum and Patton indulged in some good-natured banter about tankers and had a short exchange of views on the tactical use of armor. There was no other mention of the task force or its mission. Throughout the exchange, the ignored roommate sat nervously listening to a captain talking to the notorious "Blood and Guts" as if he were a fellow captain.

Winding up the conversation, General Patton asked, "Is there anything I can do for you, Baum?"

"I'd like to go back and finish the war with my outfit," Baum replied without hesitation.

"I see," came the thoughtful reply. "Well, there's a problem. An article in the Geneva Convention forbids the fighting of repatriated prisoners. You know you're not supposed to return to duty in the same theater of war. Technically, if you want to see more action, it should be in the Pacific."

"First, I was never officially registered as a POW by the Germans. They never knew I was there."

"That'll help."

"And second, you're George S. Patton, aren't you?"

Patton smiled wryly. He knew he was being set up, but he enjoyed his reputation for being unafraid to take unorthodox measures. And Baum knew Patton owed him one.

Patton turned and called to his aide. "Get the hospital CO in here."

The colonel appeared immediately, having obviously been waiting nearby for such a summons.

"Colonel, I'm sending one of my aides to pick up Baum tomorrow. See that he's ready." Patton then smiled at Baum again and left the room.

A few minutes later, Patton's aide returned to Baum's bedside and said, "You know that Task Force Baum has been classified Top Secret. Use discretion in discussing it."

"That goes without saying. By the way, who's picking me up tomorrow?"

"It'll be a Third Army liaison pilot. He'll fly you to your unit."

A few minutes after the aide had departed, Baum

turned to his roommate. Still recovering from the dramatic confrontation he bellowed, "Did you see what he did to me? He gives me the DSC and classifies the mission Top Secret. Do you know what that means? It means that instead of a Congressional Medal of Honor, we get no recognition at all. Congress *investigates* a Medal of Honor. We've been screwed again."

When Baum reported for duty on 14 April, the 4th Armored Division was dug in near Chemnitz, Germany, preparing for the invasion of Czechoslovakia. Hal Cohen was astounded to see Baum. Creighton Abrams, warrior though he was, was thrilled. The two sat open-mouthed staring at the somewhat thinner, more haggard looking captain.

"I told you you couldn't get rid of me," said the smiling Baum.

Abrams rose from his field table, raced around it and embraced him. Cohen, finally finding his tongue, said, "Well, you are one swivel-hipped jockey. You did one helluva job and I'm putting you in for a medal."

The three officers sat down and Baum filled them in on the details of the mission, answering questions that had not been answered in the preliminary reports they had received.

Abrams specifically asked, "Do you think a combat command would have been able to make it back?"

"No doubt about it," Baum said.

"As you know, that's what I wanted to send," said Abrams.

Soon word spread and Baum's fellow officers began streaming into the command post.

"I can't get over it," said Cohen. "We sent this son of a bitch off to certain doom and he came back."

"What's happened since I left?" asked Baum.

"We've put a couple of hundred miles between us and the Main," said Abrams. "Maybe they'll ask us to take this whole division all the way to China."

"Since you've been gone, I've been a prisoner of war myself," said Hal Cohen garrulously. "By April Fool's Day, my hemorrhoids were shrunk, and I was about to return to duty when some retreating Germans overran the hospital. They captured us, but then they let everyone else go. They kept me because I was a colonel. Now, it is one thing to surrender to superior forces in the field when there is no more food or ammo. It is another thing to be plucked from a sitz bath with your ass dripping wet."

Baum joined Abrams and the others in good-natured laughter. It was the first time he had laughed in quite a while.

Cohen went on about his twenty-four hour captivity. "I was left in a farmhouse. When a GI patrol came by, I started yelling at some sergeant that I was an American colonel and that they shouldn't throw their damned grenades in. I told them that the room was full of dyin' and wounded men and two women. German nuns."

"And you convinced them?" Baum asked.

"The door opened and this sergeant says, 'I believe y'all really is an American colonel. I'm a Georgia boy myself.'"

The day wore on and by evening the reunion had turned into a full-fledged welcome-back party.

Baum was assigned to his old S-3 position—even though the battalion had a new S-3, Major Julian "Fig" Newton—and performed various noncombat duties.

A week after Baum's return, the division surgeon, Dr. Morris Abrams, came down to see him because he had neglected to get the required medical before returning to his unit. Abrams saw that Baum was fully recovered and gave his official approval for him to return to duty.

A few days later, during an enemy artillery barrage, Baum went to the battalion's forward positions and walked from platoon to platoon, refusing to take cover. When the report of this behavior reached Colonels Abrams and Cohen, both combat veterans, they knew exactly what he was doing: seeing if he had lost his nerve, seeing if he could still be an effective combat leader.

When the battalion surgeon heard about the incident, however, he was concerned and called Dr. Abrams at division HQ. Dr. Abrams suggested that Baum undergo further examination, but he was told that it would take a direct order from the division commander, General Hoge, to get Baum to comply.

When Baum received the order from General Hoge, he complied reluctantly. At the HQ, Baum met with Hoge, Dr. Abrams and Dr. Earl Mericle, the division psychiatrist. Baum related the artillery barrage incident and explained his reasons. Hoge understood Baum immediately and with some difficulty eventually persuaded the two physicians of Baum's sanity. Nevertheless, the doctors suggested that Baum be given two weeks away from the front.

Baum objected vigorously, sure that Hoge would support his position. Hoge, however, felt that Baum deserved a vacation.

"I want to be with my men," Baum said stubbornly. "I've been with them all along and I want to be with them when the war ends."

Abrams and Mericle stared at Baum in disbelief. It was clear that they couldn't understand why anyone would turn down a chance to get away from the front. Perhaps they were even beginning to wonder if they had agreed too quickly that Baum was sane.

"I understand how you feel, Abe," Hoge replied, "but I'm ordering you to report to the French Riviera for two weeks of R and R."

When the war ended on 8 May, the newly promoted Major Baum was on a plane heading back to his unit at the front. When the pilot heard the news of the German surrender on his radio, he immediately informed Baum. Baum said only, "I'm happy this war is finally over. I really belonged with my men."

Epilogue

Task Force Baum left the American lines on the night of March 26 with 53 vehicles and 294 men. All of the vehicles were destroyed or captured by the Germans. On 12 April, the 4th Armored Division listed the 293 men of the task force (not including Major Stiller) as "missing in action." After the war ended, the 4th posted 32 members of Task Force Baum wounded in action, 9 killed in action, 16 never accounted for—a total of 25 presumed killed. The casualty reports did not list the number of kriegies who lost their lives accompanying the task force. In fact, no official records seem to exist pertaining to the POW casualties.

Patton told reporters that he ordered the raid as a diversionary tactic. Indeed, Task Force Baum succeeded in bewildering the German command, which diverted units from the north to stop it. The military historian, Lieutenant Colonel Frederick E. Oldinsky, writing in *Armor* (July–August 1976) notes that "The effect of the diversion of those (German) units on the subsequent advance of the 3rd Army was evidenced by the fact that the 4th Armored Division didn't fire a shot for the first 90–100 miles in its subsequent attack."

In his personal journal, published posthumously in the *Saturday Evening Post* in August 1948, Patton wrote: "I can say this—that throughout the campaign in Europe I know of no error I made except that of failing to send a combat command to Hammelburg."

Postscipt: Where Are They Now?

General Creighton W. Abrams, Jr., was Chief of Staff of three different corps in Korea (1953–54); Vice Chief of Staff of the Army (1964–67); Deputy Commander, Military Assistance Command Vietnam (1967–68); commanding general Military Assistance Command Vietnam (1968–72); and Chief of Staff, U.S. Army (1972–74). He died September 4, 1974.

Morris Abrams, M.D., is associate professor of urology, Washington University School of Medicine, and is in private medical practice; he lives with his wife in St. Louis, Missouri.

James D. Alger retired from the Army as a lieutenant general in 1970. He now lives in Hawaii.

Richard Baron returned to his home in New York City after living in Paris for three months. He was hospitalized at Tilton General Hospital, Fort Dix, New Jersey, for several months. When released to civilian life, he joined his family's business, Royal Paper Corp. After spending about two years in electronics research and development in Westchester County, Baron joined The Dial Press and soon became its publisher. In 1970 he left Dial to start a new publishing company.

A resident of northern Westchester for many years, Baron now lives in New York City and has a summer home on Shelter Island, where he and his wife Carole, also a book publisher, enjoy sailing with his children. He is presently writing another book about World War II.

Father Joseph Barry lives in Akron, Ohio.

Abraham J. Baum started the Major Blouse Co. with his father in New York City; because of his expertise in the use of armor, he was consulted by Moshe Dayan and assisted Teddy Kolleck on logistics during the Israeli War of Independence; helped start the 4th Armored Division Association and served a term as its president; semiretired to Florida, he pursued his passion for fishing, and later moved to Palos Verdes, California, where he is now regional manufacturer's representative for Rhoda Lee Blouse Company. He and his wife, Eileen, have four children, David, Barbara, Susan, and Eric.

Albert L. Berndt, M.D., returned to the practice of orthopedic surgery in Portsmouth, Ohio. He is now dead.

Frank Boston returned to his wife and family in Louisville, Kentucky, where he worked for a bakery. He now lives in Jeffersonville, Indiana.

General of the Army Omar N. Bradley was Army Chief of Staff (1948–49) and chairman, Joint Chiefs of Staff (1949–53). He became a five-star general in 1950 and served as chairman of the board of the Bulova Watch Co. He lived in Fort Bliss, Texas, until his death in April 1981.

Alfonso Casanova returned to San Antonio, Texas, where he married and had two sons and a daughter; he worked as a civil servant for the air force but retired recently to spend more time with his grandchildren.

George W. Casteel entered the Army in Oxly, Mississippi; present whereabouts unknown.

Colonel Charles C. Cavender became chief of staff of the

24th Infantry Division (1949–50); he retired in 1953 to live in Sun City, California.

Redo Celli married and returned to work in the steel mill in Carnegie, Pennsylvania. Retired now, he enjoys gardening for his family.

Harold Cohen rejoined his family's apparel business after the war. He is currently an executive in advertising and lives in Tifton, Georgia with his family.

John J. Cortese married while still in the service. He worked as a tractor-trailer driver until he retired. He is now a volunteer ambulance driver in his hometown, College Point, New York.

Rastovic Danitsch, M.D., returned to his beloved Yugoslavian homeland. Because he was not a Communist, he was rewarded with only a meager pension and minimal medical attention. The attempts by General Waters and others to assist him were of little avail. He died in 1976.

William A. Dwight retired from the army as a colonel. He lives in Hope, Arkansas.

Charles Eberle is a salesman of dishwashing soap to institutions and lives in Roosevelt Park, New Jersey.

John Ernest Floyd lives on a small farm in Norlina, North Carolina, with his wife of nearly forty years.

Hans Fuchs manufactures violins in Czechoslovakia.

Bernhard Gerstenberger operates a hunting lodge, "Grünenbaum" near Hammelburg, West Germany.

Colonel Paul R. Goode retired disabled from the army in 1952. He died in 1959.

Charles O. Graham later served in the U.S. NATO forces in West Germany where he often passed the Infantry School at Hammelburg. He retired and now lives in Staunton, Virginia.

Philip Handelsman, M.D., returned to the practice of medicine at Long Island College Hospital in Kings County,

New York. He has now retired to private practice.

Oberst Hoepple committed suicide.

Norman Hoffner owns a chain of beauty shops. He lives in Edison, New Jersey.

General William Hoge was commanding general of the 4th Armored Division (1945), the 9th Corps in Korea (1951) and commander in chief of the U.S. Army in Europe (1953–55). He retired disabled in 1955 to his home in Easton, Kansas, where he died in 1979.

Kenneth B. Jeffries returned to Coatesville, Pennsylvania, where he married and went to work for a local utility company. He is now retired.

Edward Jode lives in Reigate, Surrey, England.

Hugh Johnson is a publisher of Hammond, Inc., in Maplewood, N.J.

Curtis Scott Jones returned to the chinaware business as a salesman. He lives in East Liverpool, Ohio. He has two married daughters and one grandchild.

H. J. Morris Jones lives in Lexington, Virginia.

Raymond Keil lives with his wife in Dallas, Texas, where he recently retired from the motorized equipment business.

Joseph Kmetz has been in chain food-store management since returning to civilian life. He has four sons and a daughter and lives in Pittsburgh, Pennsylvania.

Richard Koehl is now dead.

Ralph Krieger, who now lives in Oklahoma City, Oklahoma, became a pharmacist and eventually owned a chain of eight pharmacies. He recently retired from the National Guard as a Brigadier General.

Nick Kurelis returned to Pittsburgh. While recuperating from his wounds at the Veterans Hospital in Butler, Pa., he was given a three-week pass to get married. An auto mechanic and, in his sparetime, encyclopedia salesman, he lives in McKee's Rock, Pennsylvania.

Harley Laepple returned to his job as a window dresser at Hess's Department Store in Allentown, Pennsylvania. He retired from his position as engineer in charge of Hess's heating and cooling system after forty-eight years with the firm. He lives in Center Valley, Pennsylvania.

Ernst Langendorf continued in the service in Europe. He then worked for Radio Free Europe until his retirement in 1974. He now lives in Grünenwald, West Germany.

Benny Lemer is in the liquor distribution business in Atlanta, Georgia.

L. T. Lyall now lives in Liverpool, New South Wales, Australia.

James Mabrey lives in Evansville, Indiana.

William Mackin is now traffic manager for Schenley Distilleries in Louisville, Kentucky.

Frank J. Malinski works in the plastics industry; he lives in Scotch Plains, New Jersey.

Joseph Matthews, retired from the National Guard as a colonel; he lives in Raleigh, North Carolina.

William Meiggs's last known address was in Cuba.

Lt. Col. Earl W. Mericle, M.D., returned to his wife and three children in Indianapolis, Indiana, where he was in private practice as a neuropsychiatrist and was elected president of the Indiana State Medical Association. He is now deceased.

Allen Moses is in the industrial laundry business in Pittsburgh, Pennsylvania.

Howard "Fig" Newton is a cotton farmer in Arkansas.

William J. Nutto recently retired from the practice of law in Corpus Christi, Texas.

Charles B. Odom, M.D., is the Jefferson Parish coroner, New Orleans, Louisiana.

Carter Ogden lived in Natchez, Mississippi, until his death in 1979.

Richard L. Pancake lives in Old Tappan, New Jersey, and works in the sales department of the Mack Truck Company.

General George S. Patton died in Heidelburg, Germany, of injuries received in a jeep accident on 21 December 1945.

Charles Paulus worked for General Motors in Dayton, Ohio, until he retired recently. He and his wife had a son and daughter and live now in Versailles, Ohio.

Lester L. Powell was awarded a second Silver Star by Col. Creighton Abrams and Capt. James Leach, his former company commander, at a ceremony at Fort Knox in 1947. A retired civil service employee who still enjoys hunting and fishing, he lives in Indianapolis, Indiana.

John Sidles returned to his home in Paris, Kentucky, where he married a girl he had known in high school. He became a successful tobacco farmer. Still an active farmer, he spends his spare time fishing.

John Slack, after the war, worked in the Army Provost Marshall's office processing German POWs in the U.S. He now runs his own graphic arts service in Philadelphia, Pennsylvania. He is the secretary of the Szubin (Oflag 64) Association.

Irving Solotoff is an electronics salesman and actor in Miami, Florida.

Donald Stewart retired from the army as a lieutenant colonel in 1968. He lives in San Antonio, Texas.

Alexander Stiller is deceased.

Elmer Sutton entered the army in Rochester, New York; present whereabouts unknown.

Adrian Tessier runs his own ecology specialty business, A & A Vacuumatic, Inc., Aurora, Colorado.

Robert Thompson returned to Hammelburg in 1967 but was unable to find the tin of diamonds he had buried there. He now lives in Tulsa, Oklahoma.

Dominique Vallani lives in Oyster Bay, New York, where

he works for the New York Telephone Company.

Robert Vannett is an automobile salesman in New Era, Michigan.

General Gunther von Goeckel retired from the Wehrmacht and now lives on his pension with his wife in Bad Kissingen, West Germany.

Robert Walborn, D.D.S., returned to the practice of dentistry in Sunberry, Pennsylvania.

John K. Waters was commandant at West Point (1951–52); chief of staff in Korea (1952–53); commanding general, 4th Armored Division (1960–62), 5th Army (1962–63), and Continental Army Command (1963); commander in chief, U.S. Army, Pacific (1964–66); retired as a four-star general in 1966. He now lives in Potomac Falls, Maryland, and Martha's Vineyard, Massachusetts. He spends as much time as possible fishing.

William G. Weaver, Jr., is Employee Development Director, Good Samaritan Hospital, Phoenix, Arizona.

Arthur L. West retired a major general and lives in Bowling Green, Virginia.

Ellis Wise is a poultry farmer (Wise Poultry Co.) in Emporia, Kansas.

Major General John S. Wood ("Tiger Jack") retired disabled in 1946; he served in various diplomatic posts in Austria, Japan, Korea, and Switzerland. He died in Reno, Nevada, in July 1966.

Walter Wrolson went to the University of Minnesota with the help of the G.I. Bill of Rights and became a Doctor of Dental Surgery. He married and had two children, a boy and a girl. In 1952 he was called up from the Reserves to active duty as a tank officer at Fort Knox, Kentucky, the home of the armored forces. When it was discovered that he had obtained his dental degree, he was quickly transferred to the dental corps but remained at Fort Knox for a year and a half until the

Korean War ended. He then moved to Warren, Minnesota, where he still practices dentistry.

George Wyatt returned home to Rosie, Arkansas, then re-enlisted for four years. As a civilian, he worked in various construction businesses in Illinois, California, and Arkansas, and as a farmer. He is now deceased.

Donald R. Yoerk lives in East Aurora, New York, where he works with heavy motorized equipment.

Dragon Yosifovitch lives in Schweinfurt, West Germany.

Robert S. Zawada studied architecture after the war and was in the construction business. He later operated his own car-wash business. He now lives in Metairie, Louisiana, and is studying real estate management.

Despite our efforts, there regretfully remain many participants whom the authors were unable to identify or locate. Readers with additional information about Task Force Baum or *Oflag XIIIB* veterans are encouraged to write the authors c/o G. P. Putnam's Sons, 200 Madison Avenue, New York, NY 10016.

Acknowledgments

We wish to thank the staff of the Infantry School at Hammelburg, West Germany, who made it possible to study the terrain of the *Lager* where most of the action took place, especially General Rupprecht von Butler, commanding officer; Oberst Hans Weberfels, area commander; Hans H. Schnebel, historian; Herr Furth and Herr Heinrich. We thank them for their hospitality and cooperation, for furnishing us with transportation and for giving us their military perspective of the action.

We wish to express our appreciation to Lieutenant Colonel Leonard T. Graham, United States Army liaison officer to the Infantry School, who not only acted as interpreter but who through dedication to our work and personal interest in our project added to our investigation and interpretation of events, often on his own time.

Our special thanks to Oberst Hasso von Uslar-Gleichen, military attaché, embassy of the West German Federal Republic, Washington, D.C., who arranged for us to enter the Infantry School and for the cooperation of the army of the West German Federal Republic, and to Brigitte Romero, German National Tourist Office.

Our deep appreciation to the following: The American

Center of Military History, whose staff supplied us with facilities, documents and leads, especially to General Hal C. Pattison (retired), ex-chief of Military History; General James L. Collins, Jr., Chief of Military History; Dr. Brooks L. Kleeber, Deputy Chief Historian and fellow kriegie at XIII B; Dr. Maurice Matloff; Charles von Luttichau, Detmar Finke, George Chalow, Janet Hargett, Sylvan Dubow, John Taylor, and Edna Finch. National Archives, Modern Military Branch, William Cunliffe and George Wagner. Richard J. Sommers, Ph.D., Archivist-Historian, U.S. Military History Institute, Carlisle Barracks, Pennsylvania; Brigadier General Robert S. Young, Reserve Components Personnel and Administration Center, Office of the Adjutant General, Department of the Army, St. Louis, Missouri; David L. Bacon and L. Kolkhurst, National Personnel Records Center, U.S. General Services Administration, St. Louis, Missouri; Marie T. Caps, U.S. Military Academy Library, West Point, New York; Senator Jacob K. Javits, New York; Ed Reavis and Ed Walker of the European edition of the *Stars and Stripes*; Fred Shaine, *Stars and Stripes*; Sam Schenker, National Secretary-Treasurer, 4th Armored Division Association; Edward Rapp, Secretary-Treasurer New York City Chapter; Lieutenant Colonel Robert A. Wilson, President 45th Infantry Division Association, Oklahoma City, Oklahoma; General Felix L. Sparks, U.S. Army (retired), Secretary 157th Infantry Regiment Association; Brigadier General J. C. Pennington, the Adjutant General (1979); Colonel James H. Leach for technical expertise in armor.

And finally thanks to: Mrs. Creighton W. Abrams, Jr.; Adolph Alcaly; Colonel Robert S. Allen (deceased), author of *Lucky Forward*; Major General Ed Bautz; Benjamin Bayliss; Mrs. Albert L. Berndt; Phillip Blanca; Martin

Blumenson, author of *The Patton Papers*; Roger Boas; Charles P. Boggess; George C. Bolz; Robert Bonomi; Glow D. Briggs; Reade C. Bush; Arnold E. Caldwell; Boyd E. Carson; George Chalow; General Bruce C. Clarke, U.S. Army (retired); John D. Coffey; Barnett Cooperman; William Craig, author of *The Fall of Japan*; J. L. Crawford; Edward V. D'Arcy; George Davis; Major General John R. Deane, author of *The Strange Alliance*; Colonel James W. deFreest (retired); General Jacob L. Devers (deceased); Colonel Thomas Diamantes; Len Feldman; John Frazier; Lester Gaines; Colonel J. W. Geer (retired); James Geer; Thomas W. Gerardi; John Goodner; Robert G. Grady; Peter C. Graffignino, M.D.; Colonel Alexander Graham (deceased); Claire Grice; Milton B. Handelsman, M.D.; General Chester B. Hansen, executive officer to General Omar N. Bradley; Glen K. Hanson; Janet Hargett; Seymour Harris; J. E. Hendersched; George F. Howe, author of *The Battle History of the 1st Armored Division*; Hugh Johnson; Roslyn Kaiser; Ralph M. Krieger; Donald Laker; Lamison; James H. Leach; Allen McCormick, professor of modern languages; Charles B. McDonald, former deputy historian, U.S. Army Military History Division, author of *Company Commanders, Siegfried Line, The Last Offensive*, and *Three Battles*; William McGovern; John McMillan; Jack McMillion; Father Alan Madden; Colonel Edward Markey (retired); Major General Raymond Mason; Jim Mills; John G. Nix, Jr.; Barney Paperman; Neil Quick; Richard Rossbach; George E. Schaefer; Joseph E. Schmidt; George Seeba; A. H. Speairs; Kenneth P. Stemmons; Frank Stinchfield, M.D., Chairman and Director of the Department of Orthopedic Surgery, Columbia University College of Physicians and Surgeons, Director of Orthopedic Surgery at Presbyterian Hospital; Clarence A.

Story; John Taylor; John B. Tettmer; Irving Thompson; John Toland, author of *Battle: The Story of the Bulge* and *The Last Hundred Days;* Jack Vaughn; Charles P. Volz, M.D.; Major General Arthur L. West, Jr. (retired); General Robert R. Wilson (retired); Colonel John S. Wood, Jr. (retired); Robert Wyley, M.D.; Colonel Hugh Young (retired); Frank Magliozzi, for his research efforts; David Baum, for research assistance; Gregor Ziemer, author of *Hitler's Children,* for his comments on the manuscript; Michael E. Monbeck, special thanks for his patient organizational help; Carole Baron, for her constant help and encouragement; and Caroline Shookhof, for going far beyond typing with her constructive suggestions.

Our thanks to Peter Israel and the staff of G. P. Putnam's Sons—especially our editor Rob Fitz; copyeditor C. Catt, who went beyond the call of duty; and Gypsy da Silva for encouragement and painstakingly careful work in the final stages of putting the book together, and Ron Lief and Angelika Marder.

WAR BOOKS FROM JOVE

07299-0	**BATAAN: THE MARCH OF DEATH** Stanley L. Falk	$2.95
07292-3	**THE BATTLE FOR MOSCOW** Col. Albert Seaton	$2.95
07510-8	**THE BATTLE OF LEYTE GULF** Edwin P. Hoyt	$3.50
07738-0	**CORREGIDOR** James H. Belote & William M. Belote	$2.95
07294-X	**THE DEVIL'S VIRTUOSOS** David Downing	$2.95
872-16597-3	**DUNKIRK** Robert Jackson	$2.25
07737-2	**48 HOURS TO HAMMELBURG** Charles Whiting	$2.95
07297-4	**HITLER'S WEREWOLVES** Charles Whiting	$2.95
867-21223-3	**I SAW TOKYO BURNING** Robert Guillain	$2.95
07618-X	**KASSERINE PASS** Martin Blumenson	$3.50
07134-X	**DAS REICH** Max Hastings	$3.50
07295-8	**THE SECRET OF STALINGRAD** Walter Kerr	$2.95
07427-6	**U-BOATS OFFSHORE** Edwin P Hoyt	$2.95
07106-4	**THE BATTLE OF THE HUERTGEN FOREST** Charles B. MacDonald	$2.95
07103-X	**GUADALCANAL** Edwin P. Hoyt	$3.25
07296-6	**WAKE ISLAND** Duane Schultz	$2.95
07532-9	**BLUE SKIES AND BLOOD: THE BATTLE OF THE CORAL SEA** Edwin P. Hoyt	$3.25
07403-9	**CLIMAX AT MIDWAY** Thaddeus V. Tuleja	$2.95
07449-7	**PATTON'S BEST** Nat Frankel and Larry Smith	$2.95
07393-8	**SIEGFIED: THE NAZIS' LAST STAND** Charles Whiting	$3.50

MEN AT WAR!

Gritty, gutsy, fascinating, real, here are stories of World War II and Vietnam—-and the men who fought in them.

___THE KILLING ZONE: MY LIFE IN THE VIET NAM WAR **Frederick Downs**   06534-0/$3.50

___SEMPER FI, MAC **Henry Berry**   06253-8/$3.95